Vacation Adventures on a Cargo Ship

ADRIAN PEETOOM

D1516097

FIFTH
HOUSE

Cover and interior design by John Luckhurst
Edited by Lesley Reynolds
Copyedited and proofread by Kirsten Craven
Maps by Paul Heersink
Scans by ABL Imaging

The type in this book is set in Minion.

The publisher gratefully acknowledges the support of The Canada Council for the Arts and the Department of Canadian Heritage.

Canada Council   **Conseil des Arts**
for the Arts   **du Canada**

We acknowledge the financial support of the Government of Canada through the Book Publishing Industry Development Program (BPIDP) for our publishing activities.

Printed in Canada

2008/1

First published in the United States in 2008 by
Fitzhenry & Whiteside
311 Washington Street
Brighton, Massachusetts, 02135

Library and Archives Canada Cataloguing in Publication

Peetoom, Adrian
Vacation adventures on a cargo ship / Adrian Peetoom.

ISBN 978-1-897252-28-4

1. Peetoom, Adrian--Travel. 2. Ocean travel. 3. Cargo ships— Passenger traffic.
4. Voyages around the world. I. Title.
G440.P395A3 2008   910.4'1   C2007-907617-3

Fifth House Ltd.
A Fitzhenry & Whiteside Company
1511, 1800-4 St. SW
Calgary, Alberta T2S 2S5

1-800-387-9776
www.fitzhenry.ca

Contents

Acknowledgements

Writing this book helped me to relive our two travel adventures and brought to mind the many people who made them such a pleasure. Some will know of their contributions, but many will not.

I am deeply grateful to the sailors of the *Ville d'Aquarius* and *Sydney Star*. Anyone on board couldn't help but admire their skills and energy. Many of them, officers and crew, invited us into their lives and shared their own stories with us. I want to acknowledge in particular Second Officer Gottfried Donnerhak on the *Ville d'Aquarius*, for his unfailing kindness and immense patience in answering my questions, especially the dumb ones. The following *Sydney Star* officers went out of their way to make our lives as passengers comfortable and rich in laughter and enjoyment: Captain Stephen R. Pridmore, Chief Engineer Nick Topham, Reefer Engineer Glen Palmer, and Electrical Engineer Keith (the record of his last name got lost). A special note of thanks must also go to our table steward, Lito Ilagan, and cabin steward, John Tefora.

Fellow *Ville d'Aquarius* passenger Daryl Curtis sailed with us through Europe and Asia. She was kind, funny, and generous, and we're in touch still. *Sydney Star* passengers enriched our lives for the roughly thirty days between Savannah and Down Under. Thank you to Martha Phelps and Clyde W. ("Bill") Halstead; Russell Albright; Michael and Roberta Broad; and Jean and David Hodder. They also freely shared their photographs, some of which enrich this book.

My wife Johanna wrote many letters to our children, her siblings, and her Dad. She also wrote a diary and took photographs. These three sources proved invaluable when I wrote this book. I also thank her for being a loving travel companion and for the ease with which she still slides into recalling those marvelous shipboard days.

P&O Nedlloyd (Rotterdam, the Netherlands) kindly provided the photographs that wonderfully illustrate container shipping industry basics. Kees Oosterhout, a P&O Nedlloyd software expert, and Peter Potts, a former merchant sailor, were kind enough to read part or all of the manuscript and check it for facts. And let me not forget to mention the hundreds of unnamed people whose lives touched ours: cab drivers; bus drivers; customs and immigration officials; local company agents; restaurant servers; bank tellers; port guards; church members;

tourist guides; sailors' centre volunteers; and the two travel agencies we used. In other words: "No man is an island."

Finally, my thanks to my publisher, Fifth House, especially my editors, Lesley Reynolds and Kirsten Craven, and managing editor, Meaghan Craven. I take full responsibility for this book's remaining shortcomings, and thank them for their enriching suggestions and professional execution.

Adrian Peetoom
Fall 2007

CHAPTER ONE

Getting Ready

A working ship is rarely silent. The noise of the main engine penetrates the whole vessel. You feel its rhythm when you touch the walls of the cabins and hallways. The noise gets uncomfortable just outside the open door that leads from the working deck into the engine room, an enormous cavern filled with pipes and wires and tanks, with the main engine, generators, a water purifier, and several refrigeration units going all at once. Here, you would soon grow deaf if you didn't wear expensive ear protectors. At full speed with all systems go, a ship's engine room is a mighty cacophony.

Even when tied up in port with the main engine shut down, a ship is not silent. Then it hums. Generators work to provide the people on board with light and heat, and to power the equipment: gauges everywhere; stoves in the kitchen; washers and dryers in the laundry room; and computers and other electronic and communication gear on the bridge and in the engine-room office. Fans stir the air inside this floating box of steel. Moreover, port means unloading and loading cargo. Huge dockside cranes, powered by mighty diesel engines or massive electrical motors fed by thick power cables, clank and crunch cargo. Stevedores yell instructions and information from ship to shore and vice versa. Mighty trucks belch dark soot and

3

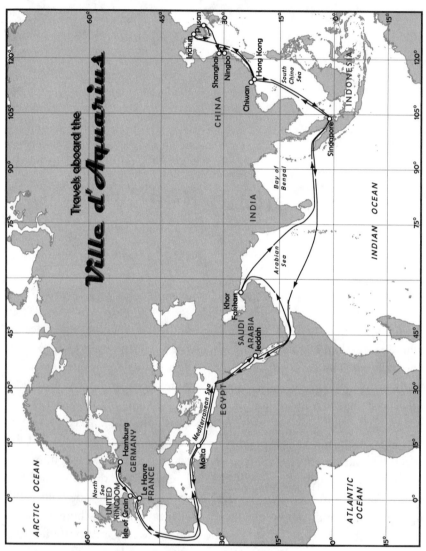

Down from and up to Hamburg, Germany, in sixty-five wonderful days.
(Map by Paul Heersink)

roar like lions as they haul containers to and from the ship. The trucks also supply the ship for the ongoing voyage with food for the people on board, and parts for the ship's equipment are all hauled aboard with noisy on-board cranes.

But there are moments when ships are quiet, when shore-loading cranes have lifted their booms high and have moved away on rails that run along the quay. Stevedores have gone home or to another ship. Dock trucks now run elsewhere or are parked for a rest. Only a few workers occupy the quay, awaiting instructions to take cables off bollards. They smoke a cigarette, sip a Coke, kick a can, and lean against the truck or van that brought them there. The ship's shore agent has gone back to his office and the gangway has been hauled up. The pilot is peering over the bridge wing railing. On the waterside, two tugs are cabled to the ship, their engines idling gently while waiting for the pilot's instructions. In the blocks waiting for the starter's gun, the ship is holdings its breath.

On one muggy day in March 1998, the giant dark blue *Ville d'Aquarius* lay poised at just such a moment in the container port of Singapore. Since departing Hamburg seven weeks earlier, it had loaded and unloaded con-tainers and supplies in London, Rotterdam, Le Havre, and Malta. It had made the slow day-long journey through the Suez Canal, and had docked in ports in Saudi Arabia, United Arab Emirates, Singapore, South Korea, and China before coming back to Singapore, one of the two main Asian hubs for container shipping. The ship, now low in the water and heavy with goods produced all over Asia, was ready to go, and officers, crew, and passengers were happy to get underway.

As soon as the dock workers got the walkie-talkie go-ahead, they flung the ends of a dozen thick ropes over the quay bollards and into the water, and able seamen (ABs) on board started winches fore and aft to haul in those lines that had held the ship tight to the dock. Other ABs coiled the incoming ropes on their appointed places on the foc's'le (a working deck at the front of a ship) and the poop deck (a working deck at the back), ready for the next port. The captains of the two powerful tugboats had already opened their throttles on the pilot's command to gently pull the massive container vessel away from the dock, a tricky maneuver in busy ports where ships are berthed close to one another and contend with strong harbour currents, tides, and high winds. Now the ship's stack belched black smoke as the engine came to life. When he judged it safe to do so, the pilot on the bridge barked, "Dead slow ahead," to the helmsman inside the wheelhouse, who repeated the order while moving the telegraph lever forward one notch. ABs began securing the gangway for safe storage until the next port. For awhile the tugboats remained attached, pushing and pulling to help the freighter into the channel marked with green and red buoys that would take the ship out to sea.

In due time, a brightly painted and speedy boat approached the vessel, the word "PILOT" clearly visible on both sides. It stuck its nose underneath a rope ladder hanging from the freighter's side, but its captain made sure that its aft stayed on an angle away from its giant friend so the two vessels wouldn't be sucked together by vacuum and wave forces, requiring both to come to a halt before letting go. Soon the pilot appeared on the freighter's deck and without any ceremony, descended the rope ladder. From its last rung he jumped down on the deck of the pilot boat. With a high-pitched sound this sea-terrier left the side of the elephant freighter, perhaps going back to port to guide another ship out, or circling around to help an incoming vessel into port.

Only after the tugs and pilot had left did the captain of the *Ville d'Aquarius* order the telegraph to "Full Speed Ahead." With a powerful rumble, the screw settled into its cruising 95 RPM. Soon the ship reached a speed of about twenty-three knots (41 km/hour), heading northwest through the Straits of Malacca between Sumatra and Malaysia, then west, eventually into the Gulf of Aden, and then north into the Red Sea to the next port, Jeddah, in Saudi Arabia. The voyage would take nine days.

Our ship leaving Hong Kong harbour. Not even fully loaded, it exudes power and might. But notice the small tug that has the power to move this giant all by itself.

That March day, my wife Johanna and I watched all this activity as we leaned on the railings of the *Ville d'Aquarius*: the tugs, the pilot boat, the harbour traffic, and the gradual disappearance of the bustling port. This time we also observed another giant container freighter, blue-gray with MAERSK prominently painted on its sides, entering the outgoing channel behind us and following us on a parallel course once at sea. For four days the two ships sailed within sight of one another, perhaps two kilometres apart in their respective sea lanes, both at full speed covering just under one thousand kilometres each twenty-four hours. Each ship's silhouette mirrored the other: a large wall of steel rising out of the water, and from front to back, row upon row of steel containers piled five or six high, with jagged gaps here and there, the cargo interrupted only by the superstructure. The slightly faster Maersk ship came closer each day, and after five days it stuck its prow just ahead of us. Later that day the two ships veered apart, the Maersk vessel turning starboard on its way to the port of Colombo, Sri Lanka.

So how do these two ships, thousands of kilometres and continents away, connect to ordinary Canadian citizens? Many consumer goods that we casually buy and take for granted are brought to us in containers carried by ships like these. No one is surprised anymore to see consumer goods labelled, "Made in China" (or South Korea, Taiwan, Pakistan, or India). Clothing and footwear, electronics, kitchen gadgets and toys, even furniture, are now manufactured for us in many Asian and Latin American countries. In Canada, summers are short and winters long, and for much of the year we eat foreign fruits and vegetables. On a recent shopping trip I spotted cantaloupes from Costa Rica, pears and apples from various South American countries and New Zealand, grapes from Europe, citrus fruits from South Africa, nuts from Brazil and China, and there isn't a Canadian banana or pineapple to be had at any time of the year. We may be weary of the global economy and have increasing concerns about its environmental impact, but we use it, wear it, and eat it every day.

Some of the container ships that bring these goods to our shores take passengers as well as freight. For sixty-five days in early 1998 my wife Johanna and I were passengers on the *Ville d'Aquarius*. Two years later we enjoyed seventy-two days on the *Sydney Star*.

At first glance we may not seem like the type of people who would embark on such an adventure. We're a typical Canadian middle-class couple. Both of us emigrated from Holland in our late teens. Johanna arrived with her large family in 1952, and I came on my own in 1954. We met in 1956 and married in 1958. I built a career in publishing, and Johanna and I raised six children on my middle-class income. Church and faith played a large role in our family life, even to the point of sending our children to Christian schools, which proved a substantial drain on family finances. Our summer holidays were limited to day trips, or a one-week stay at a cottage. In 1976 we spent ten days at Christmas time in and around San Francisco, but the whole family had earned the money for the trip by picking strawberries and raspberries for a farmer the summer before. Yet, we didn't let financial constraints limit our horizons. We were avid users of libraries and our children enjoyed music and art lessons. Moreover, over the years we welcomed many interesting guests into our home.

By the time our youngest daughter had left home, we were living comfortably in Waterloo, Ontario. As retirement at age sixty began to look like a port to which our lives were sailing, we began to think about life-after-career. I had worked for the same publishing company for over thirty years, which would provide me with a stable pension income. I discovered that the Government of Canada would give me a reduced pension at age sixty, and that there was a way to have Johanna share in it so that our income tax obligations were reduced. We figured and ciphered and contemplated, and even sweated a little. In the end, we made the decision that I would retire at age sixty, and so I did, in 1994.

It was the start of a new life with time and money for travel. My mother was still alive, and my three brothers and their families lived in Holland, so that country would be a frequent destination. We made sure that we saw all our children and grandchildren at least once a year, even those living far away. We also remained active in the church and looked for volunteering opportunities. Johanna became associated with an organization that provided home care for needy people, and I volunteered at the local hospital. I also took some courses at Conrad Grebel College at the University of Waterloo. Like many retirees, we soon were as busy as ever.

At some point during those early retirement years, we came across the information that some ocean freighters took passengers. We became instantly interested in the idea and began to talk about it between ourselves and with others. We soon found out that Johanna's only brother had lusted after this possibility for a number of years and had amassed a substantial file of information on it. Unfortunately for him, his wife wouldn't hear of it, but he loaned us his file, which we read avidly. We had many questions. Where could we go? For how long? How much would it cost? How do you find a ship and book a place? What kind of ships could you travel on? What would life be like on board? What about food? What if you got sick, or even seasick? We spent months thinking about the possibility of a freighter trip and even borrowed a library book or two about being passengers on board ships, but the books were quite old and dated, and none talked about container ships.

It wasn't until late 1996 that we became serious enough to shift this possibility to a probability. I began to surf the net, and it didn't take long before I came across the website for The Cruise People Ltd., a specialized travel agent located in Toronto. We contacted the owner, received plenty of information in the mail, visited his office, and in the spring of 1997, we made the plunge. We booked a trip on a German container freighter that would depart from Hamburg, Germany, in late December or early January 1998. We would sail through the North Sea, the Mediterranean, the Suez Canal, and then all across the bottom of Asia to ports in South Korea and China, and then back. Mind you, we were informed that the specific ship, the destinations, and the dates weren't carved in stone. Everything would be subject to change without much notice. Typically, as it turned out, the ship we boarded wasn't the one we had booked for, though it belonged to the same company. We would learn that with freighter travel comes a certain level of uncertainty.

Booked to go, we began our preparations. We were required to hold valid passports with an expiry date at least six months later than the date of our planned return to Canada, in case we became sick or hurt while travelling and had to remain abroad longer than planned. Our information package let us know where we would need visas. In early August, I visited the Chinese consulate in Toronto, but I was unsuccessful in getting the visas, being told that they would only be issued within three months of the date of our visit. I telephoned the Saudi Arabian embassy in Ottawa and was similarly unsuccessful. For all of the other countries on our itinerary valid passports were enough.

Before we left we endured immunizations to protect us against diphtheria, polio, and tetanus. The travel agent's documents also prescribed inoculation against yellow fever, but the local health authority insisted that this precaution was not mandatory for our trip, given where we were headed, and that the risk factor argued against it, so we ignored this requirement. We had to get travel medical insurance and a doctor's certificate stating we were fit enough to undertake such a voyage. Even though we were healthy and without chronic ailments, the travel insurance was expensive, well over $1,000 for the both of us.

The travel agent had given us an information package for each port we were slated to visit. It listed names, mailing addresses, telephone numbers, and the city locations of each of the shipping company's local agents, plus social, political, and cultural information that would guard us from giving offense or getting into trouble. At some point the travel agent notified us that our booking had been transferred to the *Ville d'Aquarius*, a sister ship of the original one we were booked on.

Before boarding ship we spent four months in Holland, renting a small furnished apartment close to my mother, who was almost ninety years old at the time. In total, we'd be away from our Canadian home for about seven months. At the time we lived in a house, and we knew that to leave it uninhabited would be risky. Luckily our daughter Emily agreed to live in it with her young son, and this assured us that our home and car would be looked after. Just before we left for Holland, we visited the travel agent once more to pay for the ship's lodging and transport, approximately $16,000. This amount included another mandatory insurance premium for a diversion policy that would indemnify the ship's operators for any cost involved in the aftermath of accidents or illnesses that would require the ship to interrupt its sailing progress or require it to seek an unscheduled port. This, too, wasn't cheap.

We had booked flights to Amsterdam and back and obtained $3,000US worth of traveller's cheques. (Canadian fund traveller's cheques aren't as easy to convert and sometimes require higher exchange fees.) Packing our clothes was a major undertaking as we would traverse winter, spring, fall, and summer twice during our trip, and we didn't quite trust the information that there would be ample and modern laundry facilities on board. All in all, we had three large and heavy suitcases, a box full of books, plus smaller carry-on bags.

After our preparations were complete, we flew to Holland in August. During our stay there I visited Holland's capital city, The Hague, where all the embassies are located. I managed to get our Republic of China visas, but I had to pay what felt like blackmail fees of around $350 and had to spend a whole day filling in forms and waiting around. I also visited the very unfriendly Saudi Arabian embassy, where I was told that I wasn't welcome in that country. I was told this while standing outside the building talking into a speaker. They wouldn't even let me inside.

In the last two weeks before our departure, we were telephoned four times to let us know that our boarding dates had shifted. Moreover, the original voyage length of seventy-three days would now be cut to sixty-five. We didn't mind, as we had been well prepared by the travel agency to expect uncertainty and that shifting arrangements would be part of travelling as passengers on freighters. In fact, uncertainty is part of the charm of this kind of travel. On January 2, after four pleasant months in the country of our births, we loaded everything we had brought into my brother Arend's car for the trip to Hamburg's harbour. We were ready to climb aboard our temporary home.

CHAPTER TWO

Hamburg to Malta

I don't think any first day on another ship could ever have been quite as exciting as our very first day on the *Ville d'Aquarius*. Our boarding of the *Sydney Star* two years later was much more of a familiar routine. We did the same things on both ships: unpack, explore, and have a snooze. But that first day on the *Sydney* didn't have the magic of this one.

Our first experience of a working port almost overwhelmed us; everything seemed out of control. A gatekeeper directed us to a van, which we boarded to lead the way while Arend followed us with our luggage in the car. Ordinary road trucks with containers were entering and leaving the gates. Special mobile cranes were carrying containers from storage areas to ships, and vice versa, on roads that were mere alleyways between stacks of containers. In between ordinary trucks and moving behemoths, sedans and vans bobbed and weaved their own mysterious ways. Fortunately it didn't take long before we got to the ship, its name clearly visible and a beehive of loading and unloading activity. The van driver pointed to the gangway, we got out, he drove off, and Arend stopped his car right at the foot of it. We felt like ants about to be squashed on top of the rails running parallel to the ship on which four huge cranes were lifting containers up and down. Those giants seemed to need our spot, and also looked capable of crushing every-thing in their way. Some blasted a horn, and at least two loud voices yelled at us in German. We hastily dropped the luggage at the foot of the gangway and said a quick goodbye to my brother, who got away in one piece. Then Johanna and I, bewildered, anxious, and overwhelmed by all the noise and activity, looked around for what we should do next. We looked up to the top of the gangway, from whence we hoped help would come. A gigantic wall of dark blue steel rose up high above us, stretching forever in both directions horizontally. This was the biggest sea-going vessel I had ever seen up close. How could it ever sink? I felt sure it wouldn't sway even in the biggest of storms and felt relieved at the thought.

While Johanna kept an eye on our luggage, I climbed the swaying thirty-nine steps with one suitcase in hand and two strapped bags hanging from my shoulders. The steel bar railings were oily to the touch and the stairs very narrow. At least there was a sturdy safety net stretched out on both sides along the length of the ladder. At the top I met a sailor who welcomed me aboard. He didn't seem surprised by my appearance. I pointed to my wife and remaining suitcases below. He shouted over his shoulder in a language I didn't know, which caused two more sailors to appear and go down. They carried up the rest of the bigger luggage and Johanna followed with what

Our ship being unloaded in Inchun. Notice the rail on which the cranes move at the left side.

This is not the ship we sailed on, but the photograph gives a splendid idea of the massive size of these container vessels and the height of cargo. We were awed every time we came back from a port visit. (Courtesy P&O Nedlloyd, Rotterdam, the Netherlands)

Our home away from home. Pictures, plants, drapes, (our) books, comfortable sofa, and Johanna's knitting bag. Plus three meals a day in the ship's restaurant. Sometimes it felt like paradise!

she could carry. Once all was up, the first sailor (who turned out to be the bosun—the deck crew foreman), took us to the ship's office where the captain welcomed us and instructed the ship's steward, Ariel, a skinny young man with the face of a teenager, to show us to our cabin and fetch our luggage. We climbed up four more sets of stairs, this time on the inside of the superstructure, which had the feel of a hotel. Then we reached our cabin, and while Ariel brought the rest of our luggage, we inspected what would be our home away from home for more than two months of the journey ahead. What a feeling! We were on a ship—our ship—sailing around the globe with our own large cabin. The months of planning and fretting had come to an end and we were finally here. It was almost unbelievable.

The results of our cabin inspection pleased us. In the living room were one three-seater couch and a two-seater at right angles; one easy chair; a coffee table in the centre of the room and a side table between the two couches; overhead lights and a table lamp; a wall-length credenza with drawers; and a writing desk opposite the two-seater, also with a table lamp. A key lying on the desk fit the cabin door. Left of the door was a small fridge and various cupboards. Across from them was the outside wall with two portholes, held closed with four strong clamps that smoothly unscrewed for letting in fresh air. There were even some pictures on the walls. It all added up to a neat and comfortable living room with furniture that looked new.

In the bedroom we found a queen-sized bed, the headboard hinged to reveal a handy storage area; lots of closet and drawer space; a bed-length neon reading light; and a porthole that could also be opened easily. The bathroom included a sink, shower, toilet, and a small cabinet for cosmetics and other toiletries. But this was a ship, not a hotel, and ships can be dangerous places. To get into the shower, and when walking between the bathroom and bedroom, we would need to step over tiled ridges at least fifteen centimetres high, designed to stop water from escaping into the rest of the cabin when the ship bobbed and weaved. In the living room we spotted hooks in the walls close to the floor, and bungee cords tied to them, clearly used for wrapping around furniture in big storms. A diagram and instructions were mounted on the wall explaining how to put on life jackets stored in one of the drawers. On the desk was a folder with passenger information that included safety tips.

The suitcases arrived one by one, delivered by the steward whose smile became more painful with each arrival. He was a slight young man, but the heavy suitcases and boxes didn't erase his goodwill. We unpacked as we always pack and unpack, with the rituals of a long marriage: a bit of bickering, a lot of compromise, a final place for everything and everything in its place, including an improvised bookshelf on the side table, and at the end, smiles towards one another. We were ready to go even if the rest of the ship wasn't, judging by the frequent shuddering as yet another container was wedged in place.

It was time to explore more of the ship, although we realized we had better stay away from wherever work was going on. We had seen how busy the deck at the top of the gangway was, with people loading and unloading cargo. We first walked the length of the hallway on our level, which a sign told us was the "fifth deck." It had doors to small outside decks on both sides, and an inside set of stairs. We climbed up those to a similar hallway one floor up, where nameplates on closed cabin doors told us that the captain and the chief engineer resided there. This floor also contained the captain's office, which had a red mailbox on its outside wall next to the door. The captain himself came out of his office. We apologized, afraid that maybe we shouldn't have been there, but he didn't seem to mind, and even asked, "Would you like to see the bridge?" He took us up one more set of stairs to that magic place where captains get tied to the wheel during fierce storms. (This otherwise functional wheel would have been far too small, no bigger than the ones you find in cars.) He then left us there, saying "Take your time," and didn't even warn us not to touch anything. We looked at all the instruments, dials, and signs, as well as at the busy harbour full of working ships and pleasure boats, the city up the river to the east, and with great interest at the processes of loading and unloading containers, which we could now clearly see from above.

After that we explored the rest of the ship's "hotel," (officially called the "superstructure"), always helped by door and hall signs. It all looked clean and well cared for. On our floor were two more officer cabins, one more passenger cabin, and a lounge that was locked. One floor down were crew cabins, another passenger cabin, and one that had "Owner's Cabin" written on the door. On the next level down we found more crew cabins, plus a recreation area with an indoor swimming pool, a rowing machine, a stationary bike, a dartboard, and a ping-pong table. On the next floor down were a set of smaller cabins and a locked crew lounge. Below that were two dining rooms, one marked "Officers" and the other "Crew," with the kitchen ("galley") in the middle, plus a well-equipped laundry room at the end of the hall. The working deck level was below this floor, containing the general ship's office and also a four-person room (with two sets of bunk beds) with a sign reading "Suez Canal" over the door—most intriguing. Despite the many floors there was no elevator.

During our tour of the ship, I opened the officer's dining room door and stuck my nose inside, hoping for some coffee, but I quickly closed it again when I spotted the captain at a table in deep conversation with a group of well-dressed men. We then climbed back up to have a snooze in our cabin, for in our excitement neither of us had slept well the night before.

Later that afternoon we heard a knock on our door and met a Dutch journalist who had joined the ship in Hong Kong after spending some weeks in Vietnam. She had visited the centre of Hamburg and would leave us in Rotterdam, two ports hence. Over a drink in her cabin, she gave us a lot of information about the ship and its crew, and about her experiences as a passenger. Her advice included tips on the ship's etiquette, for instance, when not to be on the bridge and when not to engage officers and crew in conversation. She took us to the dining room for the evening meal of tasty boiled smoked fish and vegetables, dessert, and coffee. We met some more officers, who came in, inhaled their meal, and disappeared again. Port time is stressful for all officers, and Hamburg was the home port for this ship, an extra burden. The men in suits with the captain were head office honchos, so we found out later, presumably informing, inspecting, correcting, and directing. It struck us that all of the officers were casually dressed, including the captain. No one wore anything that looked like a mariner's uniform, simply casual pants and a shirt.

At dinner the captain told us that we would likely leave Hamburg by 2300 hours, and that it would take at least seven hours' slow sailing on the River Elbe to reach the North Sea. He mentioned that the weather ahead wasn't all that good—"for passengers," he added with a teasing smile. By the time Hamburg let the ship go, I was fast asleep. I had tried to stay awake to experience the excitement of our first departure, but couldn't keep my eyes open. Even the constant thundering of containers being wedged into their spaces couldn't keep me awake. There were too many impressions, too much excitement, and it had been too long a day—and both of us are early to bed at the best of times. However, Johanna got up when she sensed that we were departing, went outside, and, while leaning up against a railing, watched the proceedings. When we woke up at daybreak, we were just leaving the River Elbe and entering the North Sea, the sky dark over woolly waters that would carry our ship to England. Our adventure had truly begun.

Over dinner, our fellow passenger had told us a bit about port procedures. She warned us against trying to see too much, as shore time goes by quickly, and cautioned us not to drink anything not in a can or a bottle. Her various pieces of advice about the pleasures and risks of shore visits helped us navigate our subsequent shore leaves.

I would have liked to see more of Hamburg. From the ship's railing it looked only about five kilometres away upriver, a medium-sized important city with many office towers, but none extravagantly high. At least two tall and sharp church steeples were wedged between the office towers, somehow challenging them. Hamburg is an old European city that looked to us to be prosperous and interesting, but most of what we saw was new.

Hamburg's old buildings had been destroyed by heavy and repeated Allied bombing during World War II, with tens of thousands of civilian casualties and an infamous firestorm that destroyed a large part of the city. In the years 1943-45, I lived in Groningen, a Dutch city below the flight path between England and the whole North German coastal area where important naval ports, like Bremen, Kiel, Lubeck, and Hamburg, were located. Many nights during that time I awoke to the drone of bombers on their way to these important military targets. One early spring morning in 1945, when I was ten years old, the bright sky above filled up with what seemed like hundreds of bombers flying east, and in our streets the city sirens wailed full blast to get everyone inside. Young as I was, I knew these planes were flying towards the River Elbe area, where our ship was now docked. I was afraid back then, but I also rejoiced, for Germany was the occupier of our country and the enemy. The horror of it all only became apparent to me long after the war was over. The Allied air forces had engaged in retaliatory bombing of German cities in response to the bombings of London, and especially Coventry, that had occurred earlier on in the war. Indeed, Johanna vividly remembers her personal bombing experience. She was only five years old and living in Rotterdam when the German war machine invaded Holland on May 10, 1940. Following the bombing of Warsaw in the fall of 1939 that brought Poland to its knees, the Germans also used this tactic towards Holland by destroying much of central Rotterdam. Johanna remembers how for days small bits of scorched paper descended on the city like dirty snow in winter. Both Johanna and I still get frightened when we hear the first sounds of a propeller plane at night, and this more than sixty years after our childhood experiences.

For Hamburg, a strategic city in Northern Germany with a population of well over one million, the worst came during nine consecutive nights beginning on July 24, 1943. More than 3,000 aircraft dropped about 9,000 tons of bombs, destroyed about 250,000 homes, and killed more than 40,000 people. The now infamous firestorm bombing of this city took place on the night of July 27. The combination of incendiary bombs falling close together and the hot and dry summer weather caused a three-hour firestorm that killed all within its range. Those who had not been killed outright by bombs or burned in the fires choked to death as the fires sucked all the oxygen out of parts of the city. Most of the survivors left the city right after that night. Regular bombing of Hamburg, day and night, continued until the end of the war, though never on that same scale again.

After the war, the British, who had done most of the bombing, became instrumental in rebuilding the city. The Hamburgers themselves undertook reconstruction with remarkable energy and will, symbolized by the first concert given by Hamburg's Philharmonic Orchestra on July 1, 1945, less than two months after the war had ended. In October 1945, elementary and secondary schools reopened and on November 6, the local university began its lectures once again.

I was also conscious that the horrors of that last pan-European war, so pointedly illustrated by what happened to Hamburg, were a major impetus for the formation of the European Union (EU). The Benelux, already conceived in 1944 by governments in exile as an economic union between three small countries (Belgium, the Netherlands, and Luxembourg) and implemented in 1947, had gradually expanded to take in more and more European countries, not only for economic gain but also for political tranquility. Looking out at Hamburg from our ship, it now seemed inconceivable that such a war could ever happen again. No immigration or customs officers stopped us when we drove from my brother's place in Holland to the ship. With the advent of the EU, it was as if national borders were actually disappearing altogether. The brightly lit and prosperous-looking renewed old city of Hamburg was a reminder of both the miracle of Germany's recovery after the war and Europe's sanity after a lengthy madness.

Being this close to Hamburg brought other memories back to me. In high school, I had to memorize a list of about fifteen Dutch Hanseatic towns, all of them located along major rivers accessible from the North Sea, or on the coast of what was then called the Zuider Zee, a bay in the North Sea around which much of Holland was nestled. (It's now a much smaller sweet-water lake surrounded by three large agricultural areas safe behind a huge dike built across its northern edge in 1932.) My youngest brother Bert lives in Harderwijk, one of the towns on that list, and he and I have walked along its small harbour, now only suitable for pleasure craft, with few reminders that this was once a major import and export centre. Hanseatic towns were part of the Hanseatic League of which Hamburg had been a major anchor for about three centuries, around CE 1300-1600. The term "hanseatic" is derived from the old German word *hanza* (now *hanse*), meaning "trade due" and also "trade permission." *Hanse* also came to be used for any merchant's regiment, a sort of militia.

The Hanseatic League was a vital part of the early development of Northern Europe, but it was the Vikings who first engaged in large-scale trade in these waters. Towards the end of the first millennium, sailing out of what we now call Scandinavia, Vikings began to maraud far and wide, reaching as far west as Newfoundland. At first, they simply rowed and sailed their seaworthy long and narrow boats with their characteristic high prows in order to separate settlements from their silver and gold and other treasures, especially those settlements with churches and monasteries where those items were often found in abundance. Sometimes the Vikings came for food as well: grains, cattle, and animal products like wool. However, while the Vikings brought fear, destruction, and often death, they also brought something else that would spur subsequent developments: a demonstration that it was possible to travel the always cold and often stormy seas that surrounded all those lands and the rivers that flowed into them. The Vikings certainly travelled for the purpose of looting, but they also used ships to engage in more legitimate trade.

As communities grew in Northern Europe, itinerant peddlers decided that setting up a more or less permanent shop was a smart thing to do. Merchants began to enlarge village populations. River traffic increased, as boats were so much easier and more efficient to travel in than carts. Often villages were built along rivers anyway, for protection, as well as drinking water. Some villages became towns, large enough that the inhabitants began thinking about setting up formal local law and order. The growing number of merchants, for instance, clamoured for uniform weights, trustworthy coinage, a fair taxation system, and protection of their own enterprises against raids. Walls were built around these settlements, and a system of government established, usually featuring businessmen in prominent roles. The Church, ever on the lookout for new converts, began to take an interest in these towns and villages as well.

Hamburg arose out of the amalgamation of two neighbouring villages along the River Elbe around CE 1200. Not long after, it had a bishop and a city government. Traders from what are now Poland, Russia, Germany, and Scandinavia imported grains, furs, salt, lumber, cattle, and wax into Hamburg, some for local consumption and some for trading with communities in England and what are now Belgium and France. Other cities were also established along the coasts of the North and Baltic seas, as well as up various rivers that drained into those seas. All of these cities were helped by the development of a far more efficient ship: the *kogge*. It differed from the Viking craft in a number of ways. It had a blunt and more rounded prow, and a fairly low draft that enabled it to navigate rivers, but with a far broader keel. It also had sails that could be pointed in different directions. This all added up to a cargo vessel that could hold more freight and passengers, and could even sail (tack) against the wind with a load of about fifty tons. With these ships trade grew rapidly between ports from Scandinavia to England and down the Western European coast, covering much of where the Vikings had gone before.

Just as individual merchants in a certain town wanted a system of law and order to regulate their profession, so increasingly the need was felt to have a broader system of law and order that would protect merchants wherever they went. The Hanseatic League, begun as a series of covenants between merchants in Northern Germany in the mid-fourteenth century, eventually became a series of covenants between cities large and small all along the coasts of the Baltic and North seas, as well as along major rivers. For about three centuries, the many covenants regulated weights and measures, coinage, credit, protection, privileges, import and export quotas, and all kinds of other conditions. Participants included towns from Germany, Holland, Belgium, England, Poland, and Sweden, more than two hundred in total. The league was also remarkable in that the covenants and treaties initially involved not national governments, but groups of businessmen, and then individual towns and cities, many of which were mercantile, meaning that they operated as if they were a business.

Hamburg played a major role in the league. Located on the banks of the mighty River Elbe, the harbour was deep and wide enough even for large ships like the *Ville d'Aquarius* to come in from the sea, and also suitable for large riverboats to travel all the way from the Czech Republic far to the southeast. On its way, the Elbe sucks up the waters of many smaller rivers, each one a long finger reaching into other parts of the country. Moreover,

Hamburg's inland harbour is well protected from seashore flooding and strong storm waves. Should any enemies approach from the sea, they would be exposed to attacks from both sides of the river well before they reached the city.

Given those broad historical strokes, it's easy to see that the hustle and bustle of international trade that we experienced on our trips goes back a long time. Of course, trains, trucks, and planes have been added as transportation options since back then, but doing business is still initiated by energetic and initiative-taking merchants, and regulated by forever-expanding legislation and covenants. Everything is much larger and much more complicated now, but in essence the Hanseatic League was a forerunner of the global economy of which Hamburg is such a vital component even now, and within which the *Ville d'Aquarius* plays its impressive role.

The captain had been right: the North Sea was full of strong winds and high waves the day we entered it. And I had been wrong: A ship this size *is* affected by rough seas. While we slept, we hadn't been aware of anything but a smooth river glide, but now the ship began to move in various directions all at once, and not in regular patterns. We had to be careful while walking and were grateful for railings along the stairs and in the hallways, and for sailors, officers, and crew, who would warn us when they saw us doing

The North Sea on our first day out—our storm-at-sea baptism. The white tops indicate strong waves. Notice the ship listing to the right and the wild clouds above.

something risky. By the end of the first day we had also learned that we had muscles in our feet, for they ached. Because I had experienced some sea-sickness on my only previous sea voyage, in 1954 on a small emigrant ship from Rotterdam to Halifax, I was a bit apprehensive. We had taken along a quantity of Gravol pills and I had also come across a bracelet that, loaded with batteries and placed on a strategic spot on the wrist, was guaranteed to combat seasickness in some mysterious way, although I decided not to try it yet. Fortunately, it turned out that I never needed it.

That first day, we donned our winter jackets and made our way to an outside deck, where we carefully walked around while watching the sky and water with our hands firmly attached to the deck railings, testing our stom-achs against the sea. The sea moved gray and black and wild and woolly, with the ship, now our ship, cutting through the waves with the unique musical swish that would become part of the soundtrack of the coming two months. While walking on the working deck, we heard the containers screeching, groaning, and moaning against one another and the steel bars that held them as the ship rolled from side to side. Fortunately, neither of us felt overly queasy. In fact, we loved overlooking this turmoil, especially from the railing in front of the wheelhouse, with only niggles of apprehension in the back of our heads. We had seen enough movies and read enough books about the sea to understand the explosive power of large bodies of water.

After leaving the Elbe, the ship turned west, carefully skirting a number of islands strung out along the German and Dutch coasts. In my youth I had visited two of those islands, Vlieland and Terschelling. I remembered reading a novel called *Sil de Strandjutter*, the story of a beachcomber's fam-ily on Terschelling. In the book every storm would raise the family's hopes that valuable goods would float ashore. Those islands have produced plenty of folklore about pirates, shipwrecks, and heroic islanders who risked their lives to rescue sailors of sinking merchant vessels with their own small life-boats, but who then also appropriated any cargo that drifted to the island. The islanders thus outwitted government agents intent on enforcing cargo ownership laws and customs duties, major sources of government income before income tax was invented in the early twentieth century.

It took half a day to get free of that string of islands so that the ship could swing to a southwesterly direction, heading for Thamesport on the Isle of Grain in England. The trip would take the rest of the day. The North Sea is a tricky body of water with choppy waves and challenging winds. We experienced wind force seven-eight through this leg, involving winds

This is how I saw Second Officer Gottfried many times: alert to any danger that might confront the ship, such as other freighters, fishing boats, and debris floating in the sea.

of about thirty to thirty-seven knots (55-70 km/hour), and foamy waves three to five metres high. Our first experience with stormy weather gave us confidence that we wouldn't suffer with seasickness on this large ship, unless wind speeds increased significantly. Mind you, we were careful to eat enough at mealtimes and snack in between, heeding the advice to always have something in your stomach but not overload it. In addition, knowing that reading in cars and buses upsets my stomach, I figured that a ship in a storm would have the same effect, so I didn't read in rough weather.

Clearly the main task for this day was to find our way, not only around the ship but also with respect to the routines on board. At 10 AM we had coffee, which was waiting for us with an open tin of cookies on the passenger table. Lunch was at noon, dinner at 1800 hours (ships run on a twenty-four-hour clock). Feeding times are firmly set on ships, each meal deserving one hour and no more. On this ship, the passengers ate together at one table and were served by the young steward Ariel. He also served the officers at other tables. He seemed shy and uncertain at first, and some time later we discovered that this was his first trip and he was busy learning his job. We could see that he wanted to do well, and as we were never in a rush like the officers, who would enter in a hurry, quickly eat, and get out again, we tried to make his life as pleasant as we could.

After lunch and a short sleep, I hesitantly made my way to the bridge, hoping I would be welcome there. To my relief, I was warmly greeted by Gottfried Donnerhak, the second officer, the only officer on the bridge. He wasn't "steering" the ship at all; the automatic pilot was taking care of things. All he had to do was keep an eye out for anything that might endanger the ship. Every few minutes he would grab his binoculars and survey all that was in front of him. When I asked questions he answered, in accented but perfectly adequate English, and he offered me a cup of coffee and encouraged me to stay as long as I wanted. This first visit set a pattern for many days following. Gottfried's watch began at noon and lasted four hours, and almost every afternoon I would visit him for awhile. He taught me how to monitor the two big radar screens and explained the importance of various dials and gadgets on the bridge. He also showed me the charts on a large desk at the back of the bridge. Sometimes after his shift ended he would join us in our cabin for a drink before dinner.

Gottfried talked not only about the ship and his sailing career, but also about politics, his family, the state of the universe, the changing nature of merchant shipping, and whatever other topics we both found interesting.

Gottfried was born in 1946 far away from the sea, near Leipzig. He still lived in former East German territory and was married. (We would meet his wife in Malta on our return trip.) After receiving proper training, he joined the East German merchant marine and gradually worked his way up to his present position. He told us how strictly controlled life had been for East German sailors when the Communists were in power. When they were in foreign ports, they weren't allowed to fraternize with sailors from other countries, and especially not with West German colleagues. Gottfried had welcomed the demise of the East German Communist regime and subsequent German reunification, but he was worried about the future of young people in that part of Germany. His own young adult son had trouble finding work, and if the problems of that generation weren't solved, Gottfried predicted serious social unrest. He wasn't overly tall, but his body exuded inner strength and his face was kind. Of all the German officers, he fraternized the most with the Filipino sailors on board.

Towards the evening dinner hour that first day, Johanna and I drifted into the lounge on our floor. We noticed it had a well-stocked bar with a price list for drinks (in US dollars), and sheets of paper on which to log consumptions. The invitation seemed clear: Choose your poison and be honest about recording it. The Dutch journalist joined us and confirmed our conclusions. She told us that we would be billed for consumptions once a month and would have to pay in cash, in US dollars. At dinner we were told that we would arrive in Thamesport in early morning, that loading and unloading would begin shortly after arrival, and that there wouldn't be enough time to visit anything onshore. This day, too, had made us tired, and soon after we went to sleep, well satisfied with our first full day at sea.

When we woke up early the next day in Thamesport, we soon discovered that we would be further delayed, perhaps for most of the day. The storm we had encountered had been even fiercer here and further south, and all along the coast container loading and unloading had been suspended. Loaded containers may weigh thirty-five tons, but while they hang in the air they're easily caught by winds, becoming hard to maneuver and properly place. Cargo handling had been suspended the previous night and would only resume if the winds died down sufficiently. That didn't bother us, of course, as it gave us time for some sightseeing after all. Unfortunately, we were far away from London, still close to the sea where the Medway and Thames rivers meet in a new container port that was clearly still under construction. There were no trains or buses close by to take us places, just a small village beyond the port gates, and as it was Sunday, it meant all would be quiet.

The morning became more interesting when a new passenger came on board. Daryl Curtis would stay with us for the rest of the voyage, and in the large "Owner's Cabin," if you please! Next, all passengers received an invitation from the captain to come to *kirche* at 11 AM in the officer's lounge. A welcoming smile accompanied the invitation.

Kirche is German for church and we wondered if we had been invited to a Christian worship service. But on entering the lounge just before 11 AM, we were quickly set straight—the officers and passengers had gathered for a party. With the captain behind the bar pouring beer from a keg and snacks on the counter, conversation flowed easily. Initially, we three new passengers were a bit shy and merely listened as officers bantered, mostly in German, but we soon joined in the cheerful conversation. A new face was present as well, belonging to a tall man in a suit, who turned out to be the local company agent. No one asked for money or made entries in the consumption log. We were the captain's guests, and apparently this was a weekly event.

At the party, Daryl shared news of the effects of the storms still howling outside, of damage and floods in some parts of England. This was Daryl's seventh trip of this kind, she came to tell us over time. I guessed that Daryl was in her late forties. Though very pleasant, she had known tragedy in her life. She had been engaged to an Israeli man who was killed a week before they were to be married. Though it had happened some time ago, she shared her still remaining grief with Johanna. She had had a successful career with the BBC and was still involved as a freelancer. Daryl's parents were successful British retailers who had retired to Florida, and she had one sister with whom she had good contact. Over the course of our voyage she would become a close friend, inviting us to her cabin and generously sharing drinks and whatever snacks she had purchased during port visits, where shopping was one of her priorities. She had also brought a supply of CDs, jazz and classical, which she parked in the lounge so we could use them any time we wanted to. After dinner I often played a two-handed bridge game with her. The three of us always planned our shore visits together and shared cab fares and other expenses. She now lives in Brighton, England, and occasionally e-mails us pictures of her three beautiful Cavalier King Charles Spaniels.

At *kirche* we learned that loading would resume after lunch, as the wind had died down considerably, and that the estimated time of departure (ETD) had been set for early evening. The British local company agent suggested we meet him at the nearest pub in the small village just beyond the port gates, about a twenty-minute walk. He would go there by car. The ship's four passengers left together and discovered that the old village of Thamesport was small indeed, one centre street with a small, and locked, Anglican Church at the end. Halfway down the main street were two small side streets at right angles. There were two pubs, and we found the right one. It was an entirely typical English pub with old bare wooden ceiling beams, a fireplace big enough to hold a table and four chairs, wood darkened by centuries of smoking, and a jovial publican and locals enjoying their Sunday outing. The agent's expense account paid for all our drinks, including his favourite single malt scotch, Laphroaig, for which he demonstrated proper etiquette: two parts scotch, one part room temperature water, slowly sipped. It had a wonderful peaty taste and aroma.

According to the agent, the old Anglican Church in the village had been the location for occasional trysts between the widowed Queen Victoria and her coachman, Mr. Brown, and the whole village had known about it. I had to ask myself if this agent was one of those master storytellers who never lets facts interfere with a good tale. He told us he had an offer to be an agent in Shanghai at more than 100,000 pounds a year, but that he actually wanted to quit his job and own this very pub (his wife wouldn't let him). We encouraged him to keep telling tales, and he responded with the story of a container half-filled with Brazilian beef and half with Brazilian oranges, separated by a hastily built wooden bulkhead. During a vicious storm the bulkhead had collapsed, and oranges and beef had mingled freely. After the incident, he had warned his mother not to buy Brazilian beef in the coming weeks, but when he visited her she proudly told him that with her weekly purchase of the usual roast she had received a dozen oranges free of charge.

On the walk back to the ship from the pub I got caught in a vicious hailstorm and was soaked to the skin. Johanna had been wiser in accepting a ride back from the agent. At dinner we met a Dutch pilot who had already come aboard to guide the ship all the way across the English Channel, a common practice in view of the tricky and busy crossing, one of the busiest seaways in the world. When we left Thamesport for Rotterdam that evening we were well behind schedule.

The Channel is shaped like a funnel from north to south, and when the prevailing northwest winds are hard and insistent, its waters are pushed towards its narrow end at the bottom. On January 31, 1953, about a year before I left for Canada, the combination of high tides and a fierce west-northwest storm drove so much water towards that narrow end that the sides of it burst under the pressure. Sea water gushed inland in England and Holland. Hundreds of dikes broke in the south of Holland, and about 1,800 people were killed. Others clung to bone-chilling roofs for up to twenty-four hours before being rescued. Johanna was already in Canada at that time, but I still remember radio news broadcasts filled with messages of fresh disasters, and newspaper photographs of Dutch Queen Juliana comforting people in the stricken areas.

We had been told that we would arrive in Rotterdam in the early morning, and would have most of the day available for sightseeing. However, well short of the port the ship stopped and drifted. It had to wait for a berth to become available. We had hoped to visit Rotterdam, where Johanna had been born and raised, and perhaps even see one of her aunts, but that proved impossible. The delay ate into daylight, and as the brand new container port is built right at sea, some eighty kilometres from the centre of Rotterdam,

Johanna is smiling, for the ship is fast approaching Rotterdam, the city of her birth.

a visit to the city was impossible. In fact, Europort had been wrested from the North Sea in typical Dutch polder fashion, with a strong dike anchored in the water some distance out, and behind it the land pumped dry. Gaining land from the sea is a long-standing Dutch tradition, and for years now this small country with sixteen million people has contemplated building a new airport in the sea as well. It may still happen.

With Rotterdam out as a day-trip destination, and with only about four hours to spare for a shore visit, our attention turned to Den Briel, a small city just south of the port with a history known by every Dutch school child. More than four centuries ago, on April 1, 1572, a gang of sea pirates, called *geuzen*, decided to visit the city for ship repairs and refitting, and once there they decided to stay awhile. Staying there meant defying the Spanish troops that roamed through the country chasing Dutch soldiers and leaders who were trying to get rid of their ruler, Spain's Philip II. Philip had inherited the territory that is now Belgium and the Netherlands from his father Charles V (the sixteenth-century emperor of the Holy Roman Empire, which, as Voltaire would later observe, was neither holy, nor Roman, nor an empire). Moreover, these sea brigands were known to be especially greedy for Spanish galleons loaded with silver and gold from the Americas. To the surprise of everybody, the Spaniards couldn't dislodge the sea bandits from Den Briel, which arose out of land criss-crossed with ditches and canals that provided a formidable barrier against land-based attacks. Any victory over Spanish troops had been so rare up to that point in what came to be called the Eighty-year War (1568–1648), that it turned these *geuzen* into instant patriots, however nonpatriotic and self-serving their initial decision to berth at this port might have been. To this day, Den Briel and the *geuzen* are honoured in popular old songs and by inclusion in the country's elementary school curriculum and folklore. It would be a treat for Johanna and me to walk its streets.

We had lost our Dutch journalist passenger, but walked to the port gate after lunch with Daryl, where the guard phoned for a taxi. Port gatekeepers were invariably kind and adept at getting cabs for sailors and passengers. Our cab driver offered to pick us up after our town visit at a specified time and place, and we spent three hours wandering the narrow crooked streets of Den Briel, looking at well-preserved old buildings. Den Briel's main street was still the principal shopping area of the city and the surrounding area, with stores at street level and apartments above them. Some larger old homes on the street had clearly belonged to important people: a mayor, banker, doctor, perhaps a merchant ship owner. I looked for (and found) a typical old Dutch house feature: a large hook just below the top of the gable, handy for blocking and tackling furniture up and down. The city also had a canal running right through it, with a street and houses on either side and pleasure craft, as well as some houseboats, in the water.

We enjoyed tea with fresh pastries in a deli-bakery and visited Den Briel's museum, which was mostly dedicated to the 1572 event. Den Briel had been a seaport then, but shifting soil and the Dutch skill at wrestling land from the sea made its small harbour only a haven for pleasure boats now. We returned to the ship in time for a dinner of roast duck and roast potatoes. The ship left Rotterdam's Europort that evening, and encountered more stormy weather during the night.

The following day was also filled with rain squalls and wind gusts, but we were getting used to these conditions. We sailed southwest along the coast of Holland and Belgium, right through the narrowest part of the English Channel where both coasts are clearly visible. As we travelled this route, I remembered stories of the Armada, and that grand struggle for ultimate power in Europe between Spain's King Phillip II and England's Queen Elizabeth I. In 1588, 130 warships set out from Lisbon to defeat the English fleet and land an army on England's shores. Storms in the English Channel, British sea smarts (helped by Dutch ships), and Spanish incompetence wrecked this bold venture. Afterwards, Dutch and English churches were full of Protestants giving thanks for this delivery from the Catholic threat to true and free religion.

In the early seventeenth century, this stretch of water also became the arena for sea battles between Holland and England. The wars had been one of the ten history questions asked of me when as an eleven-year-old I sat the academic high school entrance exams in the late spring of 1946. I remember the question was something like, "List and describe the four naval wars with England in the seventeenth century." At that moment I hadn't grasped the notion that the seventeenth century meant the years beginning with "16." I knew that our country and England had not fought naval wars in any years beginning with "17." Not knowing what else to do, I finally wrote down the details of the four wars I knew, and found out afterwards that my answers, offered in desperation, had been right. In the sixteenth century, Holland had been the dominant sea power of Western Europe, even though its population was much smaller than that of England. However, growing English naval power and its larger population made a clash between these

31

two countries inevitable. As we passed the northern coast of France, I also thought of the landing of Canadian soldiers on the beaches of Dieppe in 1942, a military disaster in itself, but a valuable lesson for the successful Normandy invasion on June 6, 1944.

We arrived at Le Havre, France, in the evening, the harbour just a short distance up the River Seine, but were told we couldn't get off the ship as the stay would be short and we'd sail as soon as unloading and loading were finished. All we could do was behold the lighted city from some distance away and watch the River Seine traffic. Fortunately, we would also stop here on our way back. Perhaps we would have better luck then. When we found ourselves already well underway at breakfast the next morning, we also discovered that we had a new first officer on board. The former one had left for home after four months on the ship, and Martin, the new one, had come in from Germany to take his place. We discovered that this was part of life on board: Crew members and officers come and go as their stints begin and end. Also at breakfast, we were told that another passenger would join us, but he hadn't shown up.

While we had enjoyed ourselves during the first few days of the trip, the experience hadn't felt much like the sea voyage we had looked for. We had spent more time in port than on the ocean, and when we had been at sea the waves had been active enough to restrict our on-deck activities. Moreover, the many impressions coming at us hadn't given us a handle on life on board. Most human beings look for predictable patterns in their lives—routines, schedules, and rhythms of body and soul. At least the routine of mealtimes had become well established. The food proved to be solid but not spectacular fare. For lunch and dinner we had had chicken curry, tortellini, stir fries, various soups, some stews, a lamb dish, steak and fries, and pork chops. For breakfast it was eggs in a variety of presentations, rice puddings with fruit, pancakes, and one most interesting, and to us entirely new, experience: strammermax. It consisted of a slice of dark rye bread on which were piled a slice of ham, a slice of cheese, a fried egg, and a slice of tomato. It tasted fine, but the bread took some chewing and the whole of it wasn't digested that quickly; by coffee break we still felt full. Reflecting on what we had consumed thus far, however, we felt confident that we didn't have to give quality and quantity of food any further thought.

We had seen the sailors at work on arrival and at departure, but we didn't know much about their on-board lives yet. What were they doing while we were underway on longer stretches? Did they sleep or play cards? Who worked in the engine room and what were they doing? What was life on board really like? How did officers and crew get along? Was there a culture gap between the Germans and the Filipinos?

As for ourselves, we began to long for some predictability. I was missing my usual steady diet of exercise and wondered how I could be active unless the sea was calm and I could at least walk around the working deck for longer than a watchful single circuit. I enjoy playing ping-pong, but the sailors had been too busy thus far, and I wasn't sure if they wanted passengers to muscle in on their free time. Even my reading had been sporadic because of the wild seas, and I had brought some interesting books that would need lengthy concentration. Would we ever be able to sit on deck in lounge chairs with the sun beating down on our winter-pale bodies? Even the swimming pool remained empty thus far, for had it been filled with water it would have drowned even the ceiling above it because of the rough seas. I didn't care about the pool, since I don't like swimming, but Johanna loved it. But we knew we had longer stretches ahead, and hoped for calmer seas. The itinerary posted on a bulletin board on the bridge told us that the next destination would be Malta, well into the Mediterranean and three days' sailing away. Perhaps conditions would change enough to allow us to establish daily routines and find the answers to our questions.

From Le Havre we sailed southwest, still in the Channel (or La Manche), north of the Normandy beaches and specifically Sainte-Mere-Eglise, which is mentioned in all the accounts of D-Day I have ever read. Its closeness to the beaches, its important bridge over a canal, and the church steeple as a vantage point from which to see inland made it a vital early conquest.

We sailed past the Channel Islands of Guernsey and Jersey, and then around Normandy and Bretagne. The charts on the bridge were detailed and helpful for locating these famous areas as we sailed by. After rounding the northwestern tip of France, the ship aimed straight for Cape Finisterre in northern Spain, in a south-southwest direction.

The Bay of Biscay in the North Atlantic was waiting for us, marshalling forces of wind and waves that we would never forget. The officers told me that this was almost always a rough stretch (they actually used a much more salty vocabulary). On the day we traversed the bay we experienced wind force nine, plus big swells coming out of the Atlantic—a common occurrence here, especially in winter. On the bridge I watched the ship's tortured progress through the turmoil. We passed a container vessel, drifting with engine troubles though not in danger, so the second officer told me, or else it would have called the *Ville d'Aquarius* for assistance. If it had called, our ship would have stopped to lend a hand; this is not only the law of the sea, but the *Ville d'Aquarius* is part of AMVER (the Automated Mutual Assistance Vessel Rescue System). I wouldn't have liked to be on that other vessel, for it bucked even more than our much larger ship. Our captain, now present on the bridge as well, told me that not long ago a ship had lost twenty containers in these waters, and another ship had simply broken in two, although no lives were lost. As we heard the groaning and clanking of our own containers on board, we had occasional moments of fear.

In storms like these the ocean is a sight to behold. Swells come from one direction, while the wind pushes waves from another. Wind and water hit the ship in various combinations, and sometimes the forces on the ship hold it in shuddering suspense for a moment, seemingly riding the water until the whole mass of it plunges down into a trough. It's amazing how deep the troughs between the waves can be, and how high the walls of water rise above the troughs. You don't really see that from the upper decks, but when you stand below and close to the water, it's a wild sight. At wind force nine, the tops of the crests are white, and from each crest a mat of white spray spreads out in the direction of the wind—the harder the wind, the more far-reaching the spray. Deep into the trough, the water is black, and up from the deep it becomes dark blue. As it mixes with the air, the colour of the water changes to a lighter blue, and then to various shades of green. On top, the water is white, and in high winds the surface of the sea in all directions looks like a black-gray undulating meadow with thousands of white horses galloping through it.

A high wind may not be a problem in itself, other than perhaps slowing a ship down when it sails straight into it, but high winds cause dangerous swells and waves. Waves are the hills and troughs of water you see and feel when strong winds are blowing around a ship. Swells are often long slow waves that hit a ship even when no strong wind may be around. They're usually the remains of earlier storms, often hundreds or even thousands of kilometres away, an armada of mini-tsunamis. Depending on their direction, they make a ship roll (bob from side to side) or pitch (bob up and down lengthwise). Of course, swells and waves seldom hit a ship at perfect right angles or head-on or from behind. They almost always come in at various angles.

That wind-force-nine day we experienced on the *Ville d'Aquarius* illustrated just how complex the interaction between wind, water, sea, and ship can be. On this day, big swells rolled in from the Atlantic Ocean, pushing us northeast, back towards the part of France we had left. Apparently, there had been a big storm further south in the Atlantic Ocean some days before. The strong winds from the northwest created six- to seven-metre waves that pushed us towards southern France. The *Ville d'Aquarius* had plenty of containers on board, its deck almost full and some rows stacked five high, reaching up to forty feet in the air. The wall of containers that stretched the full length of the giant ship acted like a huge sail buffeted by erratic and gusting high winds, while the large swells and giant waves pushed us towards the coast of France in two different directions.

I stood on the bridge watching the forward part of the ship dipping deep into the water, huge sprays washing over the bow. As it came up, it seemed as if the ship was being slowly wrung out like a big wet cloth, bending differently in different places, the front of it not quite doing what the back of it was busy with. The chief engineer happened to be on the bridge, so I had a chance to ask him how a ship can survive such a battering. He told me that it had been constructed with sufficient flexibility to bend with and adjust to the various forces acting upon it. A rigidly constructed ship would snap. I knew what he meant, at least in principle. Airplane wings are also flexible, as I had observed many times before while flying; sometimes they even seem to flap like the wings of a bird. I knew they were constructed to flex, or else they too would snap. Despite knowing this, it was frightening to see the ship twist and turn in heavy seas, and feel in my bones and muscles the ship shuddering under me. We were constantly cautioned about the power of the sea and wind and so didn't walk the decks that day, but even in much milder weather we learned to walk the decks defensively, expecting sudden movements, constantly prepared to steady ourselves against a wall, a railing, a door, or a piece of equipment. It's called "developing sea legs." You develop strong foot muscles at sea because of the constant adjusting that your leg and foot muscles are engaged in.

The sea is a restless play of water and wind, colours and sprays. Even calm seas provide a spectacle, especially underneath a partly overcast sky, where clouds and sun combine to create patterns of gray in the distance that become green and blue close up. Many times I saw faraway blankets of clouds from which sheets of rain reached down to the horizon. Once, while I stood on the bridge, ahead and from the starboard side a rainstorm travelled at right angles to the ship and just ahead of it. I expected it to hit the ship in a little while, but it moved faster than I had thought. It crossed our path just ahead of the ship, moving from right to left, but when we hit that spot, no rain hit the ship.

Fortunately, we avoided seasickness, although we realized it might happen during any storm. We didn't overeat, and didn't read that day. Our food stayed on the table, though the plates slid at times, and we held our cups and glasses in our hands to prevent sloshing. We stayed inside, afraid of the storm taking a personal interest in us and not wanting to be soaked by the salty spray that hit even our high windows. For most of the day we simply sat and talked, together and with Daryl, and played cards and board games. We stowed our small belongings in drawers and cupboards, since items like books were sure to fly around. Johanna was sitting on the floor sorting out some knitting needles during a particularly vicious roll and began to slide towards the glass doors of the credenza. Luckily she stopped herself against it without injuring herself, but then she slid right back to the bottom of the couch on the other side of the room. That roll came unexpectedly and scared us both.

Even sleeping proved to be a problem during our first night on the high seas in stormy weather, as the storm rolled and pitched our bodies. Pitching (head and feet up and down) bothered Johanna a lot, and rolling (moving from side to side) did me in, so we decided to try the couches in our living room. Johanna dozed on the one, I on the other at a right angle to it, our respective choices offering some compensation for the ship's movements we each liked least. We didn't do more than doze in fits and starts that night, but fortunately it proved to be the only night that stormy weather seriously interfered with our sleeping.

After about thirty-six hours' sailing, we reached the coast of Spain and turned south past Portugal. We passed the Rock of Gibraltar in late afternoon with the sun from the west highlighting this famous landmark, the shape made familiar by an insurance company logo used in television ads years ago, the high part facing the ship and behind it a slope down towards Spain.

We had been underway for seven days, and almost always had other ships in sight, even in the Bay of Biscay. The Strait of Gibraltar is a crucial crossroads, with a number of ferries going both ways between Spain and Africa, and other freighters ahead and behind us, going east or west. Meanwhile, the Mediterranean Sea didn't appear to be as busy—yet it is surrounded by a large population in two continents who need to catch fish for food and trade with one another.

We took this photograph right through one of our portholes. Notice how this ship's superstructure is right at the rear of the ship. We always wondered whether other ships also had passengers on board.

The bottom of the Mediterranean is littered with wrecks from over three thousand years of maritime activity, but the storms in the Mediterranean are less frequent and less violent than those west of the Strait of Gibraltar. And its waters are indeed a brighter blue and deeper green than the Atlantic. Going east, we hugged the north coast of Africa. Morocco, Algeria, and Tunisia slid by, all clearly visible during the day and dotted with many lights on the coast at night. Through binoculars I would look at the cities and villages perched on high hills or sheltered by rocks along beaches. At night, we saw single guardian lighthouses and occasionally a string of city lights. I wondered about the people there, and remembered tales from history of wars, conquests, and revolutions. The history of Algeria sticks in my mind, especially the 1954–62 insurrection so cruelly oppressed by its French colonial masters. I once saw a film about it and clearly remember its violence. Charles De Gaulle was appointed premier of the Fourth Republic in 1958 with the specific aim of bringing colonial conflicts to an end. Algeria gained its independence in 1962, but Algerians were given the option of migrating to France. Many did, but they have not yet fully integrated with the French, as recent unrest demonstrates.

I often thought of the people living there, human beings so different from us and yet with similar hopes and fears and dreams. I even heard their music occasionally when the small radio we had brought picked up a signal. The music sounded unlike anything we were used to—different instruments, different harmonies, and of course lyrics we couldn't understand. I'm not musically sophisticated, so I can't judge whether what I heard was North African pop music or part of a classical tradition. I'm sure the themes were the same as in Western music: love, betrayal, birth, loneliness, and if government-censored, the glories of life under whoever was the current ruler.

On this leg of the trip we became much more a part of the ship. Officers weren't as rushed at mealtimes, as they were in ports and had time to relax and socialize a bit. I had my first game of table tennis with Gottfried. As we walked around the ship we met members of the crew and soon began to talk to some of them. Some of the officers would spend time in the lounge at night or play darts in the recreation room. We began to feel more relaxed with them, as no doubt they did with us. During the day I took more time to walk the working deck right up to the bow, where I stood on a steel platform looking down a hole in the bow to the front keel bulge that parted the waters and always seemed to bob up and down. Even in calm weather

o the point of intoxicating. I also discovered that the
al exercise course. I would first descend to the work-
stairs, then walk that deck all the way around, and
the bridge deck. I was panting after the first time
etermined to gradually increase the distance and
he good food and otherwise sedentary existence
eping my shoulders and arms loose, I could use
exercise room. For hand-to-eye coordination
ed. I also began to read one of the demanding

d a lot since we entered the Mediterranean.
ed to breezes and the waves small and calm,
ed. The sun warmed our bones and made
ooked a lot brighter. Our advance informa-
ioned Malta as a destination, but rather Damietta, a port
o Egypt's north coast a bit to the west of the Suez Canal. Once on board
we learned of the switch. At first we were puzzled—what would there be to
pick up and deliver on a small island with a modest population of around
400,000? However, Malta was building a big container port to serve as a
trans-shipment point. Smaller ships would bring containers to this port
from ports all along the Mediterranean coast for large ships like ours that
regularly travelled at high speed between Europe and Asia. These smaller
ships would also pick up containers in Malta to deliver to their home ports.
Because of the large quantity of containers to be handled there, we would
have most of a day to visit. Moreover, so the captain told us, transportation on Malta was easy, cheap, and convenient. It was the last conversation
we had with this captain, as he left the ship in Malta. The other officers
had thrown him a party in the lounge the night before, and passengers had
been invited.

As we prepared to go ashore at Malta, the officers and crew were helpful
in letting us know what to expect. Throughout our trip they provided information about modes of transportation to the cities and towns, how long
it would take to get there, how much money might be needed (important
to know when exchanging dollars into local currency, which is sometimes
difficult to change back), and what there was to see within a limited time.

The routines for leaving the ship were simple. After berthing, the shipping company's local agent would come on board, and sometimes that
country's immigration and customs officers. After about an hour, the ETD

would be posted on a small blackboard close to the gangway, and that meant that we were free to leave the ship with a return deadline: two hours before ETD. The captain had already dealt with immigration and customs officers, as he held everybody's passport. We'd pick up our passports from the ship's office, which we would hand back in on our return. Some ports had harbour buses running all day that picked us up at the ship, delivered us to the port gate, and brought us back to the ship on our return. More often we walked to the gate. Sometimes gatekeepers made note of our names from our passports; other times they simply waved us through, going out or coming in. (I'm sure that after 9/11 most ports have much tighter security now.) Sometimes we walked from the gate into the port city, and sometimes we took a cab or a bus.

We were looking forward to seeing Malta, as the island promised to be much more fascinating and exotic than the somewhat familiar Northern European ports we had visited so far. Whenever and wherever we temporarily left our ship we became ordinary tourists, happy to simply taste the flavour of a foreign city and country by walking and riding around, with rest stops on strategic benches. We looked for unfamiliar street scenes and buildings, for gardens that delighted us, for anything that was new, unusual, and telling. We loved bus and streetcar tours that showed us a lot in our often limited time. We rarely used all of a full day ashore, even when we had the opportunity, invariably running out of gas after about six hours away from the ship. Of course, in conversations back home we're like all tourists, prone to brag about the far-flung places we've been to, but perhaps it's more honest to say that we "glanced" at Pusan, "marched through" Shanghai, and enjoyed "intermissions" in Malta and Singapore. We didn't stay long enough to know the real life of those cities, feel their heartbeats, experience their residential districts, their politics, their dreams, and their prospects.

CHAPTER THREE

Malta to Khor Fakkan

Malta is an island nation in the middle of the Mediterranean, around which the ancient empires of Egypt, Greece, and Rome flourished and faded. While the port is called Marsaxlokk, the town in which it's located is called Birzebbugia. The country has three islands: the main island of Malta, where the port is situated; Gozo; and Comino. Malta enjoys a pleasant climate, moderate in winter and hot in summer. There may be a shortage of well water, but with ingenuity and patience the Maltese have built cisterns and conduits that catch and preserve the winter rains. Natural coves carved out of the hills by erosion offer sheltered ports. Malta's limestone and sandstone geology is honeycombed with caves and tunnels that sheltered the island's inhabitants when under siege from nature or invaders. The land is rocky and hilly, but when carefully husbanded it produces fruits and vegetables that supplement the fish caught in coastal waters. There's plenty of pasture for grazing sheep, pigs, and goats, held in flocks and herds by rock walls. Chickens scratch a living between crops and livestock. There are perhaps a few too many mosquitoes and flies, but pests, thorns, and thistles serve as reminders that life is never completely perfect. Malta offers everything one could want to raise a family in peace. Small islands like Malta always offer a glimpse of Eden or nirvana. If only others would have left these island people alone—but they didn't. Malta has been surrounded by envy for all of its recorded history, all because of three major handicaps to its peaceful existence: location, location, location.

Malta is a mere ninety kilometres south of Sicily, a few hundred kilometres north of Africa, and roughly halfway between the eastern and western extremities of the Mediterranean. This desirable central location and the beauty of the islands arouses two kinds of lust. The first is relatively benign: others from near and far want their own piece of this paradise, so they row and sail and drift in, climb its shores, find a plot of land, build a hut, and blend in with the locals within the span of a generation or two. The Maltese are an amalgam of races. Phoenicians, Cretans, Cypriots, Sicilians, and a sprinkling of North Africans settled on the island and left their pottery and other cultural traces behind. The second type of lust is less benign, residing in those who live for power and domination. Around the Mediterranean cradle of Western civilization, power shifted regularly, and control of Malta was vital to those seeking to dominate the region.

We find a wonderfully detailed account of Malta in the Bible, written when it was part of the Roman Empire, in the Book of Acts (chapters 27 and 28). The Apostle Paul landed there when his ship was wrecked on its way to Rome after a hazardous two-week journey from Crete. In his writings, Paul described the nature of the Maltese people, noting that, "The inhabitants treated us with unusual kindness." It's what we would expect from inhabitants of an island that has so much to offer in the way of peaceful living, and we experienced the same thing during our own two visits. Actually, while probably not intended by the writer of Acts, we could read irony here. In the original account, the Greek word used to describe the Maltese people translates into "barbarian" in English, hence the Bible speaks of barbarians acting "with unusual kindness."

The Roman Empire dissolved about four centuries after Paul's visit, and Malta was subsequently "owned" by a succession of tribal kings, most of them Sicilian, who had taken possession of Southern Italy. The Muslims expanded their territory to Malta in CE 870, leaving their mark on the language and architecture, notably in the building of a beautifully walled strategic city which they named M'dina. For roughly the next six centuries, the Christian Mediterranean West battled with the Muslim Mediterranean East, with Malta caught in the middle. Every major combatant wanted, and needed, Malta to thrive and survive. In 1090 the Muslims were driven off and replaced by the latest Sicilian king. Malta fell under the control of Spain in 1282, and then in 1516 under the direct thumb of Charles I of Spain, who became Charles V, emperor of the Holy Roman Empire.

In 1530 the islands were "sold" to the Order of St. John of Jerusalem (also called the Knights Hospitaller) for the annual fee of one live Maltese falcon. Legend has it that an opulent gold version of such a falcon was made in 1539 and presented to the Roman emperor. Humphrey Bogart starred in *The Maltese Falcon*, the famous 1941 Hollywood film about the theft of the golden bird. The Maltese pay scant attention to that story—they'd rather highlight the first of their two major historical events, still celebrated on the island, if not by a festival or ceremony then by the packaging of it as a major tourist attraction. The event they commemorate took place in 1565, when the Ottoman Empire decided to take a stab at possessing Malta.

The invasion had its roots in the beginning of the second millennium, over five hundred years earlier. What we now call the Middle East was already firmly in the hands of Muslim rulers and armies, but both Jews and Christians lived in the area in relative peace until about the middle of the eleventh century. By this time, Jerusalem began to gain importance as a Holy City for the three major Western faiths. From the West came a steady stream of pilgrims, many resentful that Jerusalem was not a city controlled exclusively by Christians. Periodically, this resentment flared up and eventually led to the Crusades. During the chaotic time before the First Crusade, a group of European noblemen decided that Jerusalem needed a hospital for sick and injured pilgrims, and in 1080 they established one with their own money, as well as gifts and legacies from those left behind to look after the castles and lands. While it was a religious order, named the Order of St. John of Jerusalem, it didn't owe allegiance to local or regional clergy, but only directly to the pope.

In the beginning, the Order of St. John of Jerusalem simply provided solace and aid to the sick (becoming known as the Hospitallers), but it grew to be a military order, complete with its own army and navy. Many pilgrims arrived in Jerusalem injured by marauders along the road, so the Knights of St. John sent protective patrols up the roads, all the way up into Syria. After all, this order was made up exclusively of noblemen, whose teenage education emphasized military prowess. The next step from establishing small patrols along the roads was easy and logical: the occupation of some of the key cities between Jerusalem and the Mediterranean seaports, and further north towards Turkey, the overland route. The knights grew in number, power, belligerence, and also in wealth, as the order received many lands and treasures. They even came to own some of the cities they had occupied. In the minds of many Christians they were the vital bulwark against the infidels. However, Crusades notwithstanding, it became harder and harder to resist the ever-growing military might of the Muslims and the resentment over the attacks they had endured from fellow Christians.

In the next two centuries, the Knights of St. John were gradually pushed back to the West. In CE 1290 their city and fort of Acre, the last stronghold in the Holy Land, fell to the Muslims. At first the order resettled on Cyprus, but when that island proved inhospitable, they moved to Rhodes, another island further west. The order constantly engaged the Muslims wherever they sensed a weakness, on land by invasion, and on sea by their own sophisticated form of piracy. The Muslims fought back and finally drove the knights from Rhodes in 1522.

Malta became the next base. The first thing the Knights did was build forts and other defensive installations, for they knew that the Muslims would soon follow them. Moreover, their own ships did everything they could to harass Muslim shipping, which sometimes included killing pilgrims on their way to Mecca. (We note, in passing, that the original Maltese population, partly Arab, was never consulted about any of this.) Muslim resentment grew, and also confidence that their strength far surpassed what they perceived as a weak Christian West. Knowing the difficulty of invading this island when ships could be spotted miles away, and of overcoming a smaller army well positioned in the island's forts and on its high hills, Muslim ruler Suleiman the Magnificent assembled an enormous army and navy in 1565, perhaps as many as forty thousand soldiers, although no one is really sure of the exact numbers on either side. Against that brute force the order's Grand Master Jean de la Valette could position only about five hundred knights, with an estimated additional six thousand or so soldiers from many parts of Europe, including three thousand Maltese. That clever general stripped the island of water and food (thus anticipating Stalin's tactic against the Germans in 1941-42), and hoarded supplies in four mighty fortresses, three around the major Grand Harbour and one in M'dina.

The Ottoman forces landed at Marsaxlokk (roughly where the *Ville d'Aquarius* berthed), and had little trouble swarming the countryside. They then turned towards the fortresses with all the besieging skill and weaponry they had brought. Indeed, the fortress of St. Elmo fell after a siege of six weeks, but it cost the attackers more than eight thousand soldiers. The lack of food and water also played a role in diminishing their numbers, and dysentery claimed more lives still. The attacks on the three remaining forts were unsuccessful, and when a relieving Christian force arrived by sea in September 1565, the remaining Ottomans abandoned their attempt. The few that escaped left behind some thirty-five thousand dead. The knights lost 2,500 troops, while about seven thousand Maltese civilians lost their lives. Given the astonishing odds they overcame, it's little wonder that Malta still celebrates this victory.

The Hospitallers stayed around for a long time after 1565, rebuilding the island. They created a capital city around the Grand Harbour, which they called Valetta. They also made sure that the population eventually became Roman Catholic, and built a number of beautiful churches. Of course, they repaired the castles, especially St. Elmo. However, their prominent place in the international politics of the region slowly diminished as the Ottoman Empire weakened and major conflicts between the West and East abated.

Two hundred years later, foreigners once again eyed Malta. In 1798, on his way to Egypt, Napoleon took Malta in passing, thus preventing the island from becoming a base for a stab in the back. After Napoleon's defeat and retirement from Egypt, the English, against whose Indian empire Napoleon's campaign had been directed, took over Malta and stayed for many years. Being Anglicans, they didn't mind that it was Catholic; they were only interested in making it another extension of the British Empire and a potentially strong link in the chain of naval bases that stretched from Gibraltar all the way to the east coast of the Mediterranean.

The second major historical event that is still commemorated in Malta is the siege by Axis forces from 1941-43. When World War II broke out, Great Britain, like France and other Western European nations, was ill prepared at home and in its foreign territories, including Malta. Yet, Britain could ill afford to lose control of the Mediterranean, now even more crucial because of the Suez Canal. Italy and Germany knew that too. Hitler, who aped Napoleon in more than one strategy, saw gaining control of the Suez Canal and Egypt as critical to weakening Great Britain's control of India. With the canal under his control, Hitler hoped that his armies could penetrate India with an overland campaign through Turkey, thus starving the opposing troops in India of vital war supplies. For Italy, unhindered crossing of the waters to Ethiopia, its new colony, was a priority. To both Axis leaders, Malta loomed like a spear in their soft underbellies. The island was being prepared by the British as a submarine base for attacks on Axis naval supply lines between southern Europe and North Africa. As soon as Italy entered the war, its planes from Sicily began to make air raids and drop bombs on the island. In the summer of 1940, the British Mediterranean fleet crushed its Italian counterpart and Malta seemed safe in British hands, in spite of the bombing raids.

In early 1941, the situation began to look more desperate for Britain. In January, German squadrons of bombers and fighters stationed on Sicily began to harass the island with far greater intensity in preparation for the invasion of North Africa. Supply lines would be crucial, and British submarines stationed on Malta would be a hindrance. It didn't take long before the island began to feel the pinch of constant air raids and the increasing difficulty of getting supply ships through from Alexandria or Gibraltar. Many supply ships were sent, but few arrived. Rationing was imposed on the island in April 1941. Air raids continued, often over one hundred raids in any given month, until most of Valetta was in ruins, the ports almost fatally injured, and the people exhausted. Just outside Valetta's gate we saw big bullet holes in a wall, evidence of these aerial assaults. This destruction of buildings, airfields, and port facilities greatly hindered Great Britain's war efforts. In August 1942, the oil tanker *Ohio*, held up by destroyers on either side, limped into Grand Harbour when fuel supplies had just about run out. British warships continued to sail away and inflict serious loses on German merchant ships, thereby greatly impeding Rommel's North African campaign. Eventually, Rommel ran out of supplies and lost the war. The last air raid on Malta took place on July 20, 1943. Churchill visited the island in November of that year and the British Government awarded the whole island the George Cross for valour. The UK then helped rebuild the island and smoothed Malta's path to independence in 1964.

All buses on the island of Malta end up in Valetta, the capital, and gather in a huge square right outside the main city gate. Most of the buses are from England and all of them seem old. Posters and postcards feature them as one of Malta's attractions The buses provide efficient and frequent service and cost only eleven or thirteen Maltese cents (which at that time was about fifty cents Canadian) for a one-way trip. The bus from port took Johanna, Daryl, and me into Valetta in about thirty-five minutes. These buses are lovingly maintained and have no trouble climbing the sometimes steep hills on the island, though they sound as if they're labouring close to their engine's peak capability, like *Tour de France* racers climbing the last incline of a mountain stage. They aren't fast, but who needs speed when the longest island route only takes about forty-five minutes?

Tourism is Malta's major industry. Many British people live here all winter, rainbirds comparable to Canadian snowbirds who flee Canadian winters for Florida. The fact that Malta is developing the port we visited as a container hub reflects its long history as a vital location in the Mediterranean. We got our first taste of Malta's pride in its history by attending a theatre slide show. Aimed at entertaining tourists, the spectacular audiovisual presentation may have been of suspect historical accuracy, but it nevertheless sparked our interest and made us look forward to a planned second visit on our return trip.

Valetta has fine architecture, steep streets, a beautiful inner harbour, a welcoming climate in winter and summer, and a smallness of scale that slows visitors down. The streets were so narrow that I wondered how anyone could move furniture in and out of the houses. Two architectural details struck us especially. First, most houses had eye-catching wooden doors, often painted in vivid reds and greens. Moreover, the door frames,

A typical Malta bus, parked at the central depot, just outside the gates of Valetta. Malta's public transit (ubiquitous, frequent, and cheap), would make it easy never to own a car on the island, and I imagine many of Valetta's citizens have also come to that conclusion. (Courtesy John S. Hinchcliffe, Huddersfield Passenger Transport Group, UK)

and particularly the lintels, often had carvings and decorations, with the total effect being like the entrance to a castle: massive, defensive, and really not very welcoming. Nevertheless, we brought back a poster of pictures of the doors, framed it, and hung it in one of our bedrooms, where it reminds us of our Malta delight. The door knockers also caught our attention. Most of them were made of iron or brass, some plain, and some with intricate curlicues. Johanna spotted a pair of chickens and a pair of fish. The walls of the buildings featured light brown and tan sandstone, mirroring the island's geological formations.

We had a snack on a terrace right in the heart of Valetta, feeling the calm of it enveloping us while we listened to the many languages swirling around our ears, including Dutch from the next table. We bought some small souvenir items and in due time sauntered back to the bus terminal. Just inside the gate, a street musician was playing a guitar and singing, attracting quite a crowd. We watched for a bit, then caught our bus back to port. Between the bus terminal and our ship we spotted a street vendor with fruit, and bought a supply of apples and oranges for our respective cabins. Tired and deeply satisfied, we climbed back on board, just in time for a drink in our cabin and dinner.

In the dining room we met Captain Richter, who welcomed us to what was now his ship. He seemed as easygoing as his predecessor. He introduced us to a new passenger, Pierre, the man who was supposed to have come on board in Le Havre. Pierre spoke very little English, but between the captain's explanation, Daryl's fairly good command of French, and our smattering of French vocabulary, we learned the story of his delay. Apparently the Le Havre local agent had not kept Pierre properly informed of the ship's

Two Maltese doorknockers. (Courtesy the Malta Tourism Authority www.visitmalta.com)

48

I'm in one of Valetta's small streets. No cars here, not even bikes, just room for a quiet walk. Room and time to see massive doors and intricate door knockers, small shops, and old architecture.

schedule, and Pierre had arrived from Paris when the ship had already left. As this was the company's mistake, Pierre had been put on a plane to Malta and lodged in a local hotel at the company's expense. Pierre was a handsome silvery-haired seventy-year-old who had fought in Vietnam as a French naval officer before the Americans got involved there. After the death of his wife, he undertook this trip, partly because a ship would be a reminder of his career, and partly because it would take him close to Vietnam to revisit the old familiar places. He sailed with us all the way to South Korea, and then back to Singapore, where he met a friend and flew to Vietnam.

The thoroughly satisfying visit to Malta had made us look forward to our return some six weeks hence. At the tourist bureau just inside the city gate we had picked up brochures in anticipation of exploring even more of this fascinating island. Malta's second-largest city, M'dena, is also called "The Silent City," and we planned to visit it on our return trip, time permitting. It was also here, in Malta, that the ship made its first clock change, jumping one hour ahead. As we headed to bed early after our eventful day, our attention shifted to another much-anticipated experience: a trip through the Suez Canal.

Even before we had entered the Mediterranean, we had asked Friedrich, the chief (engineer), if we could tour the engine room. The chief had readily agreed to do this at a suitable time. After getting underway to Suez, he suggested that the next afternoon would be a good time, because on the other side of the Suez Canal the weather would get considerably warmer, and he didn't want to risk us fainting from heat and dehydration. So the day after we left Malta, we descended deep into the bowels of the ship, right underneath the superstructure.

Outside the door to the engine room, we were handed ear protectors and working gloves. Friedrich conducted the tour himself, shouting his explanations into our ears. A number of sailors were running around with oil cans, rags, and tools, and smiles that readily came our way. We spent quite bit of time in the control room, where the noise was tolerable. Large banks of dials and gauges told us nothing, but were obviously open books for the experts around us. We stood next to the massive eight-cylinder fuel oil burning engine that towered over us. The smooth two-foot-diameter driveshaft was impressive, making ninety-five revolutions per minute, completely in the open until it disappeared behind a wall on its way to the screw. Strategically placed bearings held the long driveshaft in place. We learned about ballast tanks, the problems of loading and unloading, and the difficulty of keeping the living quarters of this particular ship comfortably warm in winter and cool in summer. We were told that the *Ville d'Aquarius* was only about fourteen months old, that it had been built in South Korea for about $85 million US, and that it would only last about eight years before it outlived its usefulness (and that its quality, described in salty sailor language, left something to be desired).

The engine-room workers weren't just busy with oiling and maintenance. They had to spend many hours doing repairs in the engine room, as well as to equipment elsewhere on the ship. For one thing, the screws used to attach the cabin doors to their frames weren't long enough; Jörg Appledorn, the general handyman on board, was in the process of rehanging all the doors. It was a wonderful tour, even with the overload of technical information, the noise, the overpowering smell of oil and grease, and the heat. We left the engine room full of admiration for the people who occupied it, and for the technical marvel it represented. We also learned that the people working there drink lots of water and swallow salt pills on hot days. The chief hadn't been kidding about the dangers of the place.

Friedrich was the engine-room boss. Although he reported directly to the captain, he had the right, and indeed the duty, to refuse the captain's orders if those orders endangered the engine, and therefore the ship. From what I had seen, the first captain and he had gotten along well, and I had no reason to doubt the same would be true with the replacement master.

Reporting to Friedrich were the second engineer (also German) and the third engineer, a Filipino, the key engine-room officers. Each of them had engine-room watch duty, organized much like the watch duty on the bridge. Assisting them were three engine-room "oilers" (mechanics) and an electrician (all Filipinos), and a German engineering cadet on a four-month work stint. Finally, Jörg, the handyman, had his own workshop on the working deck. He looked after any carpentry and plumbing that might be required on board, but would also act as an AB (able seaman, meaning a licensed sailor) when required, especially when berthing and unberthing. Several times we saw him operate the anchor windlasses on the foc's'le, a dirty noisy job that caused fine rust dust to shoot in all directions. All told, nine sailors on board were directly concerned with the machinery. It seemed a very low number for keeping a ship steaming twenty-four hours a day for days on end, but I was assured it was enough.

Our visit to the engine room sparked my interest in the rest of the professionals on board and their duties, so I checked the personnel roster posted on the bridge. The captain of the *Ville d'Aquarius* was German, as were the first and second officers. The third officer was Filipino, as were the rest of the crew. The crew consisted of the bosun (the deck foreman) and five ABs, the people we had seen working during berthing and departure, and on scraping and painting duties while underway. Also on board were a cook and our steward, Ariel. There were twelve deck officers and crew, for a total of twenty-one sailors on the entire ship.

As we became comfortable with the crew, and they with us, I asked some of them why they had become sailors. Jörg grew up in a Baltic coastal fishing town. His grandfather owned a fishing boat, and on weekends the young boy loved to accompany him when he took the boat out for bunkering (loading fuel) and servicing the engine. When old enough, Jörg became a crew member himself. After he grew tired of the hard life of a fisher, he joined the merchant marine for voyages around the world. He said that he couldn't live without the sea. The officers had similar stories. Early in life something had attracted them to the sea, even though some of them had grown up far from its shores—the second engineer, Wolfgang, had come from the heartland of Germany.

Each officer and crew member had a unique story to tell about how he came to be on board the *Ville d'Aquarius.* In about half of these stories, the lore of the sea played a large role, and yet none of them sounded overly romantic about their current seafarer's life. Some mentioned that container shipping had dramatically changed merchant marine life. In the past, crews were larger and port stays much longer. On a trip like this, planned almost like a bus or train schedule, the chances were that only half of the ports you would stop in would be open to visits, and shore time would be short, that's if you were lucky enough to be off duty.

However much he delegates, the captain bears the ultimate responsibility for the ship, cargo, and crew (and passengers, if on board). The whole crew is instructed to warn him if anything nonroutine happens. Even the pilots who help the ship in and out of harbours and through the often long waterways between sea and port, can be overruled and removed by the captain if he feels he must take direct charge himself. Captains are always on the bridge when entering and leaving harbours, during big storms, during fog, or when sailing through areas where icebergs are present. I once stood on the bridge with the first officer on watch in the South China Sea. Ahead of the ship was a fleet of fishing boats, and the first officer decided to go around them. He disengaged the automatic pilot, took the helm, and changed course. Almost immediately the captain appeared on the bridge. He grabbed a set of binoculars and swept the scene in front of the ship. He didn't say a word, but clearly he had felt the maneuver in his body the moment it had been made and had come up onto the bridge to check out the situation.

Captains are also the chief administrative officers on board and they must keep various accounts, for instance, the slop chest (supplies of drinks, snacks, and other items of convenience), and payroll. Captains are the main communicators with those onshore (with pilot stations, head offices, agents at the next port, port authorities, etc.) and hold the responsibility of managing staff. The chief engineer reports to the captain with respect to engine-room matters, and the chief officer reports to him on all the other work on the ship (painting for instance). With respect to the ship's movements, the captain has three immediate assistants: the first, second, and third officers. Each officer stands watch on the bridge for two four-hour stretches every day, and during evening and night hours an AB is also present on the bridge. That makes for eight hours of watch every twenty-four hours for each deck officer, seven days a week. "Watch" means monitoring the ship's progress, watching out for possible dangers (e.g., other ships, debris in the water), monitoring weather reports, and updating the official charts and various logs (records of the ship's progress).

When entering or leaving a harbour, all three officers have specific duties, some of which concern the safety of the ship. The second officer is in charge of the foc's'le crew, responding to the pilot and captain's instructions about getting lines to the quay when berthing, and swallowing those same lines back in when leaving. The first officer keeps an eye on the crew members who were similarly working the rear of the ship. The third officer assists the captain and pilot on the bridge. Approaching a berthing position is no easy matter, and it takes the help of one or two tugs to push a ship into position without crushing the quay, sometimes in a tight squeeze between two other ships. In Rotterdam, we ended up being tightly berthed between two ships already docked there. No wonder everyone on board is involved. We learned not to engage the sailors in conversation during these tricky times, when we weren't allowed on the bridge either.

Once tied up, all three officers become deck officers on their watch times, monitoring loading and unloading procedures, and especially watching for safety hazards: For example, are the containers properly locked and lashed into place? They also keep an eye open for suspicious characters who might want to sneak on board. Stowaways are a judicial and administrative headache for both captain and company. In many ports, all doors to the decks (other than on the working deck) were locked, and on the *Ville d'Aquarius*, the crew and officer lounges also. We were instructed to lock our cabins and secure valuables in all ports.

While sailing, the first officer was responsible for organizing and supervising maintenance and repair work on deck and inside the superstructure. After his early morning watch was finished (at 800), he would talk to the bosun about what needed to be done, and often walked the decks to check and inspect them. The second officer did a lot of administration work, for instance, updating the catalogues of information about the different harbours: radio frequencies, currents, and other technical information. It's a tedious job. I often watched him cutting sections from printed sheets and pasting them into the appropriate places in the relevant books. The third officer had specific maintenance duties, for example, maintaining safety equipment, such as making sure the lifeboats were in permanent good order.

Life on board is hectic for these three officers. They never have the luxury of eight hours of uninterrupted sleep while the ship is sailing; all of them told me that they learn to nap regardless of light and noise. And they have little choice about their working conditions. Some captains will be jovial and helpful, some will be aloof and demanding. Captains don't have to accommodate themselves to their officers, officers have to serve the captain. Yet, it was also clear that "our" officers got along, drank beer and threw darts together, joked, were at ease with one another. The Filipinos we met were invariably proud of their sailor craft, proud of their reputation, and proud of the foreign currency they contributed to their country's economy. Tens of thousands of Filipinos work on merchant ships, in all ranks and functions, and Manila boasts booking agents for most of the merchant marine companies in the world. Other nations that provide sailors in large numbers are Indonesia and India.

Johanna and I have had the privilege of travelling through the world's two major maritime arteries: the Suez and Panama canals. Both represent enormous human achievement, which I reflected upon as we approached the Suez. While ancient Egyptian history makes mentions of canals, none of these had ever connected the Mediterranean and the Red seas. Until the Suez Canal was built, cargo and travellers between Europe and Asia had two choices. The first was an interminable sea journey all the way down the west African coast round the Cape of Good Hope in South Africa, and then back up on the other side of the African continent. The most frequent travellers of this route were the English, who by the early nineteenth century had the most colonies around the globe, and whose dominance of the seas was the envy of the rest of Europe. The more than eighteen-thousand-kilometre trip from London to Bangkok took about 115 days. This was the century of greatly expanding international trade and European-dominated colonies, and the Egyptian desert isthmus was a great barrier to speed and convenience. The second option was making use of the Nile River, at least partway. Cargo and passengers could travel the Mediterranean up to Damietta or Alexandria on the north coast of Egypt, transfer to riverboats to travel the almost two hundred kilometres to Cairo in the south, and then from Cairo travel by camel and donkey through the desert to the city of Suez and the north end of the Gulf of Suez, boarding another ship here for the Red Sea. While this route cut the sea distance to about ten thousand kilometres, the trip through western Egypt was anything but comfortable, especially the hundred and seventy-kilometre leg east through the desert by camel, mule, or donkey.

When we look at the map now, about 150 years after the canal was opened for business, the notion of a canal linking the two bodies of water seems utterly logical, but seventy years passed between the idea first being advanced and the first ship sailing through it in 1869. The development of the Suez Canal in the modern era began with Napoleon. Just a decade after the beginning of the French Revolution, this audacious and very successful general was starting to become too big for his britches in the eyes of the Directory, the small group of politicians who then ruled France. Who knew what this Corsican-born coiled spring might do if he wasn't kept busy with conquests? So a plan was hatched to occupy him with conquests out of the country, away from Paris. Egypt would be a good place to start. Politically, it was part of the Ottoman Empire with headquarters in Constantinople, an empire constantly subject to meddling by the ever more powerful and arrogant Western European powers of England and France, Austria-Hungary in central Europe, and the powerful Russian Empire to the north of Turkey. Egypt may have been part of the Ottoman Empire, but it was by now on its fringes, and that empire was weak. A conquest of Egypt, possible if not easy, would enhance French international influence, further weaken the Ottoman Empire, and keep Napoleon busy for awhile. Mind you, while Napoleon seemed to play along with the diversion game played by his Parisian masters, he had long-term strategies of his own. Knowing that Great

Britain would always be the mortal enemy of his own ambitions, he realized that a French foothold in Egypt could seriously damage British global interests. As in some other aspects, Napoleon anticipated Hitler's future interest in North Africa for roughly the same reasons.

In 1798 Napoleon left for Egypt, took Malta in passing, and landed at Damietta. He brought his well-trained soldiers and a number of scientists and technicians, including engineers. The goal of his mission was not just conquest and enhanced French influence; there was a typically Western-European romantic side to it. In Western minds, the East, however glorious in the past, had descended towards a more primitive existence. Europe's educated elite became convinced that it was high time for Western science, technology, engineering, and capital to restore the East to its former glory. (Not to mention, of course, the desire to open up more lucrative markets for Western goods.) Napoleon arrived in Egypt as both an old-fashioned pirate and a romantic, and while his mission ultimately ended in military failure, his return to France in 1799 had not diminished his romantic ideas about this old land. He took the Rosetta stone back with him, which would ultimately unlock the secrets of old Egyptian hieroglyphics and therefore ancient Egyptian cultures. This stela, more than one metre high, was inscribed with the same text in three forms: two Egyptian language scripts and classical Greek. Because Greek was understood, the other two unknown scripts could be deciphered. The stories about Napoleon's expedition whetted the appetite of Frenchmen and other Europeans for more information about Egypt. Talk of pyramids, sphinxes, and Egyptian arts and crafts created an "Egyptomania," especially in France. Napoleon's "visit" also stimulated the development of archaeology.

It was Napoleon who first brooded upon a canal straight through the desert that would connect the two seas and provide faster and more direct access to other romantic destinations, especially in Asia. But surveys done while he was there concluded that a canal project was impossible, as the levels of the Mediterranean and Red seas differed too dramatically (nine metres) for any canal to be feasible.

The return of Napoleon to France fulfilled the fears of the country's rulers. Soon this adventurous former Corsican was elected as consul, and then crowned as emperor of France. The Suez Canal idea was shelved for more immediate matters of state and wars, including the emperor's major miscalculation in Moscow. He kept himself and most of Europe busy until his final defeat at Waterloo in 1815.

Even after all this turmoil, a fascination with the East, and most notably Egypt, still remained part of the European soul, as did an obsession with technology and grand projects. The steam engine had already been invented, and engineers and entrepreneurs were thinking up new and grander uses for it. Railroads were one application, and Western Europe got busy building many lines at great cost. The first practical steamship had already been built, the *Charlotte Dundas*, which towed two seventy-ton barges almost twenty miles along the Forth and Clyde canal to Glasgow. The first steam-propelled ocean crossing came in 1819 when the *Savannah* made the Savannah-Liverpool journey in twenty-nine days and eleven hours. It was a new era of imagination and enterprise. In France, the government and groups of citizens were busy stimulating new inventions and developments. One Barthelemy-Prosper Enfantin became the head and guru of a large group of clever Frenchmen, visionaries in love with modernity, science, and technology. It was Enfantin who revived the notion of a canal.

In 1833 Enfantin went East, accompanied by engineers and surveyors, his head full of plans for the modernization of Egypt with railroads, canals, and dams, and mystical dreams about the meeting and melding of the East and West. After first seeking to promote his schemes in Constantinople, still considered Egypt's overlord, he travelled to Egypt, where in 1834 he met Muhammad Ali, the pasha of Egypt and nominally the underling of the kalief (ruler) of the Ottoman Empire. Even though he had been born in Albania, Muhammad Ali had risen to Egypt's top administrative position, from where he eyed with pain the economic, educational, and cultural gap between the East and West. He particularly envied England and France, and worked for his country's modernization. He used Enfantin's enthusiasm, skills, and engineering friends to promote his own projects, which included a canal linking the Nile and Alexandria. However, he didn't like the idea of a canal being built far away from the Nile, for outside a small strip on both sides of the Nile, he exercised little control over the desert where Bedouin tribes meandered at will. He preferred the traffic of goods and people to take place on and along the Nile, where he could extract revenue and control Egypt's destiny. So while he listened politely to the somewhat odd Frenchman, he nixed the idea of a canal that would link the Mediterranean and the Red Sea. In 1836 Enfantin returned to Paris disappointed, but with the canal idea still simmering on his personal back burner.

A young French vice-consul had been in one of Enfantin's audiences in Cairo. Ferdinand de Lesseps was an up-and-comer in France's diplomatic service. Following in his father's footsteps, de Lesseps served France with distinction in a number of foreign posts. He was made full consul in Cairo in 1835, and gained the trust of Muhammad Ali. The pasha asked him at one point to look after his son, Prince Said, an overweight and hard-to-control teenager. De Lesseps did, and while not succeeding in getting the young prince to control his weight, the two built a special relationship that resulted in the clever boy being educated in France. De Lesseps also spent a number of years in Spain as France's ambassador. In 1848, after the unrest in many capitals of Europe and the overthrow of France's king, he was posted to Rome, but resigned from diplomatic service in 1849 when the French government deemed him to have mishandled a situation. For five years he lived a quiet life with the wife and children he loved, until tragedy struck in 1853 when he lost two sons and his wife to scarlet fever.

In the meantime, the idea of a canal had not been forgotten. In 1845 a group of Leipzig merchants petitioned Muhammad Ali for permission to explore the possibility, but they were rebuffed. A year later, Enfantin took another stab at it. Under his direction, a group of engineer friends surveyed the desert where the canal might be built and drew up detailed plans. They concluded that the earlier information about the differing levels of the Mediterranean and Red seas had been wrong. However, Muhammad Ali died in 1849, and his grandson, Abbas, took control of Egypt. Abbas, older than Said, and therefore the natural successor, didn't show much interest in modernizing Egypt, and he soon got rid of the French meddlers. Things changed in 1854 when Abbas died and Prince Said became the pasha of Egypt. Almost immediately de Lesseps got in touch with Said. Although the two had not seen each other for about fifteen years, de Lesseps had a special relationship with the ruler of Egypt, whose Western education he had stimulated, and so discussions about the canal recommenced.

Building the canal would be a mind-boggling task. First, Said would have to be convinced and co-opted. For one thing, only he could provide the land necessary to build not only the canal itself, but a port at its north end (it would be called Port Said); the land for a sweet-water canal from the Nile to transport equipment, supplies, and personnel to the site; and settlements along the route. There were other questions: Who would own the canal? Who would share in its revenues? Who would supply the capital? Was it even technically feasible? It took de Lesseps almost five years to design and polish the scheme that eventually succeeded. He began by meeting Said in the fall of 1854 and presenting the possibility. His reasons were partly visionary and partly practical politics. He recalled the past glories of the Egyptian pharaohs, Alexander the Great, the mighty Arab invaders, and rulers over North Africa. He recalled Napoleon's dream. A canal would bring power to the East once again, and secure Egypt's independence. It would establish the reputation of Said himself as the creator of a canal that would rank with the pyramids as the epitome of human achievement. Master diplomat and salesman, de Lesseps succeeded: Said came on board.

With respect to the technical problems, de Lesseps knew of earlier plans for the canal, those of Enfantin's engineers for instance, and he trusted that their positive findings were correct. With respect to financing, the well-known "concession" route would be taken. Pasha Said would donate the necessary land and provide diggers and other workers by means of "corvée" the assignment of Egyptian citizens to do work at their master's bidding, a well-known system practiced by ancient pharaohs to build the pyramids, only one step up from outright slavery. De Lesseps would secure the capital to build the canal by means of shares in a public company. Said and the company would come to an agreement about profits.

Having the pasha's agreement, land, and access to labour in place, de Lesseps spent the next five years building the project's foundation. Using Said's money, he hired engineers to survey and draw up plans. He criss-crossed Europe to promote his plan and attract financing. He used all his diplomatic experience to tack the project through the always changing winds of European power politics, as England and France eyed one another warily. By the end of 1858, he was ready to sell shares in the Suez Canal Company. The prospectus offered 400,000 shares at 500 francs each, for a total capital of 200 million francs. Ships would be charged ten francs per ton to navigate the canal, and de Lesseps predicted that at least three million tons would pass through it each year for an annual revenue of thirty million francs. On paper, it was a profitable operation, but profit was not the only selling feature. De Lesseps argued that investors would make a contribution to "progress," that magical nineteenth-century vision so eloquently expressed in the London Crystal Palace Exhibition just a few years previously in 1851. Investing in the canal would build a better future for oneself, one's children and grandchildren, one's country, the West, the East, the world.

De Lesseps hit the European road to sell shares in Odessa, Trieste, Vienna, Barcelona, Turin, and a number of French cities, but unfortunately the response to the prospectus turned out to be less enthusiastic than expected. Only about twenty-three thousand people bought about half the available shares, and twenty-one thousand of them were French. Citizens and bankers from Great Britain, Russia, Austria, and the United States showed little interest. Fortunately, the majority of French purchasers were middle-class citizens who believed in order, hard work, saving, and progress. On the average, they owned nine shares each, and while they got irritated and scared at times about their investment and the time it took for it to pay off, they had taken to heart de Lesseps's message of business prospects and his vision for the future. They wouldn't abandon the project easily by selling their shares and thereby depreciating their value. As for the rest of the needed capital, de Lesseps convinced Said (and therefore Egypt) to buy whatever shares remained unsold. He had his initial capital.

The work began in 1859. Pasha Said provided the workers, thereby creating hardships in Egyptian villages by depriving them of vital agricultural hands. The engineers and other technicians were Europeans, mainly French. De Lesseps fought off detractors, some of whom insisted that the planned canal was too far away from the Nile. After about four years, these detractors (often orchestrated by England, which didn't want to have the canal built at all at this time) persuaded Said to call a halt to corvée, thus threatening to dry up this source of cheap and plentiful labour. However, de Lesseps turned that setback into an advantage by switching to machines that speeded up the building process and made him less dependent on manual labour. There were still many problems to overcome. The project turned out to be underfunded and new financing had to be orchestrated. Meanwhile, stringent opposition to the canal continued. In response, de Lesseps cleverly used his indirect influence on Napoleon III, the ruler of France, who was married to de Lesseps's beloved niece, Eugenie. This created the impression that the completion of the canal was a French state priority. Other unexpected setbacks, such as a cruel cholera epidemic that killed many workers, must have made completion seem out of the question at times. De Lesseps persevered and on November 18, 1869, the first ship entered the canal, which was still incomplete but ready enough to carry ships south from the now bustling new city of Port Said at the north end. Three days later that first ship sailed past the city of Suez in the south, after stopping for parties along the way. One interesting note: Verdi had been commissioned to compose an opera for the festivities, and his Egyptian opera *Aida* livened up the canal inauguration proceedings.

Some decades after the opening of the canal, Egypt sold its large block of shares to England to stave off defaulting on its massive debt. With that foot in Egypt's door, it didn't take long before Egypt became little more than another British colony. That situation prompted Hitler's attack on North Africa, his aim to control the Suez Canal, an attack halted only at Al Alamein. In the 1950s, modernization forces in Egypt engineered a military coup aimed at greater independence and the canal's nationalization. In 1956 France and England combined forces to invade Egypt and maintain control, but the power of the US made them back off. In 1967 Israel invaded the Sinai, and crossed the canal in places as part of its war against its Arab enemies. Today the canal is firmly in Egypt's hands.

Our voyage through the Suez Canal was a gentle glide with the Sinai desert on one side and bustling Egypt on the other. The serene pace belied the turmoil that has surrounded this waterway since its conception. We discovered that ships don't just sail up to the Suez Canal and go right through. They're assigned to a one-a-day convoy in both directions, and this requires that they be available many hours before beginning the trip, or pay a premium. There's a daily deadline for arrival on either side, and ships must take a canal pilot on board.

We arrived at the anchoring area outside Port Said on the north end of the canal by night. When Johanna and I woke up the next morning, we had

The Sinai Desert: hot in the day, cold at night. Even though it's all barren sand and rock, at this point our thoughts went back to its turbulent biblical and other ancient history.

A whole day of all that merchandise for just over twenty people on board, with most of them sailors for whom this journey is old hat? A tough way to make a living.

just got underway even though it was still dark outside. We quickly dressed to go outside and have a first look and were immediately surprised by the biting cold air. In winter, the desert is bitterly cold at night. After donning warmer clothing, we looked at the Sinai desert, over which the early morning sun began to glow red, and then at the city of Port Said, which was waking up to the new day. Our ship slid slowly through the water, ahead of us and behind us tankers, bulk cargo, and container ships. The ships must proceed slowly, for moving too fast will cause shore erosion, and the canal must be protected against wear and tear as much as possible. Without this canal, Egypt would be in even greater economic trouble than it usually is.

At 0730 we went down for breakfast. During the night, three vendors had come on board with all kinds of goods: copper plates, cups and wall hangings, images painted or embossed on papyrus sheets, T-shirts, of course, and other clothing, shoes and sandals, postcards, and stamps, all neatly arranged on the floor of the long hallways outside the dining lounges. Two Egyptians with broad and inviting smiles on their faces had come aboard the night before and slept in the "Suez" bunk-bed cabins we had seen the first day on board. In English, they told us that US dollars were all the currency we needed. After breakfast we looked for awhile, and later in the day we bought a parchment sheet on which was painted a typical Egyptian figure.

It takes a whole day to go through the canal. The convoy going south anchors for awhile in the largest of the two Bitter lakes that are part of the canal system, about two-thirds of the way in, for there's no room for convoys to pass each other safely in the canal itself. We waited until the northbound convoy had passed and after the last giant ship slid by, the ships in our convoy lifted anchor and proceeded south. I noticed that the last vessel of the convoy was a tug, a safety precaution if a convoy ship gets into difficulties. It was dusk already when we passed Suez, the last of the Egyptian cities we would see. Within reach of Suez, the peddlers and the pilot climbed down the rope ladders on the side of the ship and left in speedy and noisy small boats.

We spent the day rooted to the deck, absorbed by the fascinating sights and sounds of the canal as our ship slid through this ancient country. We looked at the desert on the portside, much of it desolate with a few scattered buildings and roads, connected via cross-canal ferries to roads on the developed side of Egypt. A few rusting tanks, guns, and trucks testified to the fierce fighting that had gone on here in 1956 and 1967. Some lingering war damage could be seen on the inhabited side of the canal as well, in particular one former water tower riddled with shell holes testifying to the violence. We wondered whether it had been left deliberately as a monument. That whole side of the canal was guarded by a series of army barracks, with guards constantly looking at all the ships through binoculars.

As we crept south, we passed rural areas and villages. The villages and farms were often some distance away from the canal, but we did see goats and cattle wandering between clusters of small houses built helter-skelter. Many of the houses had gardens obviously used for growing food. We even spotted the odd camel a bit further away. For a long distance, a highway ran parallel to the canal. Many motorcycles, some with a load on a carrier behind the driver, small trucks overloaded with cargo, and buses full of people shared the highway with more than a few Mercedes and BMWs, some seemingly brand new. Al-Firdan, the one major town that borders right on the canal, looked prosperous, with beautiful homes on treed lots. We saw well-dressed children in a school playground running and jumping and shouting as children all over the world will do.

One by one, we drifted up to the bridge deck to watch the whole convoy from front to back as it passed through the canal. A Suez convoy is an impressive parade of large ships sailing at precisely the same speed, each stack belching black smoke, which ships of this kind tend to do at slow speed. Sometimes you saw only the stack and superstructure of a ship gliding above the Egyptian landscape and buildings, the rest of it hidden behind a curve of the canal, for the waterway has many slight bends as it snakes through the landscape. I thought a lot about the magnificence of the Suez Canal achievement, the blessings of it to Egyptian coffers, and the former might of this ancient civilization and its relationship to the Bible. As we sailed there, I also pondered Egypt's recent problems: its already large population still growing in a land of limited resources; its periods of violence; and its snail-paced democratic developments. Thankfully, a peace treaty with Israel has held for many years. I remembered that years ago I heard an economist argue that if the West provided pensions to seniors in both Egypt and Mexico, the size of families would be dramatically reduced in one generation, and poverty alleviated. Children and grandchildren would no longer be the vital insurance policy for support in old age. An interesting idea, I thought at the time.

Dusk had begun when we reached the end of the canal, and anchored ships were already waiting for the next day's northbound convoy. After passing them, the *Ville d'Aquarius* resumed full speed, and before too long we overtook some of the slower ships that had been ahead of us in the convoy. For a few hours we sped through the Gulf of Suez and then through the Strait of Jubal until we entered the Red Sea between Egypt and Saudi Arabia. During the next day we always saw other ships on this stretch: freighters, a passenger cruise ship, and many fishing boats. We also noticed a small white ship with a large number of stacks erupting from its hold. Gottfried told me that it was a sheep ship from Australia loaded with livestock destined for Saudi stomachs and remarked that with a different wind direction we would have noticed the awful stink coming from it. In a storm, many sheep die on ships like this and the carcasses are flung overboard. We were amazed at how many islands, large and small, some populated but most barren, dotted these waters.

Also that day, as they stood on the foc's'le, Johanna and Daryl witnessed an exciting display of sea life. Johanna wrote in her diary: "Suddenly, right below us, we saw what looked like an enormous dragonfly with a fat body. It was a flying fish! And there . . . a small dolphin racing ahead trying to keep up. It jumped, arched, and swam on. Quickly others followed. I clapped my hands to encourage them. Three more jumped up. I whistled on my fingers. Each time they jumped they whistled. It must have been a pod, for I saw little ones and big ones. Such a treat! Alas, they soon disappeared to the sides of the ship. I guess we went too fast for them."

As we approached Jeddah in Saudi Arabia, the captain asked us to hide any books with provocative covers and noted that it would be wise to remove any liquor bottles from sight. The women were requested to be modest in their attire and cover their arms and legs, even though the temperature would be high in port. Apparently, the officers had already removed all of the potentially provocative videos from the cupboards in the lounge (there were quite a number!). We were told that "they," clearly meaning Saudi authorities in the form of immigration and customs officers, and perhaps medical officers as well, had the right to come aboard and inspect all parts of the ship, but they never did.

We came to Jeddah in early evening, it was already dark. The entrance to Jeddah's harbour seemed intriguingly unreal, something out of a romantic movie. The spectacular harbour commission building, which looks like a water tower, dominated the entrance, lit up and clearly visible even at night. We also spotted a high fountain of water with a spotlight playing on it. I was so surprised that I suggested to Johanna that it must be a laser-beam

The impressive Jeddah Port Authority building as we sailed into its harbour as night was falling. It is built like a water tower at the edge of the Arabian desert.

spectacle, an optical illusion. Weren't we approaching the Arabian Desert, and wasn't water scarce here? She insisted that it was real water, and she was right. We speculated together that perhaps the fountain was an act of defiance against the dryness of deserts, and a calling card for the riches oil has bequeathed on this part of the world.

As we knew already, we weren't permitted to get off the ship to explore this intriguing city, even though we had enough time and it seemed within easy reach. In fact, a series of armed guards were posted at the foot of the gangway. Johanna and Daryl noticed that the guards had their eyes on them all the time, even more than on the men. Unloading and loading took us well into the afternoon of the next day and I spent hours watching, trying to understand the processes in more detail.

We left Jeddah on January 18 and sailed south, first between Sudan and Saudi Arabia, and the next day passing Eritrea and Ethiopia to starboard and Yemen on our portside. We speculated that the Red Sea did look a bit reddish, as the scorching rays of the sun bounced off the water, but it also could have been so named because of the unprotected human skin that has burned fiery red under the fierce sun in these parts. At its south end, the Red Sea narrows enough that both continents are within sight. The link between the Red Sea and the Gulf of Aden is called Bab el-Mandeb, which means, according to one of the officers, "Passage of Tears," for here were heard the cries of prisoners from Africa captured in raids across the water. Westerners often think about slavery in terms of British, Dutch, and American slave traders bringing captives over to the Americas from Africa to work on plantations, but slaves have been kept by all kinds of people in many different periods of history, as the Bible documents.

We turned almost due east here at Bab el-Mandeb, almost always within sight of the south coast of the Arabian Peninsula through the Gulf of Aden. Through my binoculars, I saw a barren land, hot, rocky, and mostly unin-habited, punctuated by only the occasional small seaside town or village. Once out of the gulf, we entered the Arabian Sea, the northern section of the Indian Ocean. Here, the sea was calm and as blue as we saw it anywhere, and the winds were light. Johanna was again the first to spot some wild-life—more flying fish. You see them best standing right at the bow looking down into the water. The ship seems to chase them out of the sea, small creatures that soar over the water, sometimes for a hundred metres, with fins like wings spread at an angle to their bodies. The fish are gorgeously coloured, mostly in shades of blue and brown.

Gradually we turned north, curving ourselves around Oman, going west on our way to Khor Fakkan, situated in the Gulf of Oman. The heat began to bother Johanna, and perhaps because of it she became irritated at some aspects of our daily life. For one thing, the toilet seat had come loose. Moreover, both doors in our cabin had come loose because of the inadequate screws that held them in their frames. The greatest irritation was that provision of clean bed linen and towels seemed to be a haphazard affair, done only when she raised the topic. Seeing that I was regularly playing ping-pong and drinking beer with First Officer Martin by this time, I was delegated to raise the issues. Fortunately, all three irritations were solved the next day. Jörg fixed the toilet seat and doors, and Ariel apologized and promised to do better, which he did for the remainder of the trip.

We landed in Khor Fakkan in the middle of the night. It's a small but growing port on the east coast of the Arabian Peninsula, located in United Arab Emirates, south of Dubai. Unlike Jeddah, here we encountered no barriers to visiting. After breakfast we walked to the port gate, where friendly port authorities took our passports, completed a temporary visa at no cost, and waved us on our way. Daryl, Johanna, and I walked into the city. Our visit happened to coincide with Ramadan, so no restaurants were open. Ramadan is the month in which the Quran was revealed to Mohammed, and it's a worldwide Muslim month of fasting, prayers, charity, and self-examination. As much as possible, economic life slows down. In Khor Fakkan some stores were open, however. We tried to buy some apples, but found the prices too steep, about $2US per apple. I briefly considered buying a flowing Arabian robe, didn't, and was sorry I hadn't for the rest of the trip. The women of the city were dressed in a wide variety of ways, from shorts and halter tops to burkas that provided only a small opening for the eyes.

We walked through some side streets in Khor Fakkan to have a look at some ordinary houses. From the outside they looked uninviting, mostly walls and gates and no gardens. Judging by the number of BMWs and Mercedes speeding through the one main thoroughfare, there must have been plenty of wealth in furniture and art behind those austere walls. Comparing the town with the hustle and bustle of construction at the port, it looked as if Khor Fakkan had been a sleepy and small harbour city, probably more for fishing boats than for anything else, until the expansion of container shipping. However, in the sixteenth and seventeenth centuries both Portuguese and Dutch explorers set foot here, an indication that Khor Fakkan's location and harbour were internationally important at other times.

While walking back to the ship along the main road, we heard the sound of a car crash. Of course, we turned around and watched the aftermath, a loud argument between the two male drivers, both in gorgeous long white robes, standing between their large expensive sedans. The experience brought on a bit of what the Germans call *schadenfreude*, that peculiar type of pleasure people experience when they watch the bad fortune of others more privileged than they. When we continued on our walk "home," big birds with gray bodies, aquamarine wing markings, and blue crests on their heads swooped down quite close to us, making raucous noises like magpies.

As we left Khor Fakkan later that evening, the ship made its way slowly out of the harbour, carefully curving around a huge rock in the middle of it. In the distance we saw a large stadium lit up; perhaps a soccer game or horse races were in progress, attended by affluent citizens like those we had encountered that day. Of all the ports we visited, Khor Fakkan was the least familiar name, but we left it feeling that we had been given a glimpse into the mysterious and luxurious world of the oil-rich United Arab Emirates.

CHAPTER FOUR

Khor Fakkan to Pusan

When the topic of our sea voyages comes up in company, we're often asked, "Did you have to work?" Our answer to this logical question is, "No, we didn't." Going far back in history, cargo ships usually carried paying passengers. Many tales of sailing ships mention people who travelled to and from trading posts and colonial settlements. Even today some companies operate combined cargo and passenger ships, particularly in the South Pacific, on scheduled visits to the many island countries spread throughout those waters, and on Scandinavian routes to outports on the lengthy coasts of Norway, Sweden, and Finland. I have also met people who crossed the Atlantic as working passengers on general cargo ships in the 1950s and 1960s, with part or all of their fare earned by their labour on board.

Special passenger liners developed in the second part of the nineteenth century, when steam engines replaced sails, ships became larger, and passenger traffic increased. Mass migration to the North and South American continents required ships that could carry large numbers of passengers, first to bring migrants one way, and then to accommodate those who wanted to revisit their native land. Some passenger liners became famous for their size, luxury, and speed; the British *Queen Elizabeth* and the *Queen Mary* were built just before World War II for trans-Atlantic traffic. We also saw the American passenger liner, *United States*, idle and rusting in the Philadelphia harbour, and we all know the story of the *Titanic*. Of course, these ships carried cargo as well, including mail, but their main function was to ferry passengers. However, as airplanes became larger, faster, and relatively cheaper, lengthy sea crossings grew less popular. Contemporary cruise ships are floating hotels, islands of fantasy that foster the illusion that everyone on board is rich and famous and far above the humdrum routines of daily life.

As container ships became larger, and sailing technology became more sophisticated, the number of sailors required diminished. The steam engines of yesteryear required more engine-room personnel than the motor vessels of today. Loading and unloading container ships takes far fewer bodies as well, both on board and working in the port. A good sized general cargo ship would have carried forty or fifty sailors forty years ago. The much larger *Ville d'Aquarius* manages with just twenty-one. If you were to compare the profiles of a traditional general cargo ship and a modern container ship, both loaded, you would notice that most of the traditional ship lies low in the water. The superstructure is clearly visible and located well above the deck, with a clear view from the bridge. A container vessel loads half its cargo on deck and therefore needs a bridge high enough for "chauffeurs" to look over the piles of containers stacked as many as five high, up to fifteen metres tall. Its superstructure will be higher, and therefore offer more room, than old-fashioned cargo ships. For reasons of navigation and safety, the bridge also needs to stretch the full width of the ship, thirteen containers wide on the *Ville d'Aquarius*, seventeen wide on some of the newest ships. The combination of a larger superstructure and fewer sailors leaves a lot of room. Even though most freighters have already adopted private cabins for each sailor and made officers' cabins larger, some still have room left that provides an opportunity for additional revenue. The *Ville d'Aquarius* had room for eight passengers in four double-occupancy cabins. Most freighters that take passengers limit the number to twelve as, by international law, a higher number requires an on-board physician.

"So then," people asked us after we explained the nature of being a passenger on a container freighter, "what did you do all day?" First, there wasn't a single day we were bored. Novelty and excitement are fine, but only for special experiences and short times. However enjoyable the first week on board had been, it had offered little opportunity to shape daily routines.

When voyages between ports were lengthier, our days became more predictable, which suited both of us.

We slept a lot. Perhaps it was the sea air, or the fact that nothing was expected of us and our bodies reacted by letting go of adrenalin, leaving us languid. Most nights we'd be in bed shortly after nine, and we'd sleep until morning. If we did wake up at night and couldn't get back to sleep immediately, nothing stopped us from throwing on a few clothes and standing outside to stare over waters that shimmered with the reflected light from the moon and stars, or looked dark and foreboding under cloudy skies. Sometimes we'd climb up to the bridge and keep company with the sailors on duty, welcome company we discovered. When the moon and stars were hidden behind clouds, the decks would be so dark that we'd walk using our memory, step by step with arms outstretched.

We developed a daily routine. Breakfast was available from 0730-0830 and varied from day to day, as indicated by the weekly posted menus. Some mornings we had a fairly fluid rice pudding with fruit (raisins, or canned mandarin orange sections and peaches). Eggs cooked in the style of your choice were served on other mornings. We also had orange or grapefruit juice and plenty of coffee. The bread on board the ship was typically denser and heavier than we were used to, wheat or rye, typical German bread. We even got to like "strammermax"—in moderation.

After breakfast I would exercise. Plenty of food and sleep, and a daily cocktail hour plus regular beer with the officers and crew adds up to a recipe for obesity. So how do you guard against that? The *Ville d'Aquarius* had an exercise room with some equipment, including a swimming pool. It also had a large working deck that completely circled the ship. As for walking, the ship's length of 269 metres and width of 32 metres made a 600-metre circuit once around, twice around was more than a kilometre, and three times, more than a mile. It also possessed a set of outside stairs with a total of eighty-six steps. I made it a point to use all of it, except the pool. Almost from the beginning, and weather permitting, I developed a routine of walking the deck, climbing the stairs, riding the stationary bike, and using the rowing machine. As I got used to the routine, I increased the speed and duration of my exercises. As a result, I didn't gain weight and was in as good a shape leaving the ship as I was boarding it. After exercising, I would take a shower, we'd have a cup of coffee, and most often I'd read until lunchtime on the deck, weather permitting, or in our cabin or the lounge. The deck chairs and cushions were stored in a cabinet on the sixth deck and we were free to haul them to wherever we wanted, which was most often the shady side of the ship.

Lunch was served between 1200 to 1300 hours and dinner from 1800 to 1900 hours, and each meal was governed by weekly posted menus. On the *Ville d'Aquarius*, the food was plain: beef, pork, chicken, potatoes, and vegetables. The ship served salads on the whole trip out, but ran out of ingredients on the way back. (We suspected that the shipping company wouldn't buy local salad ingredients it couldn't be sure were safe. We had been warned not to eat salads in Asian restaurants.) On Saturdays a hearty soup was served at lunch and dinner, full of chunks of German sausage with all the bread you could eat. Sunday evening was the cook's evening off. The steward opened cans of fish, smoked and in various sauces, and we ate those with bread as well. Jams and peanut butter were also available, as they were at all breakfasts.

After lunch I would often have a short snooze and then make my way to the bridge for my daily conversations with Second Officer Gottfried. He was invariably welcoming, made coffee, answered my questions, and asked me about my life on land as I asked him about his career, family, country, and personal stories. Close to the end of his shift at 1600 hours, I would make my way back to our cabin for a preprandial drink with Johanna and Daryl. Sometimes Gottfried joined us, and sometimes Pierre. Occasionally we'd ask the second engineer in as well, since his shift also ended at 1600 hours. Sometimes Daryl and I played our two-handed bridge game, or the three of us played Triomino together. On occasion I would read some more while Daryl and Johanna played Scrabble.

Johanna spent much of her time in a deck chair, knitting, reading, or talking with me or Daryl. She would also go swimming in the small pool once a day, weather permitting, for the pool was filled with sea water that was warm only in the southern areas of our trip. At least once a day we would make our way to the very front tip of the foc's'le where we would stand on a steel platform looking right down a hole in the hull to where the ship met the sea, looking for sea life, talking, or simply enjoying the experience surrounded by that very particular sea symphony we'll never forget.

I previously mentioned the medical requirements passengers have to meet before permission is granted to come on board. A health certificate must be completed and signed by the passenger's physician to assure the captain that no health problems bar such a journey. Captain Richter told us that most doctors sign it without knowing anything of the conditions on

A good book, and in ten minutes or so I'll have my afternoon nap. Notice "Plato" on one of the books, a collection of that famous philosopher's complete works I had brought to finally read my way through.

board a ship. He had been faced with a number of passengers with medical problems that impeded their own enjoyment and added ongoing worries to his already full plate of responsibilities. Some panted and wheezed their way to and from dining rooms and lounges, were unable to take walks around the deck, and were slow and almost helpless in fire and safety drills. To really enjoy the trip one should be reasonably fit, and generally ships will not accept passengers over eighty years of age. In our mid-sixties, and in good condition, we nevertheless experienced the effort of all the ups and downs, especially when the sea was rough.

Like most freighters, the *Ville d'Aquarius* didn't have an elevator. Our cabin was located on the fifth deck (two decks below the bridge), and the dining room was on the first deck. Each meal and snack break required fifty-six steps down the stairs, and the same number up. Five trips to the dining room per day amounted to 280 steps up the stairs daily for a total of 17,640 routine steps up during the journey. Add to that visits to the laundry room (first deck), crew's lounge (second deck), recreation room/swimming pool (third deck), the rooms of other passengers and officers (fourth deck), the offices of the captain and chief engineer and mailbox (sixth deck), and bridge (seventh deck), and we both took well over twenty thousand steps up stairs, plus twenty thousand steps down, during our shipboard life.

Life tends to revolve around mealtimes on a ship, at least for passengers. However little communal activity there may have been during the rest of the day, meals bring passengers together. Food and drink are necessities of life, but meals are also a special kind of glue for building human communities. Guests enter your homes, and after they sit down you ask them what they would like to drink and eat. Many family tensions have been lessened around a dinner table. Johanna and I have moved around quite a bit, and in every new community we invite new friends to dinner to share our different backgrounds and identities. Unfortunately, shipboard meals aren't always amicable. One *Ville d'Aquarius* captain, Captain Anderson, told us about two couples, two sisters and their husbands, who had come on board together. One might expect cohesion from such close relatives, but instead, the couples began first to bicker, then to fight, and then to loathe one another openly and loudly in the dining room.

"What did you do?" I asked the captain.

He replied, "I told one couple they could have the first thirty minutes of mealtimes, and the other that they would have the second thirty minutes."

On the *Ville d'Aquarius*, meals with Daryl and Pierre were an almost perfect joy. Daryl's opinions were politically pretty far right and sometimes a bit of a shock to our orthodox Christian souls. Pierre carried with him right-wing views similar to Daryl's, but his were within a French context and he argued with her at times. The views of those two combined with our more left-leaning approaches to society's woes made for interesting table talk. Pierre couldn't eat dinner without wine, and so bought a bottle every night until the slop chest's supply of red wine ran out. (After we learned of his need, we three steadily refused his kind offer of sharing his bottle with us.) Daryl was fairly fluent in French, and we both knew enough words and phrases to recognize the general area of any French conversation. Body language and hand gestures also smoothed the verbal way, and timely smiles became conversational gestures of goodwill when spoken communication fatally bogged us all down.

Pierre videotaped hours of footage of the sea, ports, and containers, which he always watched after dinner; sometimes we watched with him. He didn't join in any games, nor was he seen all that much during the day or after dinner, when he usually sat in his room, reading and writing letters. He accompanied the three of us to various port cities, shared cab expenses, and drew our attention to features we may have otherwise missed. Pierre was impeded by a lame left leg and was grateful to the three of us for walking more slowly than we would normally do.

After-dinner entertainment on board a freighter differs dramatically from that available on board a cruise ship. Passengers can't count on being entertained by officers or crew, and remaining aloof from passengers is a valid option for both officers and crew. Passengers on container freighters are paying guests; however, a freighter makes its major money shipping freight. That's not to say that passengers would be dumped overboard just to save freight in a fierce storm, but in the routines of such a ship, business comes first.

Johanna and I consider ourselves blessed by our experiences on board, however. On the *Ville d'Aquarius* the officers had their own lounge, but we were invited to use it as well. It contained a bar, a card table, sofas, easy chairs, a coffee table, a TV/video set, a small library of books and videos, a radio/cassette/CD player, and some CDs. Perhaps once a week some of the off-duty officers would assemble in the lounge to watch a video and we

I'm playing with Cadet Lars against officers Gottfried and Martin in the games room. Notice the small swimming pool behind us.

would sometimes join them if the movie appealed to us. Some evenings the officers stayed in their own cabins, playing computer games or reading. They would sometimes visit one another for a beer and some talk. Many nights the officers, sometimes joined by the captain, would gather in the recreation room and play darts or ping-pong. After a few visits, I was invited to play ping-pong as well, and discovered that I could hold my own. When I had gained enough confidence, I suggested a voyage tournament, complete with a schedule and playoffs. To my delight they accepted, and up until almost the end of our journey we played regularly. We also played doubles in various partnerships. Gottfried was a very gentle man but a ferocious competitor. Eventually, Martin won the playoffs and became the ship's champion.

Germany was a participant in the World Cup Soccer played the year of our voyage and the German officers would raise the subject regularly. Some were looking forward to watching the games on German TV during their leave, so I suggested a betting pool, with each one contributing $5US, winner take all. I designed a system that would award points for accurate predictions at all five levels of the competition. Without exception, the Germans predicted their country would win. I predicted France—and won the $45. As the games were played well after we had left the ship, I asked Jörg to be the keeper of the funds. I promised to write to him to let him know where to send the winnings. When I won, I asked him to donate the money to a volunteer sea rescue operation in his hometown. Months later I received a thank-you letter with a photograph of the rescue boat and crew.

Another option in the evenings was a visit to the Filipino crew's lounge. Our first visit came by invitation to a Sunday evening birthday party for Ariel. That birthday party showed us just how much the Filipinos cared for one another. It was full of joy, laughter, beer, snacks, music, dancing, and the celebration of a "far-from-home" colleague's presence on a special day. Officers and passengers were honoured guests in the smoky decorated room, full of happy people. The music came from CDs and from a TV screen that showed music videos for karaoke singing.

I watched two sailors in the corner of the room playing chess for awhile. They asked me if I would like to play, so I sat down, played, and lost. After losing a second game, I was invited to come down more often to play chess. From then on I would drift down to their lounge once a week after dinner. I was always offered beer and sometimes brought along a case of beer myself. I played against about five different players, and won only one game

Most of the Filipino crew relaxing in their lounge in the evening. They always made us feel welcome. Notice the well-used chessboard.

the whole trip, but always enjoyed myself, even with the loud karaoke songs that filled up the room most of the time. Whenever I visited the Filipino crew's lounge, there were sailors sitting around talking, smoking, and drinking beer, playing chess, passing the microphone around for karaoke singing while watching videos, and enjoying each other's company. I noticed that social time didn't stretch long into the evening. Sleep is a precious commodity on board a working ship, and sailors also spend private time in their cabins.

Kirche was kept up after Captain Anderson left the ship. While Captain Richter clearly had no interest in this event, the other German officers, Martin, Friedrich, and Wolfgang, with Jörg also always present, continued the tradition, making sure that beer and nibbles were at hand, and we continued to have a good time together. Gottfried couldn't attend as he had to begin watch at 1200. One Sunday we asked cadet Lars, who we knew to be a PK (preacher's kid), why they called it *kirche*. It seemed that some of the officers had churchgoing backgrounds and had chosen the term to have at least a fellowship break on this day. In a long conversation with Lars and Chief Friedrich (whose best friend was a Lutheran pastor), we shared what faith and *kirche* meant to us. Both sailors were nostalgic about their childhood church time, but neither felt a strong urge to become part of the church again, even when onshore. They couldn't really say why, other than that the desire was weak.

It's high time I explain "slop chest." It's an old maritime term, which in its early days simply meant the chest in which essential tools and other items were stored during sailing. It now means the "store" of snacks, toiletries, postcards, liquor, wine, beer, soft drinks, and other items for sale to crew and passengers. Gottfried was the storekeeper. A price and supply list hung in the dining room, and on a table beneath it stood a box of chits on which you could note your order for the day. As long as you ordered at breakfast time, Gottfried would deliver your order after his afternoon watch ended. Once a month we got a bill from the captain. Prices for alcoholic drinks were ridiculously low: a case of twenty-four Beck Beer cost around $9US; a bottle of Johnny Walker scotch about $11; and red and white wine about $7. Peanuts in a can, chocolate bars, and bags of chips were about the same price as onshore, since they didn't carry the same level of "sin" taxes. We also bought 1.5-litre bottles of water in twelve-bottle cases, on the advice of Gottfried, since the drinking water on board was never to be trusted unreservedly. Postcards and letters were dropped in the red mailbox outside the captain's office, and mailed by the next local agent. You were then assessed a flat charge of 75¢US per mailing on your next bill.

By the time we had reached Khor Fakkan, we had become thoroughly settled on board the *Ville d'Aquarius*, masters of its routines and with firmly established routines of our own. We were loving every minute of our voyage and eagerly anticipating the next port. On January 23, we sailed southeast from Khor Fakkan towards Singapore, a five-day-at-sea stretch, the longest so far. At first we didn't see many other ships, but as we approached India and Sri Lanka, traffic increased again as we rejoined the shipping lane that connects Singapore with the Suez Canal. As I looked at the maps and recalled the Portuguese, British, and Dutch colonial history of the region, I thought of the tens of thousands of ships that must have followed this route from Suez to Singapore, and thence underneath the broad belly of Asia to destinations as far away as East Siberia, and back down to the multitude of islands that form the Philippines and Indonesia.

On this stretch of calm seas and placid skies, the ship left behind a prominent orange streak that hung right above the horizon. It gave me an uneasy feeling and when I asked Friedrich about it, he told me it was the unconsumed sulfur that forms 5 to 7 percent of the ship's fuel. As the *Ville d'Aquarius* consumed more than one hundred tons of fuel each twenty-

This seemingly small tugboat is just about to pull our giant ship away from the Hong Kong berth.

four hours, it emitted about six tons of sulfur daily, which eventually mixed with the sea or land. In the afternoon I hesitantly asked Gottfried, socially conscious and politically critical on so many issues, whether this kind of pollution, so visible that day, bothered him. In a previous discussion he had talked with disgust about the environmental disasters left behind by many Communist regimes, especially in East Germany. He seemed a bit embarrassed about the evil-looking trail behind the ship, but then he asked me to think about the pollution effects of alternate modes of transportation for the load we had on board, about 3,500 containers. Transporting these by rail would take about twenty-five trains of one hundred wagons each (some carry two containers), each train pulled by two or three engines, which also spew out toxic gases for hours on end. Alternatively, our load would require 3,500 smelly diesel-fuel-consuming trucks, with badly maintained trucks belching clouds of black smoke and driving on roads that have often devoured precious agricultural fields. I lack the skills to do a comparative study, but Gottfried made me think, as he usually did.

The ship curved around India and Sri Lanka, and sailed west between the Andaman and Nicobar Islands through the Ten Degree Channel. Unfortunately, we sailed too far offshore to see land. A disaster several years later brought the world's attention to this area. We were sailing through the waters of the 2005 tsunami; the earthquake that had caused it had its epicentre in Northern Sumatra, not far from where we were.

We then turned in a more southerly direction to hit the Straits of Malacca, between Malaysia on our port and Sumatra on our starboard side. Sumatra is part of Indonesia. Until 1946 Indonesia (then called Dutch East Indies) was a Dutch colony. Even before World War II, liberation movements had begun to stir, and right after the war ended, Indonesians began to fight for their freedom. At first, Holland sent an army to suppress this rebellion, but under pressure, especially from the United States, it agreed to Indonesia's independence in December 1949. Earlier that year, a good friend of mine had showed up at our house in tears one night: The family had heard that day that his soldier cousin had been killed in Indonesia.

Two of my brothers-in-law were born on Sumatra before World War II, where their father worked in the oil industry. All of the members of the family survived Japanese concentration camps, and as we saw the island in the distance we thought of them and remembered the stories they had often told us about camp life and their difficulties after the war. In 1942 Dad Stassen and the oldest son, Wim, were separated from the family and incarcerated in different concentration camps for the remainder of the war. The rest of the family—mother, sons Henk and Fred (both our brothers-in-law now) and daughter Pauline—survived the war in another camp. Henk was seven when "his" war began and as the oldest son present, he shouldered much of the responsibility for gathering food and fuel. He remembers that he often carried his much younger brother Fred on his back. When the war ended, they didn't know if Dad and Wim had survived, but they had, and the family was reunited eventually.

The Straits of Malacca are infamous for piracy. At nightfall the crew carefully locked all deck doors from the inside, and we were asked to refrain from going outside for a few nights. Pirates from Indonesia, Malaysia, and even the Philippines frequently board freighters, rob sailors and passengers, even steal cargo, and when meeting resistance have no hesitation to kill. In the dark they approach ships with small and fast boats, throw hooks over the ships' railings, and climb aboard. Our captain said that our ship would probably, but only probably, be too fast and big for any pirates to attack. During the day we saw many fishing boats, and I sometimes wondered if any of them were pirate boats planning an attack for that night.

During this stretch, the captain organized a wonderful Saturday night barbecue for all who were aboard. Only four individuals were missing: the two watchers on the bridge and the two in the engine room. Preparations had begun earlier in the week. In his workshop, Jörg had put together two crude wooden tables, which had been lifted by the on-board crane to the only deck that was big enough for the barbecue, the one we often used for daytime reading and relaxing. This close to the equator, night falls early all year-round, and by the time the cook had chicken, a variety of sausages, plus chops and small steaks ready, it was getting dark. We enjoyed plenty of salads and other trimmings, and beer and wine flowed both freely and free. Once it was dark, the clear skies and thousands of twinkling stars added to the magic of the evening. You didn't need to look up to see the stars—they crowded the sky right down to the horizon in all directions. Ancient Israelites thought the heavens were an upside-down bowl clamped over the flat earth, and that night it looked as if they had been right. Passengers and officers occupied one table and the crew sat at the other, but later in the evening Johanna and I took our dessert to the crew's table, where we were warmly welcomed. We went to bed that night stuffed with food, giddy from alcohol, and happy as a seagull full of fish. In two days we would arrive in Singapore.

One afternoon Johanna and I were visiting Gottfried on the bridge when the telex machine spewed out a printed distress signal for a man overboard from a ship some two hundred kilometres away. Gottfried then told us about other cases, and explained to us the rescue obligations of ships anywhere near a disaster. Within reach of a ship in distress, all ships are required to interrupt their voyage, sail to it, and offer assistance. "Within reach" may mean being the closest but a number of days' sailing away. Given our location, we didn't need to change course. Gottfried showed us a binder full of previous distress signals.

Another memorable event on this leg of the trip was a washing mishap. We had brought on board a commemorative towel featuring the largest church in my Mother's town. Johanna washed it, but its black dye ran and smudged our white wear. To compensate, Johanna got some bleach from the cook, and used it in a washing load. The next thing she knew, First Officer Martin came running into the laundry room and told her that the use of bleach was strictly forbidden. It had shown up in the water purification control system. Although it had been an unintentional mistake, Johanna felt awful, not only for having done what she did, but also for the cook's potential trouble. Her lesson was learned.

Singapore is one of the world's leading ports, handling every kind of ship imaginable. Its location makes it a natural hub port for containers. With rapid changes in the global economy, Singapore competes with many other ports, notably Hong Kong and Shanghai. However, it will always rank among the world's top ports because it's so well situated. We were told that during our visit a million containers were in its port, and I counted at least thirty container ships being loaded and unloaded.

For a long time, the island of Singapore was politically part of the Malacca peninsula (now Malaysia). However, in the second half of the eighteenth century, European nations such as Great Britain and the Netherlands began to eye Asia as a source of profitable markets. Singapore's strategic location made it a perfect choice for a permanent settlement, and in 1819 a British trading post was established where the city of Singapore is now located. Malacca had been captured from the Dutch in 1795, when the Netherlands was temporarily part of Napoleon's continental territory and powerless to stop British raiding. Singapore's first British overlord was Sir Stamford Raffles, after whom the famous Raffles Hotel is named. It took only three years for the settlement to show a profit, and in 1824 it officially became part of the British Empire after treaties with the Dutch, who ceded all claims to it, and with the Malaccan owners in exchange for cash and pensions. With the development of steamships and the opening of the Suez Canal, Singapore gained even more importance. After 1870 it became the major export location for rubber, and it rapidly expanded in development and population, attracting people from all over Asia, especially from China.

During World War II, the Japanese army took the city in early 1942. The British regained control in September 1945, and made Singapore a crown colony. That status opened the door to democratic movements that would eventually lead to virtual self-government. A strong Communist movement tried to take over both Malaya and Singapore in 1948, but was unsuccessful when the British declared a state of emergency and resisted the rebels. However, it was inevitable that the colony would eventually become an independent country. In 1959 the first indigenous government was elected. The first years were turbulent, as the Communists were still powerful, especially among labour unions and students, and intent on creating a Communist state. Complicating the political situation were movements to form a federation with such neighbouring states as Malaya, Sarawak, North Borneo, and Brunei, a plan brought to fruition in 1963 with only Brunei abstaining. However, because of opposition from other emerging Asian nations like Indonesia, the federation fell apart in a few years. On August 6,

1965, Singapore became a sovereign, democratic, and independent nation. Since then, aggressive economic development policies that include a stress on quality education have transformed Singapore into the thriving place we saw on our visit.

After we berthed at the port of Singapore, we were told we had about five hours for sightseeing. We four passengers were glad to have a chance to stretch our land legs again after five days at sea. We discovered from the local agent that we had come during Chinese New Year, and transit buses that normally run around the enormous port area every thirty minutes all day long weren't operating. We would have to walk to the gates. Fortunately, the city seemed to begin just outside the gates, as we could see from our ship's upper decks. After carefully walking for more than half an hour through long and high stacks of containers, keeping our eyes on the enormous smoke-belching harbour container trucks, some with engines groaning from carrying two units, we reached the gates. We also marvelled at something we hadn't seen before in any port area: meticulously maintained and colourful flower beds and flowerpots sprinkled throughout this cacophony of global trading sounds. While we walked, the gates were hidden by containers, but when we looked as if we were lost, truck drivers honked their horns and pointed us in the right direction.

After we identified ourselves at the gate and stated our plans, we walked out and found a four-lane expressway right in front of us. Even though this was a holiday for most Singaporeans, a constant stream of cars whizzed by, many of them BMWs and Mercedes, and we had to find a traffic light some distance away to cross the road. Clearly we were in the centre of this city, with major hotels and high office towers beginning not more than one block across the major traffic artery. We had been warned not to drop any garbage anywhere, not even a candy wrapper, for fines would be imposed, and we decided not to test the law. With only about five hours to spend here, we merely walked around, admiring the spotlessness of this immaculate city, and having our fancies tickled by the laundry drying on "flagpoles" sticking out of many of the apartment buildings.

At coffee time we found an Indian café open for business, light, bright, and clean, with several tables already occupied by customers. Friendly staff quickly brought the tea we ordered. All the Chinese cafés we had passed were closed. We walked by a large market complex, but it too wasn't in operation this day. We would have liked to try a lunch there, encouraged by what some of the officers had told us about the quality and low cost of the market food. Singapore has many small well-maintained parks, even in the inner city, and one large park, evidence that in this bustling metropolis the needs of human beings aren't forgotten. Flowers were everywhere in this hot and humid city, especially surrounding office towers and sometimes cascading from walls right onto the sidewalks.

Singapore is located just above the equator, with open water to its east, south, and west. While it was clear and sunny most of the day, in the afternoon clouds suddenly appeared and within minutes an enormous downpour forced us to seek shelter. Yet, the rain lasted only a few minutes, and ten minutes later the sidewalks had already begun to dry, even in the still oppressive humidity. On our way back to port, we went by a large hotel and picked up a number of tourist brochures in preparation for our return visit. There are huge benefits to being in the same port twice. Even though officers and crew provide information, and there may be a city map or tourist booklet on board, there's nothing like a quick reconnaissance visit to whet your appetite and allow you to make detailed plans before the next time in port.

We left Singapore on January 30, turning north again and passing Vietnam on our portside, although too far away to see the coastline. After a few days we arrived at the port of Hong Kong. The entry at dusk was memorable. As we sailed slowly towards our berth, the sun was putting itself to bed and lights came on in high-rise after high-rise, a spectacular sight. Hong Kong harbour waters are incredibly busy with ferries small and large, fast and faster, small container carriers with their own cranes, tankers, and fishing vessels. Hong Kong harbour looked like Rotterdam harbour with its mix of large and small vessels, sea-going ships, and river freighters that were also living quarters for families as they made their living. The hustle and bustle filled us with admiration.

Like Singapore, Hong Kong's great assets are its location, close to China and Japan in particular, and its magnificently sheltered multiple deep harbours. It's comprised of a small mainland section not far away from Canton, a major Chinese city. Hong Kong comprises one large island, called Hong Kong Island, and over two hundred small ones. Its capital, located on Hong Kong Island, is officially called Victoria. The British first occupied the sparsely populated and rocky island in the early 1840s. During the remaining decades of the nineteenth century, the colony increasingly prospered as a commercial gateway to and from South China, establishing a reputation for reliability and integrity. In December 1941, it was occupied by the Japanese, and retaken by the British in September 1945, after World War II hostilities had ended. When in 1949 the Communists took control of China, hundreds of thousands of mainland refugees swarmed to Hong Kong, making it one of the most densely populated areas in the world almost overnight. Housing, health, crime, and the provision of water were the main problems the British colonial government met with aggressive policies. However, with 98 percent of the population ethnically Chinese, the political presence of Hong Kong's massive neighbour could never be ignored. May 1967 was an especially turbulent time, with riots and strikes inspired by China's Cultural Revolution. After years of negotiations, the British government agreed to relinquish control of Hong Kong on July 1, 1997, with China agreeing to give it substantial autonomy over its own affairs. Johanna and I experienced that autonomy first-hand: For every other Chinese port we needed a special visa, but not for Hong Kong, even though when we landed the transfer of power had already taken place.

I have a special relationship with Hong Kong. In 1983 I was made director of publishing for the company I was part of for thirty-one wonderful years. I had big ambitions for producing quality children's books and a limited budget to produce them. An Australian friend, also in publishing, alerted me to the existence of a sophisticated and competitively priced printing industry in Hong Kong and got me in touch with a printing broker. Yvonne Wong had worked for a publisher in New York City for eight years, and this smart woman had returned to make use of her Hong Kong printing connections to serve North American and Australian publishing needs. Before long our company shifted a substantial portion of book printing to Hong Kong. We sent Ms. Wong the specifications, and she soon provided quotations after having contacted the various printing and binding companies she knew. After we settled on a particular project, she looked after colour separations, printing, binding, and shipping. Her price included a richly deserved commission. Over the years of our relationship, our art director visited the city twice to meet various producers and check on quality. Ms. Wong visited us every third year or so, and some of the largest producers of our books came as well. The books shipped to us always came in containers; one year we had a container on the high seas for almost every day of the year, and our total business with Hong Kong exceeded one million US dollars. By the time our ship landed in Hong Kong, Ms. Wong had emigrated back to the United States, so I couldn't meet her once again.

Because we arrived at night and unloading and loading continued in the dark, we didn't have enough time for a shore visit the next day. We were at least a one-hour cab ride away from the interesting tourist sections of the city, and so decided not to risk coming back late. We were told that Hong Kong had an interesting Seafarers' Centre just outside the port proper, a fifteen-minute harbour bus ride away, so we headed there instead. It was full of books and magazines, with a bar and an entertainment section that included ping-pong, billiards, and TVs. We had coffee and beer and read newspapers and magazines, including some Dutch ones. Johanna and Daryl spotted the multilanguage library, and borrowed a number of books each, which they promised to return on our second visit. When we returned to Hong Kong a few weeks later, we not only returned those books, but left additional ones behind.

As for available newspapers, I devoured as many as I could, both local and international. While I enjoyed being media-deprived on board, curiosity reared its head onshore and I couldn't resist pouncing on whatever English or Dutch newspapers I could get my hands on. I borrowed or purchased, often at exorbitant prices, week-old copies of such major newspapers as the London and New York *Times*, and the *International Herald*. After our visit to the Seafarers' Centre, we returned to the ship to discover that some vendors had come aboard. I bought a beautiful watch for Johanna from a vendor the captain told me was trustworthy. For the rest of the time we watched port activities. On the dockside, we observed the loading and unloading of containers, the skills of the crane operators, the constant to-ing and fro-ing of powerful trucks, the stevedores on board and below, the shouts and pointing, the occasional sedan of agents and other port officials weaving their way through behemoth traffic. On the waterside, we were fascinated by the never-ending bustle of ships large and small, sailing in all directions but never colliding.

From Hong Kong we sailed northeast again, first through the Formosa Strait between Taiwan and the People's Republic of China and then along the coast of South Korea, to our starboard side. The weather had turned much colder now, cloudy and rainy, and the force-eight wind was blowing up short choppy waves many metres high. It also seemed that the sea was never without some fishing boats plying their trade—there must have been hundreds on this leg. Not surprisingly on this busy shipping lane, we met and sometimes passed other freighters as well, container ships and slower-moving tankers.

We were on our way to Inchun, the port city for the more inland South

Korean capital city of Seoul. It got colder as we approached, though the winds were calmer than in the Formosa Straits. For the first time we also experienced fog, though not serious enough to slow the ship down. The ship docked just after midnight after going through a lock. Johanna and I woke up around that time, perhaps because of the noise through our open porthole, but more likely because of the freezing air that had entered our cabin.

We had most of a day for a visit to Inchun. No harbour shuttle bus was available, and we had long walks in and out. It was sunny, but the air was crisp and cold. Inchun is a dusty and dirty port. Large piles of fertilizer and grain lay under cover on the quays, attracting birds and undoubtedly rats. Many stevedores wore masks, making us think that air pollution was a serious problem here. In this port, the truck drivers were positively unfriendly, honking their horns and shaking their fists at us. On the way out I walked with one of the crew members who had a day off and asked him about his life at sea and back in the Philippines. He had been a sailor for twelve years and his earnings supported an extended family back home. However, he had invested money in his own trucking company, with two trucks driven by his father and a brother, which was already making money. Moreover, he had bought thirty-two acres of fertile land that his wife used to grow vegetables and fruit commercially. He wasn't going to sail much longer, but planned to buy a third truck and drive it himself. He was one of the more quiet Filipinos on board and also seemed a bit older than his colleagues, but his determination was impressive. For him the sea had had no particular pull—it was only an opportunity for building a more secure financial future for his children and extended family. Once more I was impressed by the strength of commitment shown by so many of the Filipinos we met.

Inchun begins right outside the port gates. After getting some South Korean money in a bank a block away, we walked farther into the city. Soon we came across an amazing market, a covered street full of fruit and fish and clothes. The fish displays were especially spectacular. We saw dried, smoked, and fresh fish of all sizes, some gorgeously coloured and some drab, but all artfully piled and displayed. We bought some fruit and some peanuts in the shell. Daryl and Johanna ate a freshly prepared pastry from a baker, made as they watched. I was reminded of my long-ago Dutch market experiences, where bakers would dip a ladle in a dough pot, throw a blob of dough on a hot griddle, and a few minutes later you held a hot delicacy in your hand. The women ate the pastry with gusto, and I regretted not ordering one for

A heaping helping of various kinds of fish ready for the pan. Next to this kiosk was an equally varied display of vegetables. My mouth still waters when I see the pictures.

myself. Daryl took a picture of a market-stall woman who was taking a cat-nap behind her wares, and another younger woman immediately began to yell at her in Korean with plenty of "No's" thrown in. I don't know if taking the picture was a cultural offense or if it was just a personal objection on the part of the younger woman. Perhaps the younger woman was a daughter who felt that her mother was sleeping and had no chance to give her consent for this photo to be taken.

We had lunch in a little restaurant right behind two cooking pots on the street. Each pot contained a different kind of chicken, and we thoroughly enjoyed the very inexpensive meal, chicken with coleslaw and mild radishes, plus a local beer. Since the outer layers of these vegetables had been removed, we took a chance that they were safe to eat. In fact, we saw the radishes being peeled and sliced before we ate. Judging by the growing market activity in the other streets as well, the city gets livelier as the day progresses, for many more stalls were still being set up, with clothing, electronics, leather goods, and shoes, among other merchandise. Although the faces and signs of all kinds were different, the whole scene looked familiar. I grew up when outdoor markets operated at least once a week in almost every good-sized town. On Tuesdays in Baarn, where I grew up, there was a market on the *Brink*, the square adjacent to the biggest church in town. There was always a pleasant hustle and bustle, with the merchants shouting prices and other enticements at prospective customers for their meat, cheese, fish, vegetables and fruits, clothing, household knick-knacks, and textiles. The merchants, who would find themselves in a different town six days of the week, all seemed to know each other and would carry on conversations back and forth while serving their customers. This Inchun market took me back to the wonderful human activity and interaction of the markets I had known as a child.

Over dinner the four of us got into a serious and occasionally tense conversation. The subject was the future, especially hope for the younger generations. Both Daryl and Pierre voiced their disillusionment with governments, socialist tendencies, young people, and immigration policies. I countered by pointing out that current conditions hadn't been caused by youths and immigrants, but were the products of our own generation. Gottfried, eating at the table next to us, listened attentively, and on occasion joined in the conversation. It was the most serious and penetrating conversation we had during our voyage, and civility was strained at times, I must admit.

From Inchun we sailed south again on February 5, and then east to

An improvised smokehouse. From left to right: Chief Friedrich, handyman Jörg, Second Engineer Wolfgang, Cadet Lars, and passengers Pierre and Daryl. We're sailing on a very cold and windy South China Sea.

Pusan, our second South Korean harbour. Jörg and Wolfgang, the second engineer, had managed some time off the ship in Inchun, and had bought fish at the same market we had visited. On Sunday they prepared a surprise meal. Jörg, the amazing fixer, had built a poop-deck smokehouse from supplies on board, and with help from his engineer buddies, smoked the fish for dinner. The open deck right atop the noisy screw was bitterly cold, but dressed in warm jackets, the passengers spent time talking and drinking beer with Friedrich, Jörg, Wolfgang, and Cadet Lars while the fish was smoking. The delicious fish was freely shared with us and the crew.

We berthed in Pusan early in the morning, and left the ship at about 1000 for what would be a memorable experience. We were impressed with the city of Pusan, which turned out to be more modern, well organized, clean, and pleasant looking than Inchun. When we picked up our passports, a Korean visitor to the ship's office offered us a ride to wherever we wanted to go. Thinking that the city seemed close by, we declined, but when we arrived at the port's gate, there he was waiting for us, and we were glad he was there, for the heart of the city was further away than we had estimated. We asked him to drop us off at the "old city," and he did, after a ride of about twenty minutes. He also gave us a piece of paper with writing we couldn't read, upon which he had written instructions for taxi drivers to get us back to the proper port gate. We first walked through a narrow street full of aggressive vendors of expensive clothing and leather, with prices marked in local currency and American dollars.

The signs on the street were in English and Russian. Some large Caucasian women, blonde and dark, were standing in doorways and they invited Pierre and I to come in as soon as Johanna and Daryl had stepped inside a leather store. We had landed in a street of brothels, which mostly, so we learned from the ship's officers later on, served Russian mafia figures from Vladivostok, only a few hundred kilometres north of Pusan. We had actually spotted a number of Russian ships in the harbour.

Our kindly driver had mentioned a famous park, Democracy Park, and had pointed us towards it when we left him. We began to walk in the direction he had indicated, climbing rising streets, but no park seemed to appear. After walking several blocks we gave up. We made our way back down the hill, past a small building with a swastika on the outside, a startling sight until we discovered that this merely indicated a small Buddhist temple, and Daryl told us that the Nazis had stolen the symbol. Sloping away from where we were standing on the street, we spotted a courtyard around which were built living quarters inside stark walls, a sight that brought back memories of Chinese films and books, like Pearl Buck's *The Good Earth*. We spotted a clothesline above the courtyard walls from which clothing and orange fish hung drying together.

On our way into the city, the driver had pointed out the Pusan Railway station. We now walked in that direction. We first had lunch in what seemed to be a restaurant catering to office workers, enjoying a bowl of multi-ingredient soup and a garlicky meat and vegetable dish with rice. We came by a pastry and coffee shop called La Pain D'or where Pierre bought an enormous cake to share with the officers for dessert. We left it to pick up later, and made our way to the station, the massive square in front of it a beehive of activity. A small group of people promoting some cause were singing and chanting and rhythmically bowing—perhaps they were protestors of some kind, or perhaps religious folk. A lonely woman with a loudspeaker attached to her body made a lengthy speech, but only a few people watched and listened. Unfortunately, the tourist kiosk was being remodelled and couldn't give us information, but we asked a hotel at the edge of the square for information about Democracy Park. The manager

"Old" (a traditional housing compound) and "new" (skyscrapers) Korea all in the same Pusan shot. And underwear, a towel, and fish on the same wash line. What a great setting for an intricate novel!

wrote the information on a piece of paper for us to give to cab drivers on the way there and back.

Democracy Park is partly a historical monument with large statues dedicated to South Korea turning towards democracy in the 1970s and to a famous Admiral Lee who fought against the Chinese. This elevated park was well maintained and used by many secondary school groups and about a hundred older men playing a board game with tiles marked with symbols I had never seen before. I wondered if it was mah-jong or a Korean version of the game. The players were intent on their game, didn't seem to smile much, and some had observers looking over their shoulders. It was clearly an important pastime for them all. The gardens were in early spring bloom, and there were restaurants, a gambling casino, two souvenir shops, and a marvelous view of the city and harbour. We bought some souvenirs for our children and exquisite postcards featuring the city and traditional Korean folk tales.

One can't visit South Korea without being reminded of the Korean War, officially never having ended, not even today, but with hostilities occurring between June 25, 1950, and July 27, 1953. As Europe had its Iron Curtain at that time, so Asia had its bamboo curtain. Korea had been dominated and sometimes brutally ruled by Japan from about 1910 to the end of World War II. After the USSR declared war on Japan only a short time before the end of World War II, it invaded Korea from the north, while American forces invaded it from the south, with the thirty-eighth parallel as an agreed-upon dividing line. Both invaders then proceeded to establish and strengthen a government to their liking in their respective zones of influence. Syngman Rhee ruled the south, Kim Il-Sung the north. However, permanent division of Korea had never been agreed upon by anyone, and with the active support of the USSR, the North Korean ruler planned to invade and take over the south also. In the meantime, the Chinese eyed the situation with a substantial degree of weariness, fearing that a war would bring the United States deeper into East Asian affairs, and perhaps involve them in a defense of Taiwan, considered by the Chinese as their rightful territory.

On June 25, 1950, the North Korean army, large and equipped by the USSR, crossed the thirty-eighth parallel, and in short order annihilated most of the weak South Korean army. While surprised by this invasion, US President Harry Truman decided that he needed to stand in the way of all Communist expansion, anywhere on the globe, and authorized US troops stationed in Japan to move to the Korean peninsula and engage the

Communists. Before those troops, and soldiers and sailors from other nations like Canada and Holland, were even properly organized, the Allies had been driven back to a small corner in Korea's southeast, the so-called Pusan perimeter around that city. Fortunately, that bridgehead of retreat held long enough for reinforcements and equipment to arrive and become effective. Soon the Allied troops pushed back, helped by surprise marine invasions behind North Korean lines, notably at Inchun. The North Koreans rapidly retreated to behind the thirty-eighth parallel. When Commander-in-Chief Douglas MacArthur decided that he needed to destroy the logistical and training bases of his enemy even behind that line, the Chinese joined the North Koreans in October 1950. From then until the armistice of July 1953, lines moved up and down the peninsula without either party achieving a substantial breakthrough.

While we walked in Pusan, an old man approached us, shouting loud words of welcome, mostly in Korean, while shaking our hands. His wife looked embarrassed. We wondered if he was a Korean War veteran with grateful memories of people like us whom he would have believed to be Americans.

From the hotel we walked back to the pastry store where Pierre picked up his cake. We hailed another taxi, gave the driver the written instructions, entered the gate, walked back to our ship, and had a long nap before dinner after a full and satisfying day. Pierre brought his cake to the dining room, where it was devoured by officers and passengers alike, and he made sure both the steward, Ariel, and the cook had a slice also.

In Pusan we reached the easternmost point of our journey, and our time aboard the *Ville d'Aquarius* was half-over. The ship left port shortly after dinner as the city switched on its evening lights, and a big cross beamed at us from a huge Christian church. Waiting for us were still three unvisited ports, all Chinese. The first of these would be another magical place: Shanghai.

CHAPTER FIVE

Shanghai to Singapore

Reaching and leaving Shanghai by an ocean-going ship takes proper timing. The ports are about eight hours' sailing time from the East China Sea up the Yangtze River. At low tide this river can be hazardous for a ship like ours with its twelve-metre draft. Travel in and out must be coordinated with the high tides that also penetrate the river. Local agents and captains must sometimes leave the ship before all the planned containers are on board if delaying means a twelve-hour wait. Any containers left behind are taken on board by the next company ship a week or so hence.

The river's mouth looked like a large lake; as we sailed up, the shores squeezed ever closer together. The Yangtze is fast-flowing and carries a lot of sand, often visible to the naked eye. Each direction has its own buoy-marked shipping lane, and we met a number of ships making the return journey.

Outside the shipping lanes, hundreds of fishing boats plied their trade. When they were close enough we would wave, and often someone on board waved back. In a boat that seemed to be home to a whole family, a man held up his large dog and waved its paw at us. We laughed, they laughed, and Johanna and I wondered about life for such a family. We also speculated about the health of the fish caught in these muddy waters, given the

We're inching our way towards another port berth, always a fascinating event. Notice the bumpers at quay's edge, last-second cushions to prevent damage to ship or shore.

environmental air and water horror stories regularly published in the Western press about China. One major concern was (and still remains) the Three Gorges Dam, which is being built to provide electricity. It spans the Yangtze River for 2,300 metres and towers 185 metres above it. More than a million Chinese will have to move—most already have—and no one can accurately predict what will happen to water levels and currents downstream when it is fully operational.

The container port didn't seem close to any residential or industrial area and the actual city of Shanghai turned out to be a considerable distance away. We could leave the ship at around 1100, and had the day and evening for visiting, as we were slated to depart the next morning. The company's local agent was exceptionally helpful to the four of us when we picked up our passports and visas from the ship's office. He used the ship's telephone to order a taxi, and provided us with enough Chinese money to pay for it, in exchange for US dollars at a reasonable rate. Moreover, he gave each of us a slip of paper with instructions for the taxi driver in both Chinese and English. When Johanna asked him about purchasing tea, he scribbled instructions on another slip of paper to present to a tea merchant. The taxi ride took about seventy-five minutes at a cost of $25US, not bad when split between the four of us. We were impressed by the wide thoroughfares and comparatively little car traffic on the way into the city. Shanghai was a fascinating blend of new and old. The new was evident in the impressive skyline, the traditional in a wide bike path running parallel to the road, on which personal and freight bikes were safely making their way, well protected from car and truck traffic.

The taxi dropped us off at the Friendship Centre, a seven-storey luxury department store, which used to be open to foreign tourists only and featured exquisite and expensive clothing, jewelry, and art. We saw a number of elaborate and very costly ivory carvings, including a village in miniature. At the time of our visit, the Republic of China was the only country in the world that didn't forbid the importation of elephant tusks from which ivory carvings are made. A money exchange in the store got us enough Chinese currency to cover our estimated expenses for the day, and then we ventured into the city streets. The crowds immediately overwhelmed us: sidewalks full of pedestrians, streets full of bikes, scooters, and cars, all honking, bleating, ringing, and tooting like a symphony orchestra warm-up. On one corner hundreds of bikes were waiting on both sides of the street. When the traffic light turned green, all moved forward across the breadth of the whole road, somehow avoiding one another and whatever cars and scooters came their way.

On that corner I had a personal epiphany, one I'm still reminded of regularly. While waiting for the lights to change, I happened to look in a store window and saw my reflection. It startled me. With all the noise around me and the odors of this city filling my nostrils, I remember suddenly thinking: "What's this emigrant kid from Holland now living in Canada doing in China? What's happened to me? Where have the years gone? Who am I?" It wasn't pride of accomplishment that filled my soul. I suddenly felt a stranger to my own circumstances, as if this journey hadn't been my decision but that of some other hand and mind.

Many times I had walked around the ship contemplating my own private march of achievement. Born into a poor family over sixty years ago, I had gained a university degree, finished a long and honoured career in publishing, successfully raised a large family, relished the ups and downs of a decades-long marriage, and earned enough to live comfortably in my retirement. By having lived as I did, carefully and in a measured way, this holiday was my due. But seeing myself in this window proved to be a reality check. For I saw not only the reflection of my face, but also the reflection of someone who was just one of the many people waiting and moving on this street. I was one of a large crowd, an ant with other ants, only one story among many, unique and also common. Wouldn't most of those silhouettes live much as I had? Learn a little, work a little, love a little, hope a little, adjust a little, hide a little, share a little? And weren't their own circumstances just as little under their own ultimate control as mine had been? I hadn't chosen the family and country I had been born in, nor the particular circumstances that had led to my decision to emigrate to Canada, meet and marry Johanna, or choose my career.

I had come to China as a North American, a representative of its entrepreneurial spirit: Set yourself a goal and you can reach it. By contrast, the ordinary Chinese had for millennia been tied to bits of land or river, overpowered by wave after wave of natural disasters, bandits, and warlords, who, like locusts, ate the harvests of modest achievements. This view of China had been shaped by Pearl S. Buck's novel, *The Good Earth*, a book I had often read as a teenager and young adult. Perhaps my reflection in the store window had suddenly given me a Chinese frame of thinking about myself, a frame of modesty rather than accomplishment, of gratitude rather than pride, as one of the ordinary rather than the extraordinary, of survival rather than conquest. Perhaps the Spirit of Ordinary China had made itself known to me in that window of a small appliances store in this city in this Republic of China.

These thoughts occupied my mind and stilled my voice as we made our way along the Street of the Small Appliances, where a few stores sold gauges, dials, pumps, bearings, and other miscellaneous goods displayed in their windows. We must have looked a bit bewildered, for suddenly I heard a voice behind me say, in English, "The shopping district is over the bridge." I turned to see a benignly smiling Chinese man with his arm outstretched, and when I thanked him, he merely waved his hand. We followed his directions and found the bridge just in time to see a riverboat take off, the family who lived on it sunning themselves on deck. It reminded me of similar Dutch riverboats, narrow black or brown vessels with an obviously limited draft, cargo holds covered with hatches running the length of the ship, and living quarters at the back.

The shopping street proved to be a disappointment, full of Western-style shoes, clothes, and electronics, often sold in familiar brand name outlets. We soon turned into a side street, where we found lives much more interesting: small merchants at work, children playing, neighbours chatting, an old woman knitting and dozing behind a few wares on a piece of carpet in front of her. At the end of the street we found a market. Here, as in the Inchun market, pork and chicken and fish were featured. Other stalls held fruits and vegetables, and still others clothes and shoes. The constant buzzing of flies landing on the food was a bit off-putting to our perhaps overly fastidious Western sensibilities. Johanna found a tea seller and purchased her heart's desire: jasmine and green tea.

As we sauntered back to the Friendship Centre, our city anchor, we crossed the river over a different bridge, and spotted a bird parkette, where songbird owners had hung cages in trees and the birds sang in chorus, a wonderful composition of sights and sounds. We soon discovered that all the proud owners were watching us intently. When we made eye contact with them, the owners of a specific cage we'd been looking at and listening to bowed to us. Apparently this park is full of bird owners and bird lovers every day. We then came to a busy and noisy street in full redevelopment, a jackhammer pounding the concrete, with a number of spruced up restaurants already in business and lots of construction still in progress. The panorama reminded me of Chinatowns in North American cities, notably Toronto, Vancouver, and San Francisco.

In the middle of Shanghai a daily bird concert. Most big cities have their busy streets and office/apartment towers, but if you have the time and the eyes to see, you'll find interesting oases of peace.

At the end of this busy street we turned into the Street of Textiles, indicated with a brass street sign. It struck us that these commercial streets had the same feel and appearance as similar streets with mixed housing and small shops in European cities. We enjoyed a cup of tea in a café, walked around some more, and then began to look for a place to eat dinner as dusk began to darken the day. At the mighty Whangpoo River's edge we found an obviously popular restaurant, with a large crowd already inside and many more people still arriving. Small and big fish, flat ones like sole and others like trout, some attractive and some ugly, swam in big tanks placed all around the restaurant. Diners pointed out their chosen fish to a waiter, who caught it and took it to the kitchen, from whence it returned cooked on a platter, surrounded by steamed vegetables. At the end of the meal I made my way to the toilet, only to decide that I wouldn't be able to manage the porcelain floor basin with a hole in it. After dinner we made our way back to a taxi stand in front of the Friendship Centre, where I made use of a public toilet facility much more to my Western liking. After the long drive back to port and already close to the port gates, the cab driver got confused, even with the agent's instructions. Three times he hailed a colleague, obviously to get better directions, with all four of us passengers getting a bit concerned that we would be late. Fortunately, we made it back in time, but on our arrival at the ship the driver demanded more money than showed on the meter, and he involved the guard at the foot of the gangplank to get it. As neither of them spoke English, I simply peeled off bills until he seemed satisfied. The final total still wasn't that much in dollars, and at the time I thought that perhaps there was a premium for evening travel.

It had been an interesting and varied visit, but I was a bit disappointed that we had seen little evidence of the real Shanghai of history and character. But then, I had to remind myself, what do you expect after a few hours of wandering the streets? Once again we had experienced the limits of being passengers on container freighters that are anxious to move on as soon as they're tied to shore. Ships make money sailing, not resting. Nevertheless, we revelled in the experience of being in Shanghai, a city with a dynamic and turbulent history.

Many centuries ago, Shanghai began as a mud-flat village on the edge of the Yangtze Basin, a wonderfully rich agricultural area along the Whangpoo River and the Soochow Creek, both connected to the Yangtze River and thus to the East China Sea. The combination of abundant agricultural production and access to splendid waterways presented opportunities for

The Shanghai I expected to see: alive and colourful. The scene reminded me of a similar central street in Amsterdam called the Kalverstraat, *still without car traffic, with shops and restaurants on both sides.*

economic success. However, it wasn't the Chinese themselves, but foreigners who first exploited its potential. English trading ships touched the east coast of China in 1637, at Guangzhou (later called Nanking); however, for a long time the ruling Manchu dynasty severely restricted the activities of Western traders. The prohibitions may have hindered such trading, but could never stop it altogether in this huge land where central control grew weaker as the distance increased from the seats of power. In 1832 Mr. Hugh Lindsay, agent for the East India Company, set up shop in Shanghai. Soon other traders arrived, British, and also French and American businessmen who wanted their piece of this pie. Tea and silk were exported, and opium imported from the British colony of India. Opium had been used by the Chinese as a remedy against colds for a long time, but had increasingly become a recreational drug. The British and Americans stimulated this trade, both for its huge profits and as a way to make docile the local population (making the British Empire a drug dealer). At times, the Chinese government, alarmed at this degradation of its citizens, tried to put a stop to it by forbidding the importation of opium or by levying high duties. But the occupiers, notably the British and Americans, took on the Chinese government in two Opium Wars, one in 1839 and one in 1856.

The foreign powers' superior weapons, gunboats, and warring skills defeated their host, causing deep humiliation still not forgotten in modern China. Those wars assured an ever-greater presence of Western traders in the Shanghai area. A good look at a map reveals the major reason for Shanghai's economic success: location. The city was close to large populations like Japan, and only an ocean away from that dynamically developing economic giant called the United States, an ocean that could be crossed by the steamships that now provided more rapid and reliable transport. Shanghai was also within reach of South Asian populations rapidly becoming extensions of European powers like England, France, and the Netherlands. With Russia not very far to the north, the potential was enormous. The Chinese government, weak and under pressure by the great Western powers, helped the exploiters by deeding certain areas outside the Old City to those foreigners, granting them special rights and privileges. Soon Shanghai had two areas dominated by these commercial invaders, the French Concession and the International Settlement (which combined UK and US interests), two city districts controlled not by the Chinese, but by foreign inhabitants. In 1844 China signed a treaty giving these districts "extraterritoriality," meaning that Chinese criminal law wouldn't apply there.

Towards the end of the nineteenth century, the Japanese joined the Western invaders in Shanghai. This major nation had been the only one in Asia to resist Western influences and penetration. It saw itself as a strong competitor for commercial and political power in the area. Until the end of the nineteenth century, Shanghai had been a commercial centre that imported and exported products, but didn't actually produce anything. Japanese businessmen now established factories that produced consumer items and clothing, making use of the abundant and cheap labour and access to ready markets further inland. All this business activity and the 1844 treaty made a large part of Shanghai a foreign enclave in the midst of a rapidly expanding Chinese city. No passport or visa was required to settle here, so it was no wonder that Shanghai also attracted crooks, drug dealers, and double-dealers from all over the world. They found refuge here from those who hunted them for their misdeeds and were judged not by Chinese laws, but by enclave laws, which tended to be more forgiving. Such immigrants included twenty-five thousand White Russians, who settled there after opposing the Russian Revolution in 1918.

By the 1920s, Shanghai was a seething mess of legitimate and illegitimate activities, hard at work and hard at play, the latter a sort of perpetual Mardi Gras at its worst. Along with banks, the trading company offices, and cricket grounds, there was the famous Shanghai Race Club and other places of entertainment, such as dance halls, nightclubs, brothels, gambling casinos, and opium dens. When I was young, I would occasionally hear the expression "being shanghaied," meaning being forced to become a sailor against your will, after perhaps being drugged and beaten. This expression clearly originated in this city during this lawless time. By 1930 Shanghai had three million inhabitants, with foreigners numbering about seventy thousand, many living opulent lives. The rest were Chinese peasants streaming into the city to escape a rigid rural life, where they had been tied to small plots that grudgingly yielded crops during frequent droughts or floods. Most were doomed to city lives of poverty and degradation. At that time, Shanghai was the most cosmopolitan city in the world, with many languages spoken and many races represented. I'm sure that the brass street signs we saw in English on the Street of the Small Appliances and Street of Textiles dated from those days. It was also a city of the imagination for many famous visitors, film stars from Hollywood, writers from the UK and the US, opera stars and politicians from Italy, and diplomats and military men from Germany. For Westerners, before World War II, Shanghai held an attraction similar to Egypt almost a century before: a combination of freedom, mystery, opulence, and seduction.

As Shanghai grew larger, more prosperous, and also more decadent, changes elsewhere in China began to herald the ultimate end of this stage in the city's history. In 1911 the long-ruling Manchu dynasty was overthrown by forces of renewal and patriotism. Sun Yat-sen, honoured even today by Chinese Communists, was the father of this development. His ideas were a mixture of East and West, pride in the accomplishments of ancient China combined with the Western ideas of progress, freedom, and education so evident in Shanghai, despite its sordid side.

Sun Yat-sen and his radical movement successor, Chiang Kai-shek, began the lengthy process of establishing law, order, and economic progress, supported by their own movement (called Guomindang) and the Chinese Communist Party. They had to combat and subdue many warlords who controlled large parts of the country. Their natural allies were students, labour unions, and the Communists, who had held their first National Congress in Shanghai in 1921. Strikes and other forms of unrest caused great suffering among the population.[1] Those forces steadily gathered strength, and as they did, resentment against foreign city residents grew. As Communism became an increasingly active and large force, stimulated by Russia, Chiang Kai-shek decided to go it alone. In 1927 he betrayed his erstwhile allies by taking Shanghai and killing many Communist leaders and soldiers. Typical for Shanghai, though, was the fact that the city's French Concession and International Settlement areas were untouched by the fighting, and the inhabitants were mere onlookers, safe behind their laws and barriers. But all that unrest challenged Shanghai's commercial, and by now also industrial, power.

Japan presented a second major challenge to the Western presence in Shanghai. By the 1930s, it had become an Asian empire builder, looking for areas to occupy. It had already defeated Russia in 1905 in a war that had more to do with Japan's aggressive nature than any real international conflicts over territorial or economic interests. Like Italy did in gaining a colony in Ethiopia around the same time, Japan invaded China's northern territory of Manchuria in 1931 simply to show the world it could. In

---

[1] The Pearl S. Buck trilogy, of which *The Good Earth* (1931, and a Pulitzer Prize winner) is the first volume, is set during this time. The other two books are *Sons* (1932) and *A House Divided* (1935). For her massive body of works on China, the author won the Nobel Prize for literature in 1938.

1937 the Japanese army occupied Shanghai. (Once again, the two foreign enclaves were only bystanders and spectators.) The end of this Shanghai was in sight. Japan occupied the entire city during World War II from 1941 to 1945, imprisoning any foreigners who had not left the city in time. In 1949 the Chinese Communists under Mao Zedong took over the whole country and for many years Shanghai was as closed to Westerners as the rest of China. It's only with recent Westernization of its economy that the city has regained its place as one of China's most powerful economic engines.

It was clear even from our short visit: Shanghai is once again becoming a city where East and West meet, although in very different circumstances from a century or more back. I would love to return to Shanghai one day for a longer visit to further explore the city's flawed, even evil, though fascinating colonial history.

We left Shanghai on February 10, shortly after breakfast. Before breakfast, Johanna and I stood on the deck outside our cabin and watched the tide come up with amazing speed, covering more of the mudflats and exposed dock pillars with every incoming wave. As we sailed away, we spent a lot of time simply watching the river widen, the ubiquitous fishing boats, and the freighter traffic coming in. Through binoculars, our eyes swept the shore as well, and we saw many tended fields and gardens, some terraced against the slope of the river's shore. My eyes followed a bus on the river's south shore as it made its way along a highway twisting and turning up and down hills, so its linear forward progress was about the same as our ship. I wondered about the people on this bus. I didn't see a town or city that might have been their destination, but I imagined that wherever they were going was miles and perhaps decades removed from Shanghai life. Were there village farmers on board? Children now attending a Shanghai university going home to visit their peasant parents? A new teacher for a village school? An engineer on his or her way to a Yangtze River improvement project? Wherever they were going, they were people just like us. Their lack of technology compared to ours in Canada didn't make them essentially different from us.

I thought of my grandfather, who was the sixth of sixteen children born on a small farm and who probably never learned how to read and write. He moved to the cities of Rotterdam, Haarlem, and Zaandam to scratch out a living, and his body was spent by the time I got to know him. I'm named after him, have some old photographs, and remember him even though he died when I was nine. I was probably about five when, on a visit to the primitive home he shared with my grandmother in Zaandam, he asked me to find dandelion greens for his rabbits in this industrial city where even grass was scarce in working-class streets. His rabbits were an essential means of surviving, as was his vegetable garden, for he and Grandma lived on a welfare pittance. They had no running water, and their toilet was a large vat underneath a holed plank, which would be replaced when full with an empty one by city employees through an outside wall. I walked around the neighbourhood and found enough grass and weeds to fill the container he had given me, some from small patches of public lawn, and some by reaching inside the slatted fences of private gardens. Perhaps he simply wanted to be alone for awhile, for I was a busy and curious child. Perhaps he was teaching me to explore the world myself to find what I needed. Perhaps he was glad to have someone do this task for him, giving his aching body a day's rest. It's funny how one remembers little things like that after so many years, memories triggered by watching this Chinese bus and imagining the lives of the people on board.

We left the Yangtze River, sailing back into the East China Sea and turning south. We docked in Ningbo that night to pick up only eighty-nine containers, which took just a few hours and gave us no chance to leave the ship. The next day as we sailed further south, we watched the crew paint the pool, covering up the rust at the bottom and on the sides and hiding the destructive power of salt water once again, but only for a little while. We turned past Hong Kong on our way to Chiwan, a smaller container port past the almost completed new Hong Kong airport. There, too, our stay was too short to get off the ship, even though we owned an expensive visa that entitled us to do so. After port activities in Chiwan, we slowly sailed back to Hong Kong in midmorning. There we faced the same problem as on our first visit: We only had time to visit the Mariners' Centre for a beer, a game of pool, newspapers, and lunch.

As we left Hong Kong, I was struck once again by the beauty and power of the ocean. In calm blue skies and seas, the wake is visible for a long time, with a multitude of colours, from white to intense blue, and green patches as well. Standing right above the wake on the poop deck, the noise is quite overwhelming. Johanna and I also noticed the hypnotic effect of standing at the tip of the bow and seeing the ocean split below your feet as the bottom-front bulb of the keel hits it. (That funny-looking bulb apparently increases a ship's speed by one knot.) When standing alone in the extreme fore or aft spots of the ship, the waves' rushing noises reached up to envelope me completely, and I sometimes had the feeling that I was cut off from the rest of the world, from life itself. I actually thought at times about what it would be like to jump in. Other passengers have told me they have had the same feelings.

Most of our conversations with other passengers, officers, and crew were civil but on the whole superficial, chit-chat and only a bit deeper, with occasional hesitant hints at greater intimacy, like sharing feelings about the hypnotic impact of rushing seas. But sometimes genuine connections were made. Johanna and I were invited to have a drink in the cabin of Second Engineer Wolfgang, together with Pierre, who would leave us in Singapore. With Wolfgang doing most of the talking, we discussed the effect of global trade on people. Wolfgang shared with us how he had changed since the beginning of his career, from a strongly patriotic German to more of a world citizen. He hoped that his own place in the scheme of global trade made some contribution, however small, to a better understanding between people, and he had shared what he had learned with his family and friends back home. Pierre also gave evidence of being changed by travel, at least by his contact with the people on the ship. We noticed that he gradually become less aloof as the trip progressed, and more solicitous towards Daryl and Johanna, smoking less when they were around, and closing or opening windows in the dining room when they were cold or hot.

During *kirche* we had another moving conversation. Jörg began to talk about his town and youth. He mentioned his beloved Grandpa, captain of the fishing boat that took him to sea for the first time, and his Grandma, who called him *mien jong*. That expression of endearment, "my dear boy" in dialect German, is exactly the same expression, to the letter in print and in pronunciation, as that used in some Dutch rural dialects by mothers for their sons, and grandmothers for their grandsons. Jörg, that bear-like and beer-drinking superb fixer, was as moved by the moment as we were.

We arrived back in Singapore on February 16. We would have a full day here with plenty of time to make use of the tourist brochures we had picked up on our last visit. Before we left the ship, we said goodbye to Pierre, who was leaving us to fly to Vietnam. Daryl had lost a filling and had asked the captain to make a dental appointment for her. We would meet her later in the old and famous Raffles Hotel. We had decided to take a four-hour bus tour that promised to show us some of the major sights: old Singapore and government buildings, the Indian sector, the Chinese sector, a jewelry factory, and a botanical garden.

We boarded an air-conditioned luxury bus at Singapore's Convention

Centre for the tour. The guide was funny and entertaining, but clearly the tour was subsidized by various merchants. At the Indian and Chinese districts, as well as at a location advertised as a jewelry studio, we were let off the bus for about forty-five minutes, an invitation to spend our money. At 1030 in the Indian district, a merchant offered to custom tailor me a suit for one hundred dollars, to be delivered to the ship by 1700, guaranteed to fit. He showed me hundreds of business cards from previously "satisfied clients," and when he heard that my English had a Dutch twang, he picked out cards from Dutch men. Even when we declined his clever pressure, he retained his good humour. He did sell us each a beautiful silk shirt, plus a silk scarf for Johanna. In a tourist boutique, Johanna spotted small tins of tea packed by Stassen Tea Company. She bought one to show our two brothers-in-law who had survived Japanese concentration camps in Indonesia during World War II, for their surname is Stassen. In the Chinese district, we resisted all temptation to purchase anything, as I was beginning to worry about being able to pack our suitcases, especially on our way back to Canada.

Next, we visited an exuberantly colourful temple, followed by a jewelry studio, which turned out to be a hard-sell retail outlet, so we walked around the neighbourhood instead. Both the Indian and Chinese districts were tourist-trap markets, partly indoors and partly outdoors. There were sunglasses galore, plenty of electronic goods, and colourful dresses, shirts, skirts, and scarves, which seemed cheap enough, although I found the merchants tended to be aggressive. I get a little anxious when bombarded by pushy sellers who want my money and whom I'll never see again.

The botanical garden, which featured many orchids, was a treat, with sloping acres of colourful and fragrant flowers. It was a restful place after the noise of the merchants. The many paths curved past all kinds of flora, the plants labelled with little signs. With ever-changing fragrances and birdsong from all directions, it seemed a paradise to us.

The bus dropped us off in time for a quick lunch at the Convention Centre before we walked to the famous Raffles Hotel, where we had arranged to meet Daryl, who had promised to treat us to the drink invented there: a Singapore Sling.

Raffles is a huge white three-storey hotel in the heart of Singapore. It has an impressive pillared entrance attended by a doorman dressed in white with a red sash worn diagonally across his body and a sort of pith helmet on his head. The gardens were immaculate with tall tropical trees and dense flowering shrubs. Raffles has recently been completely refurbished, and it now costs over $450US per night to stay here. It's still *the* place to stay and has been ever since Singapore was a far less sophisticated outpost of the British Empire. Here, short story writer Somerset Maugham drank at the Long Bar, and also E. M. Forster, the novelist. The Long Bar still exists. It's air-conditioned now, but many ceiling fans connected with steel bars waft the air to and fro as well, just like in earlier times. The window shutters and the beautiful dark wood everywhere, as well as the tiled floor, made us think of Somerset Maugham short stories and the quiet elegance of British colonial times. Indeed, the hotel looks like something out of a movie set during those times, like *A Passage to India*. Adding to the tropical ambience were birds freely flying around in the bar. Daryl was waiting for us and we ordered drinks: beer for me and Singapore Slings for the two women. We peeled peanuts from the full bowl on the table and threw the shells on the floor, as everybody did. The visit to Raffles was a grand way to end our time in Singapore and we returned to the ship by cab in a steamy outburst of rain.

While waiting for the loading to finish and the ship's departure later that day, I stood on the bridge deck with Chief Engineer Friedrich. I had noticed a small tanker lying next to our ship on the harbour side, and asked him about the process of getting fuel on board. It's a slow job, because fuel must be heated to 135 degrees Fahrenheit in order to travel through pipes into our ship, and even then it's thicker than water. In front of us, about seventy ships were at anchor in the large bay. He told me that some were without a charter and were hoping for one. Some ships with serious engine problems were waiting for parts, while some had finished their last voyage ever and would be scrapped or beached somewhere soon. Friedrich lent me his binoculars so I could spot their names. For almost every ship he had a story: who had built it, approximately when, what it had been called on its maiden voyage, who had owned it and who owned it now, what names it had sailed under—an incredible wealth of details. He told me that ship identification was his hobby and that at home in Germany he had three thousand slides of merchant ships. He was building the museum of his career. It was incredible, yet he was almost shy about it.

That moment caused me to reflect on the business of shipping, on ships and what happens to them, on officers and crew. I had learned a great deal about shipping while on board both by asking specific questions and noting what various posters and plaques on the bridge and elsewhere revealed about this particular ship, and merchant shipping in general. I knew that a ship was both a village and a business. As a business it's a travelling warehouse, with a CEO (the captain or master), middle management (the officers), and workers (the crew) looking after the plant and facilities, keeping it in good order and running it for profit. But because the employees live on board for twenty-four hours each day and for many weeks at a time, it's also a village with homes (cabins), recreation areas (lounges, pool, and deck chairs), a store (slop chest and food storage areas), and a restaurant (kitchen and dining rooms). The captain, who can be seen as the mayor, is also in charge of the village, together with a village council (his officers and perhaps the crew's bosun). Occasionally, the whole village gets together for a party. During life on board the ship, the aspects of business and village are intermingled, but keeping them both in mind helped me to understand how the ship worked.

The *Ville d'Aquarius* had "Hamburg" painted prominently above its screw. However, information posted inside the wheelhouse indicated that this Hamburg ship was registered in Cyprus. Why was it registered in that small country, not known as a modern seafaring nation? As we learned during both our trips, many merchant ships fly "flags of convenience." Shipping companies, forever on the prowl for cost-saving initiatives, register their ships in whatever countries offer them the fewest restrictions and lowest tax liabilities for a fee. The more restrictions a country imposes on its merchant shipping fleet, however valid and protective of ship, crew, and environment those restrictions may be, the more chances that the owners will find another country of registration, one with fewer restrictions (which really means fewer safeguards). Traditional maritime powers, such as England and the United States, could once boast of having the largest merchant fleets in the world, but now England has only a few hundred ships officially registered, and the United States not many more. Judging by official registrations, some very small countries seem to be major maritime powers these days. The International Transport Workers' Federation (ITF) lists such unlikely "powers" as Cook Islands, Gibraltar, Lebanon, and Netherlands Antilles.

After the sinking of the oil tanker *Prestige* off the coast of Spain in November 2002, the media discussed these flags of convenience (FOC) as dodges for escaping inspections and regulations, resulting in old and unsafe ships causing environmental disasters. The media were also beginning to echo what the ITF has been exposing for a long time, much of it discussed in a booklet, which I picked up in a seaman's centre. It tells how sailors are exploited by low wages for long hours, and how there's minimal maintenance of the ships, poor on-board conditions, little shore leave, inadequate medical attention, and lack of safety procedures. In *Flags of Convenience—The ITF's Campaign*, the ITF argues that, "In some of the worst cases, seafarers are virtual prisoners on the ship, unable to earn enough for repatriation home which the company demands they must pay." In theory, the countries whose flags these ships fly should monitor them, but they don't. It's entirely likely that a ship registered in Malta will never dock in that country.

Some things may have escaped our attention, but from what Johanna and I saw, the *Ville d'Aquarius* looked well maintained, with on-board conditions that were far above a spartan level. Each sailor, no matter how low his rank, had his own cabin with a bathroom, a small desk, and a chair. By the time we left the ship, we had seen the inside of most of the cabins, either by looking through an opened door, or as guests having a beer and a chat. Each sailor took care to make his cabin a bit of a home, adding a calendar, one or more photographs of loved ones, or a few books. As for medical care, several sailors visited dentists in ports after the captain requested appointments by radio in advance of arrival, which were then made by local agents. Second Officer Gottfried of the *Ville d'Aquarius* also served as the ship's medical officer. He told me the story of a sailor on board who had broken a hip and a leg in an on-board accident. With the help of satellite telephone instructions given by a doctor onshore, Gottfried had administered immediate medical care, and as soon as the ship was within reach of shore, the patient was lifted from the ship by a shore-based helicopter.

However good the sailor's lot aboard the *Ville d'Aquarius*, we also saw rust buckets in various harbours and wondered about conditions on board those ships. In the fall of 2002, Johanna and I decided to undertake a six-week volunteer stint at the Montreal Mariners' Centre. Each day I was on duty, I would drive a van throughout the port area for picking up, and later in the evening taking back, sailors who wanted to visit the centre for making telephone calls, playing pool or table tennis, or sitting around and talking, sometimes with clergy, and attending the daily chapel service in the evening.

I climbed aboard many ships, and conditions on board varied greatly. Some ships were well maintained and seemed clean and comfortable places, much like the *Ville d'Aquarius*. Others made me feel uncomfortable. I regularly visited a dilapidated Egyptian ship, where even senior officers lived in small, graceless, and dirty cabins. They welcomed me on board, and were grateful for the facilities at the Mariners' Centre, where they headed every night while in port. After I told them that I had sailed through the Suez Canal twice they became especially friendly, and often invited me to their table for a beer. I also became involved with a small cruise ship that normally sailed between Montreal and the Caribbean that had been detained for a variety of infractions and nonpayment of debts. It had been tied up in Montreal's harbour for almost a year. The centre made an effort to gather an extra supply of mittens, coats, and hats for the crew, who had not counted on being in Montreal in cold November.

The 9/11 terror disasters have also had their effects. I read in the papers that right after the attacks, many crews weren't allowed to leave their ships at all in American ports, robbing them of a welcome break from on-board routines. While the initial restrictions may have been lifted somewhat, leaving ships for a land break is still subject to more security checks and restrictions than before 9/11. The life of a sailor is challenging under the best of circumstances, and can be hell under the worst.

Ownership of the *Ville d'Aquarius* might have been in Cyprus, but much of the ship's destiny was clearly in the hands of the bureaucrats at the company's head office in Hamburg, the people we had spotted talking to the captain the first day we were on board. While sailing, the *Ville d'Aquarius* captain and his officers had plenty of head office forms to complete, and when the ship finished its round trip, it was inspected by technical as well as administrative people, overseers and controlling managers. The operations of this ship and a number of others in the same fleet were in the hands of a major German company called Niederelbe Schiffahrts Gesellschaft mbH & Co. KG (NSB for short, the "B" stands for Bremen). The head office is now in Buxtehude, conveniently located between Bremen and Hamburg, both ports used by the company's ships. I was told that NSB had leased the *Ville d'Aquarius* from the Cypriot owners. "Leasing" means operating and maintaining the ship, staffing it, sailing it, and looking after it.[2] In turn, NSB had leased the ship to a French-Arabian company now called CMA CGM, which sold space on board to companies that needed to ship goods around the world, and then looked after all the port and documentation arrangements. The agents we met in various ports were in fact CMA agents.

[2] The NSB pennants the ships flew gave Johanna and I a funny feeling. "NSB" had been the initials of the Dutch Nazi party before and during World War II (the Nationale Socialistische Beweging).

Clearly the officers on board and their crew had direct responsibility for ship maintenance on behalf of their employer (NSB). This often means solving problems far from the safety of port. Storms are always a threat, even when all ship systems are performing as they should. On three occasions we noticed the engine of the *Ville d'Aquarius* no longer turning over in the middle of the sea (the sudden silence is deafening), twice with a storm raging around us. The first time we were told that a fuel-supply pipe had burst, spraying oil through part of the engine room before it could be shut off. It took a couple of hours of hard work before a new pipe was put in place, while the ship seemed to drift out of control on the choppy waves. It was an uncomfortable and anxious time for the passengers, and we never did discover why the engines stopped the second and third times. The second pause occurred in calm weather, but the third took place back in the stormy Gulf of Biscayne, and lasted at least two hours.

Collisions are another hazard. Traffic rules on the high seas are very precise, and not based on the importance of any ship or its size. A small fishing boat in the right position takes priority over a giant freighter like ours. But collisions occur, even in open seas with lots of visibility. Especially difficult are fleets of fishing boats crowded close together trying to take advantage of a large school of fish enjoying life in a shipping lane. I noticed how tense the bridge officers became when they spotted these fleets ahead of the ship. Whenever other ships, large or small, were visible to the side and ahead, the officers would constantly scan the scene with their binoculars and peer at the radar screens. The screens not only showed the course and speed of the *Ville d'Aquarius*, but also those of any ship within its range, instantly plotting whether the current speed and current course would risk a collision. Ships this large can't stop on a dime. I was told that a fully loaded 250,000-ton tanker destined for Rotterdam already begins to slow down when entering the English Channel just north of Le Havre.

Entering and leaving ports was always hazardous. Many ports are a bit inland, perhaps some distance up a river, such as Hamburg, or in a bay that provides shelter from storms, like Hong Kong. Getting to a berth in such ports requires the ship to substantially slow down on the way in and out, both for safety reasons and to prevent shore erosion. Even in calm waters, a ship as large as the *Ville d'Aquarius* throws up a substantial wake that can swamp small boats and erode riverbanks. The sheer number of ships at port means that collisions are always a possibility, especially when visibility is poor. Moreover, the tides, currents, and winds peculiar to any location aren't always known by even the most experienced captains, so local pilots who know the area well come on board to guide an ocean traveller in and out.

Tugboats are used close to berthing positions and sometimes for longer treks on the way in and out of ports, especially when the entry and exit channels are narrow. We never tired of seeing tugboats working around our ship, sometimes one, but mostly two. Some were much larger than others—perhaps the strength of the wind and currents in various harbours makes a difference—but all looked tiny beside our ship, and yet they exuded raw power. The tugs began by pulling slowly until the ropes were taut, and then opened the throttles wide with a mighty roar and a wild churning of the waters. At first the ship didn't seem to move, but when we looked at the dockside, we could see the very first detachment. However small these workhorses looked, they got the job done. On the way to a berth, these mighty mites help retard the speed of their big cousins. I once read a story of a heavily damaged Japanese aircraft carrier, which, during World War II, had limped into a small port without the help of tugs. The ship's own engines couldn't retard its speed sufficiently, so when it hit the quay at a speed of about five knots (9 km/hr), the quay was completely destroyed by the large and heavy ship. The dangers of a ship damaging its berthing position were demonstrated by the rows of heavy truck tires hung from the quays in all the ports we visited, to cushion any contact between the shore and the ship.

Apart from the ship itself sustaining damage from some external force, life on board is full of hazards as well. A ship is a moving steel box, filled with machines and tools, with moving parts in greasy engine rooms and ropes and cables that snake and wind their way across decks and up and down the ship. There are bollards and winches and steel parts that stick out everywhere. As if that weren't enough, down below loom dark deep restless waters. It all adds up to danger for the workers (and unsuspecting passengers). I once slipped while on a walk, smacking my body hard against the deck; I hurt for two days. A ship moves in mysterious and unpredictable ways and anyone walking aboard ship needs to exercise care, even on a relatively calm sea.

The other major threat on board is fire. Even a large ship is a small territory when on fire, with a limit to how far one can run away from it. Moreover, fuel, wood, and synthetic materials are highly combustible and can produce potentially deadly fumes. On the *Ville d'Aquarius*, fire hoses were prominently displayed throughout the superstructure with instructions in big print. At least once a week during our trip, fire alarms rang throughout the ship for a safety drill. Passengers and crew put on their life jackets and reported to their assigned lifeboat (there were two), with the captain in charge of one boat and the first officer in charge of the other. Each had a roll-call list for checking if anyone was missing.

However, the most constant and ultimately most persistent danger to a ship itself is salt. When we boarded the *Ville D'Aquarius*, the ship was only thirteen months old, but it already showed plenty of rust on the hull and the decks, and it was almost completely repainted during our sixty-five-day trip. What surprised me even more was that it had already been painted twice before we got on board. The captain told me that a new ship is delivered almost as spanking new and gleaming as a car just out of the showroom, but the appearance fools no sailor; unless two more coats of paint are applied in the first few months, the ship will rust so quickly that it will look aged long before its time. Even with those two immediate extra coats, rust will eventually win. When we climbed on board, it didn't take us long to find rust everywhere. The power of the salty sea is also evident in the feel of the ship during and after a storm; everywhere your hand touches on the outside of the ship, on the railings, stairs, and machinery, even high up, you'll feel a coat of grainy salt.

While at sea, and sometimes in port, the sailors were busy chipping rust and repainting—a dangerous, dirty, and noisy job. I saw sailors dangle along the superstructure and from masts in safety harnesses on ropes, with their heads covered in kerchiefs and old shirts, and wearing safety glasses. They worked for hours on end, chipping rust and painting, while the ship rolled and pitched. Rust on the decks is especially hard to control, and was removed with powerful pulsating and rotating steel brushes that clattered with an insistence heard halfway up the ship, even when the wind and waves were making their own commotion. I was amazed at how cheerful the crew members remained while working, always ready with a smile and a wave to us as we watched or walked by. They worked for six days most weeks and often on Sundays as well, and had already started by the time we had breakfast, continuing past our cocktail hours.

Chief among the deck workers (ABs) is the bosun, the foreman who gets his instructions from the first officer, and who organizes the actual work (he also participates in it). The ABs do more than chip and paint, they also repair anything that gets broken on the decks and in the cabins. On entering and leaving port, they operate the winches and ropes that tie the ship to the berth and the tugs to the ship. They lower and take in the gangway and attach or remove the safety net around it. There's always supposed to be one AB on watch at the top of the gangway during time spent in port. Often after we left a port, and certainly after travelling through the Panama and Suez canals, the ABs washed and power-sprayed all of the decks. Soot (carbon) builds up inside the ship's stack, especially when it travels at less than maximum speed. "Blowing the stack" ignites some of this soot, and it's a spectacular affair, especially at night, a virtual trail of fireworks hanging in the sky. However, the process usually leaves a layer of soot clinging to the ship's surface, which must be washed away or the inside of the ship will soon become filthy as well. Clearly the crew of the *Ville d'Aquarius* took pride in its appearance, whether driven by company pride or their natural sense of neatness. It certainly looked better than many of its peers in the various harbours we visited.

I had assumed that there were rules about the maximum number of working hours for ABs, perhaps stipulated in union and governmental contracts (thinking that perhaps forty-eight hours per week would be a reasonable figure, although clearly these ABs worked more hours than that). I was assured there were such rules, but when I asked one of the officers what would happen to a captain who strictly enforced them, I received a stare and a long hesitation before the answer came, in a tone that indicated the problem. "That would be that captain's last voyage." He explained that there were two reasons for the overlong workdays. First, transporting containers is a brutally competitive industry, and shipping companies look at payrolls as places to save money. It's better to pay some overtime than to have too many bodies on board. Second, most Filipino sailors want to work the hours, since after a certain number of hours per day, overtime rates kick in. Many of these sailors told me they counted on the extra income.

In the discussion above, the business side of shipping figures large, but now when I see a merchant ship I always wonder what life is like on board that particular ship. Where has it been and where is it going, and with what cargo? What's been done on board to give a human element to daily work that is demanding and dangerous? For as much as we could, Johanna and I tried to hear the stories of the people who worked on board the *Ville d'Aquarius*. Most of our contact with them remained formal and only occasionally did we get to know a bit about the real pains and joys in the lives of the people on board, for people don't easily bare their souls. When they do, the impact is lasting.

When I think back to these sailing experiences and to our volunteer work at the Mariners' Centre in Montreal, moments of intimacy stand out. At the centre in Montreal, a ship's bell rang at 2100 hours every day, announcing a brief Christian worship service in its small chapel. These were conducted by clergy, one on staff and two volunteers. I was asked to conduct these services a few times, when the other three were unavailable. One night a sailor stayed behind after the service and came up to me to ask for a special blessing. He wanted me to put my hand on his forehead, for, he said, he had a strong headache. I did, prayed over him, and then we sat at a table and talked for awhile. He was a Hindu with two teenage children at home in India about whom he worried. He wanted to quit his job that took him away from his home and family, but knew he couldn't because an extended family was dependent on his income. He freely shared his pain and worries and told me that he felt better at the end of our conversation. I felt humbled by having been able to help this man. Every sailor has a story.

CHAPTER SIX

Singapore to Hamburg

The voyage between Singapore and Jeddah, our next port, took nine days, the longest uninterrupted stretch of the journey. It was a marvelous time of rest, sunshine, meals, games, exercise, conversation, and time spent watching ships. We enjoyed a second Saturday night barbecue, this time with a roast pig as the centrepiece, carefully and slowly prepared by the cook on an improvised spit over a barbecue tub on the poop deck. Once again, all officers, crew, and passengers were invited, beer and wine provided, and all the food you could ever want to eat. The Filipino officers and crew sat at their separate table, but there was plenty of kibitzing flying in all directions. It was another magical evening: the stars all around, the ship plowing across the water, dim lights on deck, the food, talk, laughter, leisure, lack of care, fellowship, and conversation, or just sitting and drinking it all in. Johanna had brought with her a richly illustrated stargazing guide, plus a flashlight with a red filter that would enable her to walk around and read the pages in the dark. After the barbecue, Gottfried went with her to the bridge deck and helped her spot the constellations. It was a marvelous experience for her.

One day, Chief Friedrich spotted porpoises, and another day he saw two whales. On both occasions, he quickly alerted the passengers. The weather

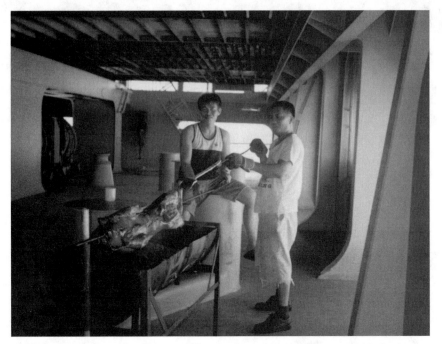

This pig had been slowly roasting all day for the evening BBQ party on deck after we left Singapore on our way to Jeddah. This is the same deck on which fish had been smoked a few thousand kilometres to the east and north.

was calm and hot on this leg, though big swells were constantly rolling the ship from side to side. Even though there was hardly any wind, the sea never seemed entirely restful. We couldn't sit on deck every day—at least twice the ship was washed down with power hoses from top to bottom, and the decks were out of bounds for passengers. While in our cabin reading one morning, we heard the sound of rushing water coming from the hallway. We discovered that a toilet pipe on the bridge deck had burst, and water was running down to the bottom of the staircase. Water on board is kept under pressure, for it has to be pumped up from storage tanks in the engine room, a long way below. Hence it came out of the broken pipe with force and in quantity. The water on the entire ship was shut off for the hours it took to fix the pipe, and an AB was busy rest of the day mopping up the deluge. When we met Jörg the fixer later in the day, he merely shrugged his shoulders about the workmanship on board this "piece of junk" (he actually used an equivalent German phrase that sounded much more contemptuous). This long stretch at sea was also used to repaint most of the outside of the ship, including the decks, railings, and walls. We were careful wherever we walked about the ship, but even so, Johanna got some gray paint on her clothes.

On February 25 we came in sight of Jeddah and were once again warned to hide any liquor and books with covers that might be deemed provocative. The captain had tried to persuade the agent to issue shore passes, not only for us but also for any crew members who had a day off, but his request was denied. Once again an armed guard, relieved every two hours, stood at the foot of the gangway. This time we were able to meet the principal agent when he came on board after berthing. I asked him to bring us some English language magazines, starved for news as I was after nine days of being incommunicado. He brought three, one a woman's magazine in which a number of ads had been blacked out by hand. The agent told us that he had come from Somalia, and he talked about his life in Saudi Arabia in guarded but unmistakably critical language. Though a Muslim himself, he had not been able to make local friends and couldn't become a citizen, therefore his children were only allowed to attend inadequate schools. For political reasons, he couldn't return to Somalia. It was clear he enjoyed talking to us, an interruption to what he gently communicated as a tough life. He also surreptitiously handed us two addressed envelopes and asked us to mail them for him to his friends, one in Canada and one in the United States. We refused his offer to pay for the postage, and were once again glad to leave this place.

Out of Jeddah, we turned north again on our way to the Suez Canal. Sailing closer to the Saudi Arabian coast, we saw many oil-well platforms rising out of the water. We arrived at the south end of the canal in late afternoon, and anchored for the night, the city of Suez within sight. More ships approached and anchored behind us. We woke up the next morning to the loud noise of the anchor lifting as the ship prepared to enter the canal. Just ahead of us and leading the convoy were three French warships. Throughout the day, we used both our naked eyes and binoculars to watch the sailors busily moving around on board the closest warship. Warships or not, these ships were beautiful in our eyes, elegant and slim, looking like race horses barely held in check.

Two Egyptian merchants with their wares had come on board early in the morning. This time their small boat had been hauled up by our on-board crane and was hanging alongside the ship. The two men provided Johanna with a few anxious moments. One cornered her and wanted to kiss her, and the other told her how beautiful she was and that he loved blue eyes. Despite this, we did buy a well-crafted copper plate and a small copper vase. One of the merchants asked Johanna if she had any cakes of soap she would give him, which she did, having brought lots on board. When Johanna discovered that she had left her camera somewhere and we couldn't find it, we had another anxious moment. Fortunately, the captain had seen it and put it in a safe place. When he gave it back he gave her a warning: No stranger on board could ever be trusted. At one point, one of the merchants, perhaps not satisfied with the extent of our purchases, came up to the deck where we were sitting to persuade us to come down and examine his wares some more, promising us real bargains. When we refused, he told us that his daughter was a coin collector and asked if I could spare him some coins from the countries we had visited. I gave him the Singaporean coins I had in my pocket, not believing a word of what he had told me about his daughter.

For most of the day we sat in our deck chairs watching the two continents go by slowly, the Asian desert on one side and Africa on the other. I also climbed up to the bridge deck to view the landscape and the convoy from a higher vantage point. The Egyptian pilot sometimes wandered out of the bridge. He didn't look like a typical pilot, who was usually weather-beaten, with the rough wind, sun, and sea having carved their marks on his face. He looked more like a traditional college professor, well dressed in a suit and tie, with his shoes polished, hair carefully coifed, and the look of a gentleman of leisure on his face, which seemed strange given the responsibility he bore for guiding this huge ship through the narrow watery artery. His English was not only immaculate, it was literary and poetic.

With considerable pride the elegant pilot pointed to the developments on either side of the canal close to its northern exit. Just south of Port Said, an enormous agricultural land development was almost completed, with some farms already in operation. The soil was black and fertile, with drainage ditches marking workable plots. On the desert side, across from Port Said, construction was underway on a new container port, one now in full operation. Just before we reached the end of the canal, the pilot and merchants were taken off the ship and ahead of us the warships accelerated. Although our ship was faster than most freighters, it was no match for these thoroughbreds. When we woke up the next morning, they were nowhere to be seen. Our ship was washed down once more that day after another fiery stack-blowing spectacle, needed after the slow Suez Canal trip.

Once clear of the Suez Canal, we began to make our way back to Malta. Gottfried was looking forward to arriving there, since his wife would be waiting for him. She had flown in from Germany and would sail with us all the way back to Hamburg. We docked at about 1100, had lunch on board, and then left by bus for a brief repeat visit to Valetta. There Johanna bought some famous Malta lace in a boutique. On our way back, we left the bus at the far edge of Birzebuggia for a leisurely walk into town. With the end of the trip in sight, Daryl wanted to buy us a farewell restaurant dinner and together we consumed delicious pizzas with a fine bottle of red wine. Stuffed and happy, we walked back to the ship on a trail that meandered along the bay in which our ship was tied up further down, past elaborate buildings on the right and small fishing and pleasure boats on the left. Some boats had a high curved prow with a horse's head figurehead and paintings of birds on their sides in red and green. Daryl thought these were old Phoenician motifs. In town we spotted Gottfried and his wife dining in a restaurant, and we went in to greet her and introduce ourselves. Happy and tired, we made our way back to the ship for a good night's rest in preparation for another full day in Malta.

When you approach Malta you first see water on both sides of the island, indicating that it's not all that large. Yet just as our ships' crew stirred up bottom sand docking, so too has this small island stirred up the Mediterranean throughout history.

For sheer tourist pleasure, the next day was perhaps the highlight of our whole journey. In the morning, Daryl, Gottfried's wife Hannelore (Gottfried had to work), and Johanna and I took a bus to the Valetta bus terminal and found another bus to take us to M'dina, another forty minutes away. The bus stopped outside an entrance built into a mighty wall behind which this old city rests in peace. No vehicular traffic is allowed within the city walls, only pedestrians, bikes, and horse-drawn carriages. We visited a museum that displayed beautiful historical tableaux portraying life in the sixteenth century. Below M'dina's fort, rural Malta spread out in a panorama of small farms and villages. This was one of the strongholds the Saracens, the Muslim invaders, had besieged in vain in 1565, and one could easily see why they had failed. The surrounding walls seemed at least two feet thick and it was a forbidding climb before even reaching them.

We witnessed the changing of the guard at midday, and Johanna almost got into the act herself. She told me that she could easily imagine stepping back in history, walking through the narrow crowded streets, and shopping in the market square surrounded by merchants, sheep, and goats, while church bells tolled, pigeons flew and pecked, and soldiers marched. The sandstone buildings looked like those in Valetta and featured more gorgeous doors that evoked images of how life was lived behind them centuries ago. The decorative door knockers were of the same designs as in Malta's capital.

Fort M'dina's changing of the guard is a daily re-enactment spectacle. Johanna simply had to see it up close. That's not the sea behind her, but Malta's blue-hazed farm area.

After lunch in an Italian restaurant, we took the bus back to Valetta, and on the way Johanna and I discussed, not altogether unseriously, the prospect of living on Malta for four months during our Canadian winters. After all, we were retired and why shouldn't we live in elegant surroundings in a decent climate? But we knew our children and grandchildren would be cut to the quick if we moved this far away. We shall have to live with only the memories of Malta. In Valetta we found telephone company offices where I bought the first telephone card of my life. I needed to call Arend to let him know when we would be arriving back in Hamburg, since he had promised to pick us up. I also wanted to phone our daughter Emily, who was living in our home back in Canada. We got back to our ship in time for supper, and late that evening the ship left for our penultimate port, Le Havre.

On the way to Le Havre, the captain told us that passengers might not be able to go ashore there this time either, as port time would be fairly short. The weather began to turn positively nasty again and we wondered how rough the Gulf of Biscay would be this time around. We saw schools of fish and even some large tuna in the Mediterranean. Then fog appeared for a day. While the ship didn't slow down, we found fog, even this relatively transparent one, an eerie experience, especially at night. The Gulf of Biscay was rough, with big swells once more making the ship roll from side to side. It's especially intimidating to stand on the poop deck, the lowest open deck of the ship, and see water higher than the top of your head only a few metres past the edge of the ship, now at its lowest dip. While in the Gulf of Biscay, the ship stopped once more, the engine silent. For some hours we simply drifted on the waves and swells, perhaps the most uncomfortable few hours we experienced on this ship. The engineers talked about "some maintenance," but we never found out what that meant, or why it was done at this particular time.

We reached Le Havre safely on March 7, arriving very early in the morning. At breakfast we were notified that we would have enough time for a shore visit after all, as the ship wouldn't leave port until the very late afternoon or evening. After breakfast, Daryl, Johanna, and I walked to the port exit and took a taxi, which got us into the city in about twenty minutes. The taxi driver, a fine Le Havre promoter, told us about the Saturday market and the cathedral. As we had no French money at this point, the driver named a US-dollar fare, which we gladly paid him on arrival. The cathedral was new, the old one having been destroyed in the aftermath of D-Day in 1944. The new cathedral made me realize that we hadn't seen any ancient buildings in this old European city. Once I began looking, I spotted three older buildings that clearly predated D-Day, two of them with bullet and shell holes still visible. The impressive cathedral had a high tower rising out of the centre of the sanctuary, and along all its sides right to the top were pebbles of coloured glass that reflected the sunlight in ever-moving ways, a wonderful sight. The cathedral didn't have a pipe organ, only an electronic one, an anomaly we thought.

From the cathedral we made our way to the indoor market, which was a feast for the eyes and nose. At the market were bakers, cheese merchants, fishmongers, greengrocers, wine merchants, chocolatiers, and butchers. Each one of them seemed to display their wares as if creating a painting; there were mosaics of meats, cheeses, and chocolates with carefully balanced sizes and colours. Meats came in dainty portions and the cheeses looked as if they had just been released from ripening storage, and then only reluctantly. Fish in great variety and size appeared to merely rest from the struggles of sea life, cool atop beds of ice. Bakers had worked magic with flour and butter and creams in many colours. I thought Dutch food merchants were good at displaying their wares, but these Le Havre artisans royally surpassed them.

We both felt that buying any of it would destroy these works of art, but that didn't stop the Le Havrians from buying left and right. Johanna bought a fresh baguette, which we picked at while walking until it was consumed. Volunteers were handing out pamphlets and engaging shoppers in conversation about an impending municipal election. I was approached by a volunteer, but before she could say anything I said, "*Nous sommes Canadiens*," the very first genuine French phrase I had ever offered in earnest. I got a smile and a nod in return, but luckily no verbal response, which would have left me floundering. After the market, we had lunch at a restaurant close to the ferry and fishing harbour. We also quietly watched a fellow diner with a long bushy beard, a small but obviously wiry body, a wrinkled forehead, and a sailor's cap. Perhaps a fishing boat or coastal freighter captain, he clearly relished his meal and the bottle of wine that accompanied it. Afterwards we wandered the streets until we found a taxi and made our way back to the ship. While we had been enjoying ourselves in the city, the Le Havre cranes had unloaded the hundreds of brand new reefer containers, which were now standing on the quay in a long row four levels high—an impressive sight.

The *Ville d'Aquarius* left Le Havre while we slept that night. Around breakfast time the next morning we found ourselves already in the Channel. While it was a dark and dreary day, with wind and rain gusting, we had a whole day of watching Channel traffic. It was busy indeed, with tankers and all kinds of other freighters competing for space with cross-channel ferries between England on one side, and France, Belgium, and Holland on the other. Some ferries, hydrofoils, and catamarans were going at very high speeds. The captain was on the bridge for the whole day, and both he and the officers on watch seemed tense and extra alert because of the traffic. As we sailed past the coast of Holland, the captain offered me his cellphone to call Arend as we passed close to his village. He would pick us up the next day in Hamburg.

That night we had our last canned fish and bread Sunday night dinner. Afterwards we shared the last of our liquor with the officers in the lounge, paid our last bill for slop-chest goodies, and began to pack our suitcases. We left many of the books we had brought in the lounge's library.

We went to sleep knowing that we would arrive back in Hamburg at breakfast time. We woke up early, got dressed, and watched our ship's entry into the Hamburg harbour, where it made a complete 180-degree turn before being berthed. We spent the morning finishing our packing and waiting for Arend, who had promised to be there around noon. He arrived in the same van that had guided us to the ship nine weeks ago, and I asked the van driver to come back in an hour as I wanted to show my brother how we had lived. After our final lunch on board, we said goodbye to Daryl and to the sailors and officers who were within reach. The bosun and Ariel the steward got our luggage out of the cabin and down the stairs and gangway to the van, which drove us back to my brother's car in the gate area. That night we slept in a nonmoving bed for the first time in more than two months. We stayed with Arend and his wife Betsy for about three days, and then he drove us to Schiphol airport for the final leg of our journey home.

During our voyage, I came to realize how much my childhood and youth, family, country, and schooling had shaped my feelings about the sea. As Canadian writers have given voice to the geography and culture of their childhood, telling of prairies and mountains, forests and tundra that are part of their very being, so my psyche has the sea imprinted on it forever.

There are many splendid books on oceans and seas that provide answers to such questions as how big, how deep, how much, how far, how warm, or how cold. History books describe sea travel, from rowing and drifting long distances in primitive crafts to manning giant container vessels and equally

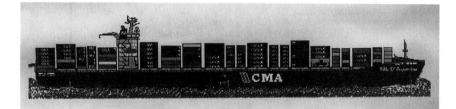

MV „Ville d' Aquarius"

Statement of Miles

for Mrs. *Johanna Peetoom*

After 874 Rivermiles and 23966 nm Seadistance
We Neptune, King of the Sea,
confirm that you was living in good harmony with all my vasalls
and respecting the sea
From now
We command all whales, sharks, finny monsters
and dolphins to aid and comfort thee on thy
voyages. All periwinkles, shrimps, bloaters, kippers
and sea kale to nourish thee. We forbid all jelly
fish to sting thee, lobsters to give thee nightmare
and sirens not entice thee from thy course.

Neptune

Chief Off.	Captain	Chief Eng.

MAX. EAST:	$\varphi = 35° 07'\ N,\ \lambda = 129° 02'\ E$
MAX. SOUTH:	$\varphi = 01° 03'\ N,\ \lambda = 103° 39'\ E$
ONE NAUTICAL MILE:	$40000\ KM / 360° / 60' = 1852\ M$

*The total distance is more than once around the globe. We both got a certificate,
a much appreciated gesture on the part of the ship's owners and captain.*

giant cruise ships, in which the number of employees roughly equals the number of passengers on board. Mine is a more personal account of what I saw, heard, smelled, felt, and thought about while at sea. It's about the dialogue between the sea and myself as I stood on deck and stared at the waves. The trip brought back scattered memories of history and geography lessons from school and books I've read about storms, pirates, and admirals.

I had been a passenger on a sea-going ship once before. In early March 1954, I boarded the Dutch emigrant ship *Waterman*, destined for the port of Halifax, Nova Scotia, Canada. This former Liberty ship had at first been a ten-thousand-ton floating truck ferrying war goods from North America to Europe during the second half of World War II. After the war, the *Waterman* had been rebuilt as a troop and emigrant carrier for the Dutch government. I remember the choppy Atlantic under fast-moving March clouds, a queasy stomach, and an overcrowded and shuddering ship, all sailing under a cloud of emigrant uncertainty. It was no romantic sea voyage, merely eight days to be endured.

My previous experience had left me somewhat apprehensive about possible seasickness. However, I discovered I'm not prone to seasickness (strange for someone who easily gets carsick), and I survived a number of storms and one wind-force-nine gale in the Bay of Biscay in midwinter. But apprehension about *mal de mere* wasn't the only thought about the sea I carried with me as we climbed the thirty-nine wobbly steps onto the ship in Hamburg. Even though I've lived in Canada since I was nineteen, the memories of my youth are Dutch, not Canadian, and inextricably connected to the sea.

Holland is so small a country that it's possible for almost every Dutchman to set out for the seashore in the early morning, enjoy many hours of relaxation, and get back home the same day. The proximity of the sea makes it culturally and psychologically a part of the Dutch soul. Much of my elementary and secondary school education consisted of learning the names and deeds of famous admirals and captains, famous sea battles, and famous expeditions. Dutch school children rejoiced that in the sixteenth century our country, then only about 2.5 million people, owned as many merchant and warships as all of the rest of Europe put together. We knew about scurvy, lost sailors who miraculously reappeared after many years, the four naval wars with England in the seventeenth century, and perfidious Albion (England) stealing our colonies in the early 1800s when Napoleon had us in the palm of his hand. Those vague memories took on an almost tangible shape as we travelled the string of Asian ports that were so often the result of British imperialism. Other flashes of memory surfaced: the national ritual of catching a new crop of herring in May, which we ate salted but otherwise raw all year; and the building of the Afsluitdijk, that more than thirty-kilometre-long stone and sand barrier that transformed a dangerous inland salt water sea into a more placid sweet-water lake in 1932, two years before I was born.

I left school knowing that my forebears practically invented long-distance merchant shipping, then post-Renaissance sea warfare, and then colonizing. Only later did I learn that Greece, Phoenicia, Portugal, Italy, and Spain had been no seafaring slouches themselves, all of them at it much earlier than Holland. But what you learn in school is also patriotism, and patriotic stories seem more important than facts. When Dutch parents took their children to photographers for childhood pictures, almost invariably the boys were dressed in little sailor uniforms. I have such a photograph of my Dad, taken about 1909.

Even today Holland possesses one of the largest port complexes in the world: Rotterdam harbour, a gateway to all of Western Europe. Holland's *polders*, diked lands often wrested from the sea, are reminders of what Napoleon is reputed to have said: "God created the earth, except Holland: Dutchmen did that themselves." The sea, so I surely knew at the end of my school days, was both friend and enemy. It brought riches, but always threatened to take back the land by breaching the dikes. I'll never forget the terrifying floods of January 31, 1953, when 1,800 Dutchmen died.

In school we learned more about the location of lands formerly part of Holland's trading empire than about the rest of Europe: Malacca and Ceylon (now Sri Lanka), New Amsterdam (now New York), Madagascar, Tasmania, New Zealand, Indonesia, Curacao, and the Antilles. Ours was a seafaring nation, so our geography lessons attended to what was most important.

Many of the novels that captured my attention as I grew up had maritime settings. *Holland's Glory*, a story of Holland's tugboat industry written by Jan de Hartog, was full of tough men and sturdy ships on wild seas. I brought it with me when I emigrated, and read it regularly until it fell apart. For years I also treasured *Het Fregatschip Johanna Maria*, by Den Doolaard, the "biography" of an early-nineteenth-century sailing freighter from its construction to its final resting place in a Dutch port.

No wonder I was interested in travelling on a freighter. The sea held the promise of excitement and undiscovered horizons that were part of my heritage, presented to me mostly in stories and books. Now I had a chance to travel the seas of my imagination, and what a pleasure this first experience had been.

CHAPTER SEVEN

Container Shipping

As Johanna and I settled back into life in Canada after our two-month absence, we were happy to be back with family and friends, but soon realized that our urge to travel had only been fuelled by our trip on the *Ville d'Aquarius*. Another freighter voyage appealed to us, but we would be boarding the next ship as passengers much more educated in the business of container shipping.

When Johanna and I had climbed aboard the *Ville d'Aquarius*, we hadn't really given any thought to the fact that this was a container ship. We knew it was a freighter, but what kind of freight the ship would carry and how it would carry it wasn't a factor in our decision to book. We certainly weren't prepared for the energy, noise, and confusion of the Hamburg port. While the essence of what we were seeing was soon clear enough, we needed time to sort out the details of this complicated business. After hours of looking at what was going on in the ports, we began to see things we had missed earlier, and we learned even more by talking to the officers and crew.

The photograph of a container port on page 133 records a scene much like that we experienced in Hamburg. Underneath the dangling container, we see the sun's reflection on the ship's steel hull. Right above the forty-foot long container standing on the dock, a bit of the working deck is visible, with its walking path around the ship right underneath the outer containers. (The *Ville d'Aquarius* had a similar design.) Above the rows of containers, two crane arms are busy placing, or taking away, containers. The dangling container is being lifted by a third crane, not visible on the picture, except for the reflection of its cables on the side of the standing container. The crane installations are massive; they have to handle loads of over thirty tons right to the edge of their arms. These cranes move parallel to the ship on rails to where they need to be for the proper placing and pickup of containers on the ship. They pick up containers by means of an adjustable clamp that grabs the container at its top four corners. To the centre of the clamp are attached strong cables that raise or lower the container to the desired height. Those cables are attached to the bottom of a carriage that slides to and from just underneath the crane arm. Inside the carriage, an operator controls the loading and unloading, observing through its glass bottom

Most of the time we would leave the ship and come back to it in the middle of loading and unloading. Who would not feel a little frightened having to walk through this? (Courtesy P&O Nedlloyd, Rotterdam, the Netherlands)

while his hands and feet operate various controls. The open-sided yellow "box" is actually a "container" to move stevedores and their equipment up to and down from the various levels of containers already on the ship. They simply step in and hold on, and the crane operator does their bidding, setting them down on top of the containers. The container standing on the dock seems to be a reefer (a refrigerated container), judging by the large dial on its upper left and the access opening for attaching cooling systems.

My *Collins English Dictionary* defines "container," in a shipping context, as: "a. a large cargo-carrying standard-sized container that can be loaded from one mode of transport to another. b. (as modifier): a container port; a container ship." Loading from one mode of transport to another is a simple idea. Instead of handling goods in small quantities from source to destination over long distances, we pack goods in a container, and simply shift the whole container from truck to train, from train to truck to ship, from ship to truck, and so on. Many containers are fully loaded right at the producing plants or farms. In large warehouses, loads that occupy less than a whole container are packed together with similar small shipments in containers destined for the same general area.

Not long after we returned to Canada, I bought a pair of running shoes that were produced in Indonesia. I imagined the voyage those shoes would have taken had container shipping not been developed and transportation of goods been as it was forty years ago. For the purposes of my story, somewhere on the outskirts of Malang in Java, Indonesia, is an imaginary shoe factory specializing in the manufacture of running shoes for the Western European and North American markets. Each pair is packed in a box printed with the brand name and other information, and two dozen of those boxes are packed in a large corrugated shipping carton. One of those cartons is going to a sporting goods store in the Conestoga Mall in Waterloo, Ontario, Canada, but how does it get there? Air freight is too expensive, so it has to be carried by ship for part of the way. But between Malang and Waterloo lie many long stretches of water, and a tortuous route and set of handling procedures.

At Malang, which is about seventy-five kilometres away from the nearest sea port, Surabaja, our carton is placed on a skid with other large shipping cartons containing boxes of shoes also destined for Canada, perhaps for the same store or other stores in the same chain. Ropes or metal straps are used to hold the cartons together and attach them to the skid. A small forklift places the whole skid onto the back of a truck. The truck is driven to

Surabaja, where it's lifted off the truck and placed in a dockside warehouse to await the arrival of the ship that will carry it away.

In preparation for the ship's imminent arrival, the skid is moved from the warehouse to the proper quay location (let's hope that rain doesn't soak the cartons). A special cargo net is wrapped around the skid, the ends of which are attached to a hook at the end of a cable that's part of the ship's own crane, or a dockside crane, and the skid is lifted up, moved above the proper hold (cargo bin) of the ship, and lowered into place. Once in place, the net is removed and hauled back up and out for the next load. It requires at least two people on the quay to handle these tasks, and at least two in the hold of the ship, plus the crane operator and the forklift driver. It takes about eight minutes to lift and lower one skid, and a long time to fill up a ship one skid at a time.

Once all the Surabaja cargo for this coastal vessel is loaded, it sails along the north coast of Java and picks up more cargo in places like Semarang, Tegal, and Tjirebon, before it reaches the major Indonesian seaport and capital of Djakarta. Here, the ship unloads its cargo, once more skid by skid, onto the dock. Forklifts place each skid in one of the warehouses, awaiting the next ship that will carry them further. It takes plenty of time, plenty of stevedore power, and plenty of paperwork and label-checking, to make sure that our carton keeps moving in the proper direction.

In the Djakarta harbour, the skids await the arrival of a freighter that will sail directly to North America (New York, Halifax, or Montreal), or sail first to Singapore to be transloaded again. If going to Singapore, the cargo would then wait for another ship that planned to sail the route the *Ville d'Aquarius* had just covered. In either case, our carton could easily have been unloaded in a European port once more (Antwerp, Rotterdam, or Hamburg) before finally being loaded onto a ship that would take it to a North American port. In each harbour the whole loading process is repeated. Each skid is taken from the warehouse, placed on the dock, put in ropes or a net, hauled up by the ship's crane, and lowered into the proper cargo hold. It would take days to do, and many strong hands and arms.

Once our carton finally arrives in Canada, say in Halifax, it must still travel to Waterloo, Ontario, about two thousand kilometres. The skid is loaded on a truck (together with other skids that are going to Ontario), and the truck drives the load to the railroad freight platform, where it's placed inside a railroad boxcar. When the boxcar is full, it becomes part of a large freight train that eventually goes north through Nova Scotia and New

Brunswick, then west through Quebec and Ontario, and after a number of days, arrives in the freight railway marshalling yard north of Toronto. There the boxcars are emptied. Our skid is placed on a truck, and driven to a Toronto warehouse of the footwear chain store that owns the Waterloo store. There it's unloaded and our carton is put on another truck for the one-hundred-kilometre drive to the Waterloo store.

How often has this box been picked up and put down during its long journey? How many human hands have touched the carton between Malang and Waterloo, and how many times has basic shipping information been recorded on different forms? It's clear that a container carrying many skids going in the same direction is a better way to ship goods. Containers can be placed on ships, trains, or trucks without anyone ever opening them (except for customs inspections) or unloading and loading their contents until they reach their final destination. Containers must still be lifted on and off ships, trucks, and trains, but fifty skids, and maybe thirty-five tonnes, are lifted at the same time inside one box, rather than lifting fifty skids individually. Also, there's only one set of papers required to document the entire container. It's no wonder that the time spent in ports is cut down, not just by hours, but by days.

The inspiration that led to today's container shipping industry came from truck driver and later trucking company owner Malcolm McLean in the mid-1950s. He had the idea to take the body of a tractor-trailer and place it fully loaded on a ship, a railroad car, a loading dock, or even an airplane. This would keep shipments together, protect the goods from the elements, and save all kinds of handling and paperwork. In 1956 McLean piggybacked fifty-eight truck trailers onto a ship in Newark for delivery in Houston, and his idea, though not immediately embraced by everybody, took root. By the late 1960s, container ships were crossing every ocean, and now about 90 percent of the world's goods moves in containers.

There are two kinds of steel containers designed to be carried safely by trains, trucks, and ships: the 1 TEU (Twenty Equivalent Unit), 20' long, 8' wide, 8' high; and the 2 TEU (or Two x Twenty Equivalent Unit), 40' long, 8' wide, 8' high. Some 2 TEU containers are 45' long, and some may also be 8'6", 9', or 9'6" high.

On one side of each container, doors swing out for loading and unloading, each door held in place by two strong vertical steel bars that keep them secure even in rough seas. Often these doors are sealed for protection against theft. For containers that are slated to cross borders, the seals may also mean that they have been inspected by customs officials and are now in bond.

In the photograph on this page numbers and letters are visible. PONU identifies P&O Nedlloyd as this container's owner or lessee. The numerals 123430 7, with 4261 underneath, identify this particular container and will be listed on port documents and bills of lading. Underneath those numbers, weight and volume capacity are listed: "Max" (32,500 kg), "Tare" (3750), and "Payload" (28750), as well as "CUB" (67.2 cubic metres), and imperial equivalents.

There's little danger that a single container on a flatbed truck would slide off, but containers are sometimes stacked five high on a ship's deck. Without securing them in some way, it's possible that at least the outer layers of the containers could drop into the sea as the ship pitched and rolled in heavy weather. The bottom layer of containers must be anchored to the ship, and subsequent layers to the layers below. Therefore, on every corner of each container, bottom and top, there's a steel bulge with three holes in it: one towards the side, one towards the front or back, and one towards the top or bottom. The top and bottom holes are made to fit a "twist lock," a

The "administrative" end of a container, with capacity and identification numbers clearly visible. This one looks new, but it will soon be rusty and dinted. (Courtesy P&O Nedlloyd, Rotterdam, the Netherlands)

steel gadget of which the lower "bulge" fits in the hole below, and the upper part will fill the hole of any container dropped on top of it. When inserted properly, a small steel bar sticks out from it, away from the container.

When we had been confined to the ship at the port of Jeddah, I had watched this part of the loading and unloading with rapt attention. Three cranes were busy all day, each able to handle from twenty to twenty-five containers per hour, and for each crane a stevedore danced on the ship below its arm. The stevedores in Jeddah were Pakistani. They would come to Jeddah for three months, be housed in Spartan barracks, and work long hours, but at least go back to their families with pockets full of money. For awhile I watched a slim and agile young man hopping across the container layers putting twist locks in the four holes on each container below his feet, until more containers covered the layer he had completed. Another stevedore on the ship's working deck used a long slim pole to hit each small steel bar of each twist lock to turn it ninety degrees and thus lock the two containers together (hence the name "twist lock").

It's heavy work, for these twist locks weigh about five kilograms, and the steel poles are hard to control when held well above the head. I wouldn't like to run on those steel surfaces as the stevedores do, especially in wet weather and close to the container's edge. I never watched the process without admiration for the workers. I remember two special moments. It was Ramadan in Jeddah, a time for intense Muslim devotion. The young man I was watching had a folded-up magazine page in his back pocket, and when prayer time came he stopped working, took out the magazine page, unfolded it, placed it carefully on top of a container, and knelt and prayed. Sweat was pouring off him most of the day. He was aware of me watching him and in midafternoon he made a drinking motion and looked at me. I threw him a cool can of Coke across our divide. He drank deeply and waved his thanks.

Containers stored below deck (about half the load) don't need twist locks. The ship's holds have four ninety-degree-angle steel bars placed so that containers fit tightly in transit. For unloading and loading below deck, a massive steel hatch is lifted from the working deck and deposited onshore with a massive clanging sound, no matter how carefully the crane operator lowers it. Whenever those hatches were put back on while we were asleep, we invariably woke up from the noise and the shuddering of the ship. Some of the container ships we saw in the ports had a similar system of steel frames above deck as well, thus eliminating the need to anchor each container with twist locks. However, those installations seemed to take up considerable deck space, perhaps making the ships less efficient cargo carriers.

In Australian and New Zealand ports a slightly different system was used. Dockside cranes lifted up the containers and then paused so that a stevedore could insert twist locks at the bottom of each container. Then the crane would lift the container to put it in place, drop it on a container below, and the locks would engage automatically. That process was less dangerous and also more efficient, as it eliminated the job performed by that young man in Jeddah.

Even twist locks on all four corners of each container aren't sufficient to hold in place containers stacked up to six high on top of the decks. More protection is needed, and is provided by long steel bars that connect layers of containers to the ship, and to one another. The ends of these bars consist of thin plates that are inserted in the side container holes; the middle of each bar is a screw arrangement that enables stevedores to tighten the bars once they're attached. Sometimes even the bars aren't enough protection. In Hong Kong I picked up a container shipping magazine that featured a

You would swear that with all these strong steel bars ingeniously placed no container would ever fall overboard. Alas, some do: the power of the sea when riled. (Courtesy P&O Nedlloyd, Rotterdam, the Netherlands)

photograph of a ship that had limped back into port with at least one hundred containers barely on board and all on a slant, the top ones hanging over the water. I wondered how they would ever fix that problem without damaging the containers, quays, and especially the stevedores, and without some containers going overboard.

For loading and unloading, container ports use custom cranes, huge steel structures anchored in rails. The cranes are powered by diesel engines, or by thick electrical cables that unwind from steel drums and are protected in grooves next to the rails. The cranes' movable arms are lifted at an angle when not in use, and lowered above the ships and across their widths for loading and unloading containers. The various cranes hold containers tight with a similar twist lock, except that these are part of the grabbing carriage itself, and are twisted mechanically by the crane's operator. The operator hanging in the movable carriage underneath the arm has excellent visibility through a glass bottom, and each operator we saw at work was a master at his trade. I never ceased to admire them as they aimed the carriage over the top of the containers, connected with them, and deposited them at precise spots on a ship or truck on the quay. Some were so skilled that they seldom had to give it more than one try, although windy weather increases the difficulty, as the large hanging containers are easily blown around.

In addition to the big custom cranes, mobile harbour cranes, powered by diesel engines, pick up containers from trucks and trains and deposit them in their assigned storage locations. In some ports, containers were stacked five high, so you can imagine how big and high those mobile cranes have to be. The basic system of lifting and placing containers remains the same; twist lock mechanisms are attached to the appropriate container corner holes, but controlled by the crane driver.

Not all cargo fits a 1- or 2-TEU container. The two ships we travelled on sometimes had oversized cargo on board: a heavy mining dump truck, a massive tractor, lumber, yachts, and storage tanks. These are placed on container platforms, which are container bottoms with the proper twist lock holes, but without sides or with partial sides. Cargo can then exceed the dimensions of the platform, and be lowered onto a ship as a top layer, often by ropes attached to each of the four corners of the platform. Some containers have sides but no fixed top and are sometimes protected from rain by a canvas cover. However, these covers soon get torn by high winds, as we saw ourselves.

Containers can hold anything that can be stuffed into them, and no

One kind of port container carrier. Think of it: This one carries a twelve-metre container weighing perhaps more than thirty tonnes! (Courtesy P&O Nedlloyd, Rotterdam, the Netherlands)

doubt some cargos exceed the weight limit. A heavy equipment dealer told me that his company once stuffed a container so full of spare parts that the crane couldn't lift it up from the dock. The ship left without that container, the contents of which had to be repacked in two separate containers for the next ship. Companies and individuals can either lease containers from shipping companies, or buy them and paint their own names and logos on the sides. Prominent shipping company names are P&O Nedlloyd, Evergreen, Cronos, Maersk, and Haspag-Lloyd. This isn't to say that, for instance, a P&O Nedlloyd ship only carries its own containers. All the ships we saw carried containers from many companies. Unfilled places on ships, like unfilled seats in airplanes, are lost revenue forever, so shipping companies will try to fill a ship as full as possible with whatever containers they can contract for.

Steel containers may look indestructible, but I saw many that had been damaged. I've not seen it happen, but it stands to reason that occasionally containers drop to the ground while being unloaded. I've watched containers being lowered between two rows, with not much room to spare, and bumping a few times on the other containers before hitting the right spot.

A different kind of port carrier that lifts the load up high. A truck drives underneath, receives the load, and then drives off to the container's final destination. (Courtesy P&O Nedlloyd, Rotterdam, the Netherlands)

In heavy seas I've seen containers constantly hitting their neighbours on either side. The long steel bars screech their own melodies. All those noises, plus the sound of the wind and the waves, make for a unique symphony, one with many discordant notes, and the whole of it ominous and disconcerting. Containers are also constantly exposed to salt water. The majority of containers I've seen on board and on docks show plenty of rust. In fact, some containers had steel patches, repair work for spots that had rusted through.

Loading and unloading isn't a matter of first come, first served. Even before a ship arrives in port, many sheets of paper document the intricacies of this process. There are many factors that enter into the equations that produce those loading sheets. First, where do containers have to be unloaded? Ideally, a container is placed on the ship and not moved until it reaches its port of final destination. Planners don't always succeed, for we have seen containers off-loaded, piled onshore, and then reloaded just because containers destined for this particular port had been placed underneath others in some previous port.

Second, a ship must be balanced while sailing, with the weight properly distributed between fore and aft, port and starboard. A container full of pillows weighs much less than one filled with automotive parts. The *Ville d'Aquarius* carried eight hundred brand new reefer containers from South Korea to Le Havre, France, a very light load as the containers were empty. Each container is accompanied by a bill of lading upon which is recorded its estimated weight. Those estimates are used to place containers in a location that will help the ship remain balanced. Weight factors are the reason why container ships are often loaded and unloaded at the same time, one or two cranes lifting containers on board, one or two others lifting them off, in order to keep the ship on an even keel. If all the fore cargo was taken off first, the ship's aft would sink down. There's another problem: Officers have told me that bills of lading cannot always be trusted. Some containers carry far heavier loads than officially recorded, which is another reason why there are a large number of ballast tanks deep in the holds of freighters. These tanks are filled with sea water and emptied as required to help stabilize the ship while unloading and loading and also while underway at sea.

Third, container ships often carry dangerous cargo, such as chemicals. It would be disastrous to have a collision at sea and have containers burst and their contents mix into a killing chemical soup. Any chemicals that would be potentially dangerous if combined must be kept apart.

Finally, some container ships carry loaded reefer containers. Full reefer containers must have access to cooling energy, via brine conduits or electrical cables, and these have their own deck and below-deck locations.

All these and other factors go into the loading and unloading sheets produced by computers with sophisticated software. At each crane, a stevedore uses these sheets to check the numbers of the containers going up and coming down. I also saw deck officers with sheets in their hands. An extra container or one not accounted for can be a major problem. In fact, the *Ville d'Aquarius* was held up for an hour in Jeddah before a missing container was found and hauled aboard. It can also be a costly mistake, since ships have to pay fees for the time they're tied up in port.

The more I learned about container traffic, the more I felt the great contrast between our quiet life as passengers with no access to computers, TV, or telephones, and the exciting hustle and bustle of international trade that opened up before our eyes every time we went into a port. I began to understand that the seas and oceans aren't just bodies of water connected eventually to all other bodies of water, but channels of communication for diverse human communities. I saw the vital roles played by ordinary people in physically demanding jobs all linked together so that I can enter a store back home and casually buy a new pair of runners produced on the other side of the globe. Behind these factory workers, truckers, stevedores, and sailors, one also finds entrepreneurs, bankers, insurance companies, shipping agents, ship owners, politicians, financial journalists, and economists. We buy a pair of shoes and pay for them with Canadian dollars, but that pair of shoes has been passed on in many other currencies already: Indonesian rupees, Singaporean dollars, Dutch guilders, and US dollars.

Freighter travel made me feel small, insignificant, and modest at times, and grateful for what others contribute to my life. But I also felt uncertain. How much were Indonesian factory workers paid for the shoes that cost me $100? I read somewhere that only a handful of rupees went to them. Then again, that small amount might contribute more to the welfare of some Indonesian family than the $100 would detract from mine. The Pakistani stevedore in Jeddah worked and lived like a slave, but after three

This "sight to behold" could be the scene at 0200, with us fast asleep in spite of the noise of containers being dropped in their places, diesel engine trucks to-ing and fro-ing, and stevedores shouting. (Courtesy P&O Nedlloyd, Rotterdam, the Netherlands)

months he went home with enough money to feed his family for many more months than the three he worked under abominable circumstances. Filipino crew members earn a low hourly wage, one that would be unacceptable to Canadian sailors, but they told us that their income made them financially privileged in their own country.

I'm too far away in distance and circumstance to make informed judgments upon the fairness of the situation. I know that greed often rules the world of international trade, but I also know that trade is a legitimate part of human existence. Our freighter cruises taught me to look at labels and discover where things have been grown and produced. In this sense I have become a materialist: I have developed a sense of gratitude and appreciation for things, realizing much more now that faraway human beings have a hand in making and bringing them to me. And one more thought: Stop all container shipping and the economies of the world will grind to a halt.

CHAPTER EIGHT

Savannah to Panama

We were barely home after saying goodbye to the *Ville d'Aquarius* when we set in motion plans related to further freighter travel. First, we sold our split-level house and bought a condo, which brought with it much less responsibility for maintenance and would be more secure while we travelled. After we were established in our new home, we were ready to plan our next trip.

Using the Internet, we discovered a vital source of freighter travel information: *TravLtips*, the official publication of the TravLtips Cruise & Freighter Travel Association. This well-illustrated magazine contains articles on ships and trips, letters to the editor, ads for particular cruises, and listings of companies in the business of providing passenger space on their vessels. It includes articles written by former passengers, so it's a valuable resource for avoiding potentially bad experiences. The magazine enabled us to relive our first experience and imagine the satisfaction of a second. After reading three issues and talking to a TravLtips representative on their toll-free number, we decided that our next trip would take us through the Panama Canal, a second vital artery of merchant shipping. We booked a voyage from Savannah, Georgia, across the South Pacific to Australia and

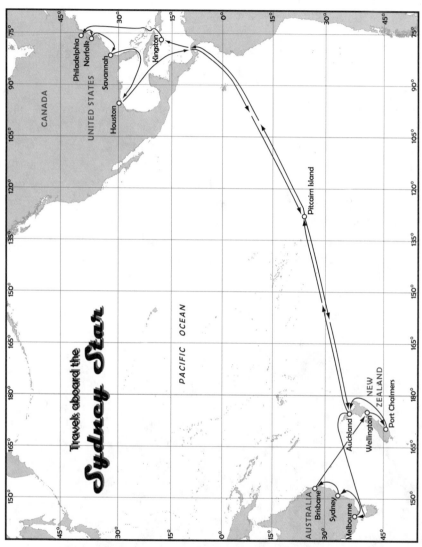

A massive piece of ocean on our second trip. Twenty days without a port to visit each way. (Map by Paul Heersink)

New Zealand and back. The trip on the *Sydney Star* would begin in early March 2000, and take about seventy-three days.

We decided to drive from Ontario to Savannah, and on the way visit friends in Connecticut and New Jersey. In Savannah we'd park our car somewhere for the duration of our trip. We could leave our heaviest and bulkiest winter clothes at home, since in March, Savannah would already be much warmer than Ontario, and from then on we would sail towards the equator and even warmer temperatures. We would hit Australia and New Zealand in their fall season, and the climates of both those countries don't require real winter gear. One roomy suitcase each would do. Remembering that ship decks attract dirt like light attracts moths, we each brought three pairs of footwear for daily use: nonslippery walking shoes for the decks, sandals for inside, and plastic slip-ons for inside our cabin. We now knew how easily dirt gets tracked where you don't want it on a freighter. We also decided that we would need more books than we had taken before, as the itinerary included two uninterrupted stretches of twenty days at sea, one in each direction between the Panama Canal and Auckland, New Zealand. Johanna bought a supply of wool and yarn to occupy her during her time at sea. We took along serious literature, including poetry, nonfiction, and George Eliot's lengthy nineteenth-century novel, *Adam Bede*, which I would read aloud to Johanna while she knit. We knew that there would

Some container ships do dock at Sydney Harbour proper, which is near the opera house. Notice the two tugs that watch their big brother like hawks. (Courtesy P&O Nedlloyd, Rotterdam, the Netherlands)

The superstructure of our second ship. Our cabin was on the starboard side (not seen), one of the top windows level right underneath the open boat deck. This picture offers a good view of the always wobbly stairs.

be plenty of lighter reading—mysteries, spy novels, and romances—already on board.

Australia required visas; TravLtips got them electronically as part of their booking procedures after we provided a photocopy of our passport identification page and their fee. Medically, no additional inoculations were required, not even against the yellow fever that had slain so many Panama Canal diggers. Our physician once more supplied a signed letter declaring us fit for freighter travel. We also decided to bring a radio/CD player and plenty of our favourite CDs.

In early March we loaded our car, locked the condo door, and drove to Connecticut. After a two-day visit with friends there, we began the trek southwards towards Savannah. Once in Savannah, we booked a motel for two days, nailed down a safe parking spot for the next ten weeks, and called the local Blue Star Line agent to let him know where we could be reached. We used the two days to explore Savannah, a fascinating city. It has a rich history, well represented in its major museum. Savannah is the birthplace of jazz pianist Johnny Mercer, whose memory and work is still celebrated there. A Southern cotton-producing slave-holding state, Georgia was conquered by the Northern armies during the Civil War. The Savannah River runs right through the city, with former riverside warehouses now transformed into boutiques, bars, and restaurants. A cobblestone and brick road with a small park at the end of it makes for a great riverside walk.

As the city's port is located farther inland, mighty freighters sail through regularly, catching the attention of the city's many tourists. Uphill from the river is the heart of the city with its banks and offices. Fortunately, commercial buildings share this district with apartment buildings and even some stately homes that are often built around small lush parks that invite walking tourists to sit a spell and enjoy the view and the people. Many of these homes have intriguing family histories that are featured on plaques and in tourist brochures. We took a tourist streetcar ride through the city, getting off and on at will along the route to take a closer look at some of the homes the streetcar guide had mentioned. The climate was as good as it gets for March——sunny but not hot. The only pests were hordes of mean gnats, little biting insects that thrive in the mild climate. Since our first visit, our only son Albert and his wife Monica have decided to make Savannah their home, and we look forward to visiting the city again. Occasionally we rent the movie *Midnight in the Garden of Good and Evil*, which is set in Savannah and features a number of locations we visited.

On Friday, March 10, the day of boarding, we parked our car at the boat building wharf where Albert was about to take a job as a designer of the interiors of pricy pleasure boats, and headed to Savannah's container port. At about 1000, we climbed the long way up to the working deck once again, two ABs helping us get our luggage to our cabin. We unpacked, and then got ready to explore our temporary home.

It was unavoidable that we constantly compared our experiences on board the *Sydney Star* with our first voyage, at least in the beginning. This time we inspected the ship with a far better understanding of passenger life at sea, and were much more aware of factors that could make our trip either more or less enjoyable. We especially hoped that we would be compatible with the other passengers, because the percentage of days at sea would be considerably higher than aboard the *Ville d'Aquarius*.

Our first impression as we climbed aboard was that this was a much older and smaller ship. There was plenty of rust everywhere and our cabin was considerably less spacious, with only a combined bed-sitting room and a bathroom. There were two single beds separated by a fixed bedside cabinet, which had switches that controlled all the cabin lights. On the other side of each bed was a smaller cabinet with a table lamp. Along the wall opposite was a credenza with desk space, two clothes closets, and plenty of drawers, one of which contained two life jackets. In the corner against the outside wall two comfortable armchairs and a small coffee table were placed underneath a ceiling light. On the desk we found a three-ring binder with on-board information, including mealtimes, safety procedures, instructions regarding our use of on-board facilities, and mail procedures. There was a list of items available for purchase from the slop chest: a selection of wines, liquor, and beer, as well as snacks, chocolate bars, toothbrushes and toothpaste, shaving items, and writing paper and envelopes. There was also a most welcome present: two pairs of brand new white cloth working gloves; ships are always dirty to the touch and I wore mine out before the end of the journey. The portholes provided plenty of light, but only one could be opened, and that with difficulty because of advanced rust. The bathroom had a deep bathtub and a shower head. Although the cabin was smaller, it was less sterile in terms of colours and materials and the whole of it felt a bit homier.

The decks on the *Sydney Star* were named, not numbered, as indicated with appropriately placed signs. We were housed on the starboard side of the Officers' Deck, the fourth one up from the Working Deck with inside stairs going up and down. On the portside, seven officers had their cabins. Both cabin hallways shared an exit door to the outside, where a set of open-air stairs also connected all decks. Passenger accommodation was provided by six cabins, two singles and four doubles, accommodation for a maximum of ten people. Between our cabin and the exit door were three more compartments. Next to us was a roomy and pleasant passenger lounge with hundreds of books in wood and glass bookcases along one wall, a TV and VCR, a radio with a cassette player, games, jigsaw puzzles, videos, a games table, easy chairs, couches and coffee tables, and a bar and counter on which was set a bowl of apples, oranges, and fresh grapes. There was a binder with sheets numbered for each cabin for marking down consumptions and a little box with chits for ordering slop-chest items. Drinks were cheap: beer, shots of hard liquor, vermouth, liqueurs, and cans of soft drinks, including cocktail mixes, were all 50¢US. Three large windows gave plenty of starboard-side light. Across from the passenger lounge was a laundry area. The small passenger pantry also across from the passenger lounge contained all the supplies and equipment to make tea or coffee at any time. The fridge held a selection of fruit juices and cartons of milk and a loaf of bread, butter, jam, and peanut butter for snacks. On the pantry counter stood three containers of cookies and crackers, while the cupboards contained cups, plates, and cutlery. Cleanup supplies were also provided (a poster suggested we wash up after use). Last but not least, there was an ice machine grinding out cubes all day. We happily concluded that we wouldn't lack for creature comforts.

We climbed the outside stairs up one floor to the Boat Deck. Johanna's eyes lit up when she saw the small outdoor swimming pool at the top of the stairs, but she was dismayed to see the amount of rust on the bottom and sides of it. We noticed more rust on the steel railings and at the edges where the floor and sides of the ship met. In comparison with the *Ville d'Aquarius*, the deck area was huge, three wide expanses in a U-shape around the ship's stack. Most of this deck was open, but on each side towards the front was a small alcove with windows to the front and sides that would provide a place to look out to sea while protected from the wind, rain, and sun. On one side of the deck were wooden tables and benches and a number of deck chairs with removable cushions. The deck had beautiful white pine floors; we could see that we would spend most of our routine days at sea here. On the Boat Deck were two large lifeboats hanging in davits just above it, one on each side, and also steel tubs, which contained inflatable life rafts, lying horizontally on stands. Around the hot and dirty stack were metal screens to keep people from harm. We later discovered that the captain, the chief engineer, and the chief officer had their cabins on this deck, right underneath the bridge house.

Johanna and I climbed up one more deck to the Bridge Deck. The gleaming wooden sliding doors into the bridge house were locked, but standing on that deck leaning on the beautiful mahogany rail called the taffrail, we had a fine view in front of the ship. We discovered another set of stairs going to the top of the bridge house, an area that we later learned is called Monkey Island (not every ship has a monkey island—the *Ville d'Aquarius* did not). With safety ledges at the front and sides, it was obviously the best place from which to observe the ocean world around us. When the ship rolled and pitched in swells and waves, from here one would see the bow waves shoot spray over top of the containers, the changing water colours under a sky filled with broken clouds with sheets of sunshine raking the sea surface.

There was much more wood on the *Sydney Star* than on the *Ville d'Aquarius*. The newer ship had been steel and plastic; this older vessel featured steel and wood. The deck floors, the polished taffrail on top of the steel fence around the Bridge Deck, and the mahogany doors into the various superstructure floors were all evidence of an older more traditional ship. Even though we learned that this ship wouldn't be much longer in service, all those doors and railings were carefully refinished once more while we were on board.

From the Bridge Deck we made our way to the level immediately below our cabin, called the Crew Deck. It contained the kitchen, two dining rooms, and two large lounges, one for officers and one for crew, and an elaborate sound system with large speakers. On the wall hung plaques and other items commemorating the ship's milestones: its launch, its maiden voyage, its major Japanese refit, and port honours, which included a Rotterdam plaque. A beautiful brass clock and brass lanterns were spread throughout this area, giving it a traditional ship's atmosphere. Easy chairs and couches arranged around coffee tables invited conversation. The room reminded me of descriptions in novels of passenger lounges on ocean liners: dark wood and soft lights, with an aura of relaxation and hints of luxury. We immediately expected that passengers would be allowed here only by invitation, for didn't we have our own lounge? At the back of the officers' lounge a hallway led to two additional bedrooms for guests and special assignment officers, four additional crew cabins, the officers' laundry area, and the set of inside stairs. For the Filipino crew, a lounge and dining room was located on the other side of the kitchen. Although not as luxurious as the officers' lounge, it too had a bar, easy chairs, sofas, and coffee tables, and benches along large tables for dining. This section also contained a ping-pong table, a dartboard, and a set of drums plus sound equipment.

The Poop Deck was located one more level down at the ship's aft. The rear part was open around the ship's superstructure. A wide steel deck curved around the top of the engine room, with one door giving access from the outside. There were no cabins on this level. The floor below was the Working Deck, which looked to have a walking "path," similar to our first ship. On the Working-Deck level and below the steel Poop Deck, thirteen crew members had their much smaller cabins, a laundry area, and a small workout room.

After our quick tour, we concluded that the *Sydney Star* would suit us well and returned to our cabin for a quick sleep before meeting the other passengers, none of whom seemed to be on board yet. They would certainly return soon, for the ship was scheduled to leave at about 1700. Indeed, barely dozing, we heard voices in the hallway and left our cabin to introduce ourselves to the others. We all went outside to watch the ship's departure from high up on Monkey Island. Two tugs guided it into the river shipping lane.

The Garden City Port, Savannah's container port, is located northwest of Savannah along the wide and deep Savannah River. It's a slow three-hour sail to the Atlantic, first right through the city and past an old warehouse area. As we had discovered on our day in town, it's now a tourist area filled with boutiques and restaurants. Many people onshore watched us as we slowly

A splendid view of Savannah as you sail on the river from its port to the right to the Atlantic on the left. Its riverside of former warehouses is now a mosaic of tourist boutiques, bars, and restaurants.

drifted by and when we waved to them they waved back. A street trumpet player spotted us and played "Popeye the Sailor Man" as loud as he could in our direction.

After sailing through Savannah, we passed oil refineries and other industrial plants, then marshes and lakes. Unfortunately, at this point I suddenly began to feel unwell. It wasn't the ship, for it moved placidly and perfectly horizontally on the river. I excused myself, and went back to our cabin where I was violently sick to my stomach. I was forced to miss dinner and dozed and slept for the rest of the evening and night. The next morning I woke up early, hungry but otherwise fine, sorry that I had missed our entry into the Atlantic Ocean. We were now underway at full speed to our second port, Houston.

Johanna had already learned the dining routine. Shortly before every meal, Lito, our dining room steward, would walk by our cabins while playing a tune on a little hand-held xylophone, a signal for passengers to come down. We were seated at two different tables, with our places indicated by name tags. At breakfast we were handed a menu to place advance lunch orders, and at lunch we ordered our four-course dinner. During breakfast time, the captain came by to say hello and give us the weather forecast. He had met the other passengers already and made it a point to welcome me on board. He must have been relieved to discover that I wasn't seriously ill.

This was my first opportunity to observe our fellow passengers, who had joined the ship in Philadelphia. Bill and Martha were a Pennsylvania couple in their fifties, both of them still busy with careers. Bill was a partner in a firm specializing in providing used large construction and other equipment to customers all over the world. Martha had been a senior executive at a hospital, but she would join her husband's firm after their return home. This was their first such journey and they didn't know what to expect. They brought on board seventeen pieces of luggage, most of them boxes full of delicatessen foods and champagne, and a wealth of ideas for parties. They were open, embracing, gregarious, funny, and sharing folk. They planned to leave the ship in Melbourne, travel in Australia for a bit, and then return home by air.

David and Jean were a British couple, both retired and on their second freighter cruise. David had been a pharmacist. While enjoying the trip, they regretted being away from their two young grandchildren, who were the most handsome grandchildren ever—well, at least in the UK, in their immediate area, maybe even on their street. We soon saw pictures. They planned to leave the ship in Auckland, having reserved a camper for a two-week vacation in New Zealand, after which they would fly back home.

Michael and Roberta were brother and sister, also British. Michael was a retired aviation engineer who had worked on the Concorde, while Roberta was a retired administrator. Neither had ever been married and so they were spending their retirement years together. They had met David and Jean on their only previous cruise, remained friends afterward, and had booked this cruise together. Michael and Roberta would also leave the ship in Auckland, but then fly home almost immediately. They had bought a house and were anxious to get started on remodelling and redecorating it.

Russ was from Sacramento, California, and was also a retired pharmacist. He had long wanted to make this kind of journey, but his wife's stomach couldn't bear even the thought of riding waves, so he had come on his own. In Sacramento he was part of a writing group and he hoped to spend many hours on board ship pecking away on his laptop. He would stay on board until Melbourne, spend a few days in Australia, and then fly home.

A diverse group: three nationalities, different backgrounds, and about twenty years difference between the youngest and oldest. Three were on their first trip of this kind, six on their second, but none had sailed this particular route, or with this company.

As we knew from our previous trip, and also from reading *TravLtips*, passengers come aboard with diverse agendas and backgrounds. Well into our voyage, the *Sydney Star* chief engineer, Nick, a reflective person experienced in passenger matters, provided all of us with an interesting analysis. In terms of wealth, he said, he had met four kinds of passengers. Some had scraped together savings for a lifetime adventure. Invariably they enjoyed each day and event and were appreciative of kindnesses extended to them. They didn't complain, even when things went wrong. Some passengers were wealthy, but came aboard with realistic expectations about life on a freighter and didn't demand to be served as if on the luxury yachts they or their friends owned. Most passengers were between the rich and the "scrapers." The kind ones among them behaved much like the first two groups—grateful for what they enjoyed and patient with annoyances.

But then there were those who should never have come on board. They wanted everyone to know they had paid for this trip and expected to be served beyond what was offered. They didn't like doing their own laundry, found fault with their cabins, and wanted to use the phone, fax, and telex as if they were at home. He told the story of a British couple on board one of his ships who reminded him of the British TV sitcom, *Keeping up Appearances*, the ongoing adventures of the Bucket couple (pronounced "Bouquet"), where the wife forever manipulates circumstances in order to appear upper middle class or better. The female passenger bragged about her mansion on the seashore, but her accent made the engineer believe that she lived quite close to where he lived. When he asked her where she lived, he discovered that it was along a canal in a very modest and not at all prestigious housing development.

"What did you say?" I asked.

"I told her where I lived." Nick replied.

"What happened?"

"She shut up."

He told us this story well into our journey, after letting us know that we were easy passengers, that we weren't giving anyone any trouble, and that he enjoyed having us on board.

After leaving the Savannah River, the ship turned south towards Florida for the three-day sailing journey to Houston. For much of that stretch land remained within sight, and at night lighthouses and large cities beamed their presence our way. Once we had travelled far enough south, the ship turned west into the Straits of Florida, past Key West and into the Gulf of Mexico. While the Atlantic had been placid, we were now in a gigantic basin known for its swells. Going due west, the weather turned decidedly colder. The ship began to roll, slowly but incessantly, and once more we had to use all our leg and foot muscles to stay upright and remain in control when walking and climbing stairs. A moving sea reaches right into your body, and I noticed that sight, sound, touch, even the smell and taste of salt on your lips, help you to prepare for what the ship is likely to do in the next second or two. However, you never totally rely on your instincts, no matter how honed by experience. "One hand for the ship, the other for yourself," was a slogan on board the *Sydney Star*. But you quickly become accustomed to rolls and pitches, and to those moments in rough seas when the ship seems suspended between contrary forces.

Johanna and I explored the ship further that first day. We noticed that the Poop Deck was used as a storage area for a number of items, including the ship's garbage, which would occasionally be burned in a steel drum, leaving stinking smoke to waft everywhere, including sometimes towards us in our cabins. We walked the Working Deck, where rust was everywhere to the sides and underfoot, towards the most forward area of the ship, the foc's'le (short for "forecastle"), which on this ship was uncovered and open to the wind and sun, and one set of stairs up from the Working Deck. We were pleased to discover that at the most forward point of the foc's'le we had a fine spot from which to look down at how the ship's storm-trooper bulb cleaved the waves.

Foc's'le is such an interesting word, steeped in maritime history. Pictures of old ships show us two "castles," that is living quarters. Officers and privileged passengers would reside aft above the rudder, while the low-ranking crew and more modest passengers resided fore above the bow. The forecastle was also the place from which sailors would launch attacks on other ships, at first with bows and arrows. Later, ships would fire cannons to cripple enemy ships and then from the forecastle launch rifle and pistol fire, and even invasions from enemy vessels. The name has remained, but the function has changed. Now a foc's'le is a working deck used mainly for handling berthing ropes, and a place from which anchors are dropped using large windlasses. It still has a high foremast with a place for a watchman (the crow's nest), used when fog holds the ship in its grip, and it carries the most forward navigation light as a signal for other ships and ports, as well as a brass fog bell. The *Sydney Star*'s foc's'le, we noticed, was the most rusted place on the whole ship, particularly the crow's nest mast.

This first leg of the trip became the time to sniff out the particular culture on board the *Sydney Star*. It takes a few days to find out what's entirely acceptable, somewhat acceptable, and unacceptable. A ship's culture is made up of many subtle behaviours, especially when the ship's primary function is to carry freight. When are you welcome on the bridge, for how long, and how much conversation can be had with the officers on duty? At dinnertime, the nine passengers were divided between two tables, with specific seats indicated by place cards. The captain was the host at the largest table; the chief, assisted by the chief electrician, at the smaller one. The deck and engine-room officers were Filipino, as was the whole crew, and ate Filipino food at their own table. The groups didn't mix at mealtimes. Unlike on the *Ville d'Aquarius*, at dinner the officers wore their traditional uniform: blue pants and a white shirt (but no tie), while passengers were asked to abstain from shorts, T-shirts, and other casual attire. Deck officers also wore their uniforms while on watch. Fortunately, everyone began to relax in the few days between Savannah and Houston, and conversation became less formal.

We reached Houston three days and nights after leaving Savannah. Even though Houston is listed as one of the largest American ports, especially for tankers, its harbour isn't located right at the seaside, or even very close to the city itself. To reach its berth, the ship sailed into a bay protected by a string of small islands. My youngest brother, Bert, had been here in the early 1960s, when he spent eighteen months at sea as a sailor on Dutch general cargo ships, travelling mostly between Galveston and Rotterdam/Antwerp. Now that I realized how hard sea life is for lowly workers, I thought of him, all of sixteen then, and how difficult it must have been for him. Some of the other passengers planned to visit the Houston Space Center, not far away from where the ship was berthed, but Johanna and I only visited a mall for some forgotten items in Bay City, the closest municipality.

The captain had recommended we walk to the Seaman's Center, just outside the port gates. This well-equipped and well-staffed centre provides many services to sailors, including minivan transportation to all parts of the area, free of charge (although donations are welcomed). We were dropped off to where we wanted to go, and picked up again at a pre-arranged place and time. The centre had a small chapel, lots of telephone booths, clothing and souvenirs for sale, and recreational facilities. It was a splendid facility, and memorable for the helpfulness and kindness of the people there, most of them volunteers. Remembering our enjoyable Houston experience, we looked for such centres everywhere we went on the trip, but found that in smaller ports, centres were oftentimes only open in evenings and on week-ends. In larger centres maintained by faith communities, chaplains conduct church services for visiting sailors. Visitors' books reveal how much these centres are transit points for the seafaring community.

After leaving the port of Houston on March 14, we sailed for the Pan-ama Canal, another three-day journey. We entered the Gulf of Mexico once more and sailed southeast between Cuba and Mexico's Yucatan Peninsula, although we saw neither country as we made our way through the Yucatan Channel. Once past Cuba, we found ourselves in the Caribbean Sea. Around it the various West Indian countries are neatly placed, like spectators around a bullring. To port, well beyond the horizon, were Cuba, Jamaica, Haiti, the Dominican Republic, and Puerto Rico. Even further east were a multitude of smaller islands curving around to the north coast of South America, including Netherlands Antilles and Aruba, both former Dutch colonies. I recalled that my Uncle Henny had been a school principal in Aruba. To starboard, Mexico, British Honduras, Honduras, Nicaragua, and Costa Rica slid by unseen. We sailed near the Swan Islands, three of them formerly owned and used for an airbase and weather station by the United States. The islands are now owned by Honduras, which maintains a weather sta-tion there staffed with a few personnel. We also saw many islands simply consisting of sandbanks, uninhabited except for birds.

As we sailed through the Caribbean, I thought about Columbus, of course, and the old Spanish, Dutch, Portuguese, French, English, and later, American explorers, exploiters, and buccaneers who plied these waters fight-ing each other, claiming ownership, setting up trading posts, and bringing trinkets and communicable diseases to the original inhabitants. Many of these lands are beautiful and lush, but devastatingly poor—mere minnows in the sea of international politics. I remembered an economist's recom-mendation that Canada should offer Jamaica status as a Canadian province, a holiday land for the winter in exchange for assistance in increasing its standard of living to our level—a good idea, I thought at the time.

We arrived outside the Panama Canal at night, and docked in the Port of Cristobal, first to unload a small number of containers and then to welcome Reefer Engineer Glen on board. When we woke up the next morning, we discovered that we were already through the first set of locks, and anchored in Gatun Lake. The ship had been elevated eighty-five feet in the middle of the night, and we hadn't felt a thing.

In some ways, the history of the building of the Panama Canal repeats

159

that of the Suez Canal. Both were founded on similar creative visions. Not only were they expected to yield immediate economic benefits for their respective countries and the ships that would sail through them, but they were symbolic of nineteenth-century Western faith in the universal progress of the human race. They simply had to be built. There was one other element in common between the two canals: the skillful French diplomat and promoter Ferdinand de Lesseps.

The history of the Panama Canal really began in 1513. In that year, after a horrendous march overland from the Atlantic Ocean, the Spanish captain, Vasco Nunez de Balboa, became the first European to cross what is now Panama and see the Pacific Ocean on the western side of the Americas. An engineer in Balboa's company, Alvaro de Saavedra, suggested that the two oceans should be linked, and Balboa passed the idea on to King Ferdinand of Spain. But that suggestion remained dormant in Spanish civil service files for more than three hundred years.

The idea was kissed awake again in the nineteenth century. The Suez Canal had opened, and since then major advances had been made in the technology of digging ditches, especially large ones. Instead of thousands

One of the locks of the Panama Canal, with a "road" each way. Worth noting is the optimistic sign, and the mule (locomotive engine) used to hold ships safely in the narrow locks.

of ant-like human diggers, large construction companies operated dredgers, drillers, spreaders, and cranes. Moreover, it was a time when Western societies were striving to build bigger things, railroads and bridges certainly, but also buildings like the Crystal Palace in London and the Eiffel Tower in Paris, less for long-term practical use than for their sheer spectacle. Spanish control and influence in Central America had weakened considerably during the nineteenth century, causing all kinds of adventurers and entrepreneurs to nose around. One of those was Lieutenant Lucien Napoleon-Bonaparte Wyse, a French army officer and descendant of Napoleon the Third (who had been a power behind the creation of the Suez Canal and was the nephew of Napoleon Bonaparte). In 1876 Wyse and some engineering and surveyor colleagues explored the potential for a canal in this area. Wyse wrote a report for the French government, making sure that a certain person of his acquaintance saw it as well. That person was Ferdinand de Lesseps.

De Lesseps was now in his late seventies, and for all anyone knew was retired and looking after his dozen children, nine of whom he had fathered after his sixtieth birthday. However, he found the challenge too much to resist. Building a Central American canal should be a cinch. The Egyptian isthmus had been split for one hundred miles, but the distance across this one was only a little over forty miles. And didn't the French have a prior claim to build it? Others thought so too, for before long, acting on behalf of the French government, Lieutenant Wyse had in his pocket a concession contract for building the canal. The Colombian government, which controlled the area then, was the other party to the agreement.

The job sounded simple; a railway built in 1855 was already in place roughly parallel to where the canal would be built, so transportation of men and supplies would be easy. In 1879 de Lesseps, full of confidence and held in high domestic and international esteem, called a conference in Paris. Engineers, diplomats, and promoters from about twenty countries attended. A few engineers suggested that building this canal might be more difficult than digging the Suez Canal, but de Lesseps wouldn't listen. This charmer and high achiever, confident to the point of arrogance, knew what could be done. He received the overwhelming approval of the delegates who agreed the canal should be built with de Lesseps in charge. The process would follow that of his earlier project: raise funds, visit the site to settle the preliminaries (surveys, drafts, and logistics), and make an overall plan for the work, modelling it after the Suez Canal. He knew that the waters of the

Pacific and Atlantic oceans were at the same level and would as easily merge as the waters of the Mediterranean and Red seas, so a simple ditch would do and no locks would be required.

De Lesseps founded the Compagnie Universelle du Canal Interocean-ique in 1879, for which he envisaged attracting equity capital to the tune of 400 million francs. When only an initial thirty million was raised on the first share offering, he travelled to the United States for a promotional tour in the major cities, and on his return also visited important European cities. It had worked for the Suez Canal, and it would work again. Indeed, using all the spin he could think of, de Lesseps managed to raise 600 million francs.

The first construction efforts began in the early 1880s. Ports were built on either side of the projected canal route, excellent surveys were produced, a trail was hacked out through the jungle, worker housing projects were erected, and hospitals were built for the wounded and ill. But that was the end of the good news and soon optimism began to swim upstream against reality. In truth, the building of this canal presented technical and health problems almost totally unforeseen, except by a few isolated and ignored voices. First of all, the route passed through hills and mountains thrust up by volcanic forces that had created rocks of varying composition, each mountain likely to present unique engineering problems. Moreover, almost the whole route was covered by a dense and relentless jungle. That abun-dant growth could count on a phenomenal tropical rainfall of well over one hundred inches per year. Those rains didn't come down gently—tropi-cal rainstorms seldom do. When the deluge came, rivers quickly grew five and tenfold, causing huge floods and threatening construction. Finally, the swamps and jungles bred mosquitoes hungry for the blood of man and beast, carriers of malaria and yellow fever. Unknowing workers streamed to the construction sites, where they were housed in barracks that had no window screens. In fact, when canal building began, no one had made the connection between mosquitoes and these two diseases.

By 1882, troubled by these bad omens for the project, the two major French contracting firms withdrew, using escape clauses in their contracts and citing that they had done what they had promised thus far. They knew that the project in its original form was doomed. A canal dug straight through from one end to the other would be impossible. Moreover, already more than a thousand Compagnie employees had died, most of them suc-cumbing to malaria or yellow fever. But the work went on with many new construction companies, some more honest than others. In 1885 the following pieces of equipment were grinding it out along 260 miles of track: 99 steam shovels; more than 10,000 flatcars and trucks; 147 locomotives; 206 drills; 34 dredges; 357 boats and barges; and 324 pumps. It was a formidable technological assembly, operated by people from many parts of the globe, but notably from the nearby West Indies, especially Jamaica.

Despite the increased amount of machinery, the problems mounted also, and the canal wasn't being built as fast as planned. For one thing, the immense amount of rock and soil was being deposited as close to the excavations as possible, to spare expense and fill up otherwise useless valleys. Moreover, the slopes of the canal were made quite steep. When the deluges came, the waters undermined the unstable heaps of excavated rock and soil that then slid back into the trenches. Worker strikes took place in 1885, escalating to almost a full-blown revolution, and US troops invaded Panama to restore order. By 1886 the project was in deep trouble. The board of directors encouraged the eighty-one-year-old de Lesseps to visit the project once more, to take stock and encourage the troops. Following his visit, he raised another 385 million francs through bonds, and also tried to start a lottery, a proposal initially rejected by the French government. He still insisted that a single straight ditch would do, but this last effort to salvage the project in its original form was doomed. In 1888 the Compagnie suddenly ceased operations, having run out of funds. De Lesseps had failed. He died five years later, his spirits low and reputation damaged. He also died poor; his wife and children were rescued from destitution by a pension awarded by a grateful Suez Canal company.

For the first decade after the collapse of the Compagnie nothing much happened. A few French workers stayed around to make sure that the now idle equipment was properly greased and oiled, expecting that it might be used again one day. Some of the Compagnie shareholders hoped that Americans would take over the project. American construction companies had already been involved, and the American invasion of Panama in 1885 was a clear indication of the country's interest in the region and the canal, which was essential to shorten the distance by ship between the east and west coasts of the United States. The need for a canal was made even more urgent by the Spanish-American war of 1898. The battleship *Oregon*, needed in the Caribbean, had to be brought from San Francisco, taking sixty-eight days to travel thirteen thousand miles around the bottom of South America.

Some Americans had decided that Nicaragua would be the place for a canal, as it was much closer to the North American continent. In 1899 Congress passed a bill paving the way for a canal, with Nicaragua as the preferred location. The way was still open for a Panama location, however, for the bill included a maximum $40 million available for the Panama assets of the Compagnie. After much behind-the-scenes maneuvering, the US Senate voted for the Panama route in 1902. A contract was negotiated with the Colombian government, and when its legislative body stalled approval, Americans, and perhaps the US government itself, fomented a revolution that resulted in Panamanian independence in 1903. The US purchased the Compagnie's assets, which included the original concession, the railroad, and much machinery, a lot of it in good condition. It also signed the contract with the new Panamanian government. The US government took control of a six-mile strip across the whole of the width of Panama for a term of one hundred years, in exchange for ten million dollars in gold and an annual payment of $250,000 when the canal was in operation. The US was now in complete control and construction could begin.

Digging began in 1904 using the old plans, but progress was still slow, even with the addition of up-to-date equipment. Logistically the project was chaotic. There was still insufficient provision for the earth removed, and workers were still dying of disease. A major outbreak of yellow fever caused fear and hampered the recruitment of new workers. The need for new project management and better planning was crucial if this project was ever to be completed. The US government appointed engineer John F. Stevens as the new canal czar. He took the job on the condition that he'd be in charge without being second-guessed by government committees. Stevens stopped the digging in order to lay proper foundations for productive work later on. He needed to put in place four crucial elements: sanitation, housing and food, transport, and equipment. He couldn't afford to lose another twenty thousand workers to disease. Already present in Panama was a physician, Dr. William C. Gorgas, who had learned that controlling or eradicating two types of mosquitoes would get rid of these plagues. Stevens gave him his head. By 1906 yellow fever was defeated, and while in 1906, 82 percent of the workers had malaria, by 1913 only 8 percent were afflicted.

With respect to housing, mass-produced and not altogether unpleasant barracks were erected for forty-two thousand workers, while a system for producing and distributing food was put in place. Stevens also dismantled the existing rail system and rebuilt it with universal standardized track widths and modern stock, so he could get equipment from wherever he wished. The dug-up earth and rock was moved away from the canal works, so the project wouldn't suffer from cave-ins and mudslides. He assessed what equipment he had, discarded what was no longer needed, and ordered more modern and suitable new equipment.

The first year of chaotic US involvement in the canal brought back the realization that a straight sea-level canal connecting the two oceans wasn't feasible. What loomed as a major handicap was the erratic nature of the Chagres River. After regularly gorging on monsoon-type rains, it flooded not only its banks, but construction sites and the planned location of the canal. The answer was clear: the irrepressible river had to be tamed once and for all. An enormous dam was proposed, behind which would be created a large lake as a catch basin for all the water from the Chagres River. The lake would serve as part of the canal system, reducing the total amount of digging required. But this solution could only work if ships were lifted eighty-five feet up in the air by means of locks, and then let down again on the other side. After plenty of dispute, not free from political skullduggery, the decision to build the dam was made in 1907, approved by Congress and signed by President Teddy Roosevelt.

It seemed like the canal was finally going to become a reality, when out of the blue, John Stevens quit. Highly popular with his workers, a superb organizer and leader, and committed to the project, he nevertheless threw in the towel. No one ever knew precisely why he quit. The US government reached back into the army for the next czar, George W. Goethals, a splendidly competent but otherwise unknown engineer. The new boss divided the total project into three parts—the Atlantic side, the Pacific side, and the middle—and gave the manager of each part wide latitude to get the work done. By 1911 the following equipment was in daily use: 111 steam shovels; more than 5,000 rail cars; 369 locomotives; 26 (soil) spreaders; 14 piledrivers; 553 drills; 20 dredges; and more than 100 boats, tugs, and other watercraft.

While Goethals was faced with many unforeseen problems, the outer edges of the world's largest ever construction project proceeded steadily. The central part, the excavation of a canal through rock, was the most demanding. For one thing, the rock wasn't of uniform composition. Each section presented new problems, threatening cave-ins, slides, death, destruction, and failure of the project. From 1908 to the end of 1913, 6,500 men worked every day for ten hours, often in temperatures of 120 degrees Fahrenheit. Every night, five hundred workers repaired and serviced the machinery that would be needed in the morning. The magnitude of the project had grown from the original French plans that specified a steep-sloped canal width of 670 feet and depth of 250 feet requiring 23,000 cubic yards of material to be excavated. The Americans widened the canal to eighteen hundred feet, and even though the depth required because of the eighty-five-foot lock elevation would be close to one hundred feet less, the total excavation now amounted to fifteen million cubic yards!

In 1912 Dr. Gorgas paddled a canoe the length of the canal and in August 1914 the first merchant ship, the ten-thousand-ton *SS Ancon* made the trip from the Atlantic to the Pacific, taking nine hours and forty minutes to do so with a canal pilot to guide it. The last superintendent of construction, Goethals is reputed to have said at one of the opening ceremonies on August 3, 1914: "Gentlemen, the two consuming ambitions of my life are fulfilled on the same day. The first, to see an ocean liner sail through the Panama Canal: the second, to see France and Germany at war." However strange that last observation, the truth is that the opening of the Panama Canal was overshadowed by the outbreak of World War I—a most interesting juxtaposition of events.

For decades the Americans operated the canal and reaped the financial rewards. However, in the post-World War II anticolonial atmosphere this

Our ship in Panama Canal's Gaillard Cut, named after engineer David Dubosi Gaillard who engineered and supervised its digging. He died suddenly while still on the job. The white shore markers are navigational aids.

situation couldn't last forever. In 1979 the United States and Panama concluded a treaty that paved the way for the canal to be handed over to the
Panama government in 1997, one hundred years after the original covenant
between the Colombian Government and Napoleon's descendant had been
signed. In those twenty intervening years, Panama would gradually take
over the control and operation of the canal. On December 31, 1989, a Pana-
manian citizen was appointed as chief administrator. When we sailed the
canal, Americans were no longer involved at all.

Though both the Panama and Suez canals are equally vital to the economic health of their countries, and still important for global trade and
communication, the Panama Canal is the far more spectacular sight. The
Suez Canal is a rather boring ditch dug in flat ground between two waters
of equal level, but every ship in the Panama Canal is lifted eighty-five feet
into the air on one end, in three stages, and let down the same distance at
the other side. Once through the Atlantic Ocean locks, our ship waited for
others to join it after it was locked in. As in the Suez Canal, ships travel in a
convoy, a whole day carefully planned and scheduled. It cost our ship close
to $50,000US for a one-way fare through the canal, so Captain Pridmore
told me. Waiting in Gatun Lake for the convoy to form was a pleasure. The
lake isn't simply a large body of water with all of its shoreline clearly visible.
Like many Canadian wilderness lakes, it's dotted with islands, the tops of
flooded hills that are still covered with lush trees. We saw one speedy pleasure boat zigging and zagging between the islands, like a boat on a lake in
Ontario cottage country. It was a beautiful spot, full of greenery and colourful birds flying hither and yon. It's hard to believe that this is an artificial
lake; all that remain to tell its history are a number of markers indicating the
tops of long dead trees. The weather was sublime, sunny and comfortably
warm with no mosquitoes.

By about noon the convoy got going, each ship finding its assigned place
in the line. The captain had arranged for lunch to be served on the Boat
Deck. On this beautiful Sunday we ate and drank, but never sat for long.
There was too much to see on either side of us. Roads led up from the canal
and disappeared behind forests and hills. We saw various construction sites,
one a massive dredging operation. To port we saw the remains of the train
tracks that had been built to connect the two oceans before the canal. Old
passenger cars sat on the tracks, perhaps awaiting a future in a museum.
We passed a jail and two villages that were just clusters of houses on both
sides of a dirt road. At the Pacific side we saw obvious remnants of the

long-standing American occupation of the Canal Zone: beautiful housing developments and extensive barrack areas. During the canal passage, we constantly roamed the ship trying to find the best place to observe all that surrounded us. When we reached the end of the canal, it was especially fascinating to watch our ship being let down to sea level.

About a dozen Panama Canal employees had come on board and were posted both fore and aft to attach and control the cables attached to loco-motive engines (called "mules") that run on rails along both sides of the locks. Four mules for each ship, two at the front and two at the back, keep the gigantic freighters straight in the locks, and also pull them through, a tricky task when high winds hit the ship's side. The locks were only a few metres wider than our twenty-five-thousand-ton ship, so there was little room for error. We had a glimpse at the size of this engineering miracle when we spotted a sizable yacht with about eight people on board in the lock next to us (each lock has two parallel sections). It looked tiny com-pared to the huge lock and the *Sydney Star*.

Once we passed through the last lock, the evening darkness fell quickly, and while at dinner we sailed underneath the Bridge of the Americas, which not only connects rural Panama with Panama City, but is also the sole land link between North America and South America. It's a mighty structure that towers high over the canal, as busy as any urban bridge anywhere. Even from this far below its pavement we saw a steady stream of cars, buses, and trucks going both ways.

I asked Captain Pridmore whether things had changed after the Panama-nian people took over the canal. "For the better," he replied. Improvements are being made all the time. Indeed, we saw construction from one end of the canal to the other, building and facility construction at both ends, dredging, strengthening banks against erosion, and widening of the canal itself. But this canal, too, is no longer as vital to shipping as it once was. It's too narrow for the new generation of container ships and huge tankers, and its high fees make sailing around the continent an option once more. As early as the 1970s, plans to enlarge the canal were considered, including, believe it or not, serious discussions about excavating by means of nuclear explosions. Another idea, since rejected, was to build a new double-track high-speed railroad alongside the canal, unload giant container ships on one side, transport the containers to the other side by rail, and load them back on another ship.

CHAPTER NINE

Panama to Auckland

As the *Sydney Star* gunned its engine on entering the South Pacific, we were sailing into the blue waters of history. Even though the Pacific Ocean covers about one-third of the globe, it wasn't until the eighteenth century that this enormous body of water was extensively explored, surveyed, and mapped by Western European sailors. Around twenty-five thousand islands dot the South Pacific, some so small as to be mere rocks or sand dunes rising barely above the water's surface.

No one can consult a history of the region without coming across three famous names: Captain James Cook, Captain William Bligh, and the scientist Charles Darwin. The British government dispatched Captain Cook (1728–80) three times to explore, survey, map, and name whatever he found. Cook was born into a working-class rural family. He landed in the seaport of Whitby in his teens and found himself instantly attracted to the sea. He used his free time to teach himself navigation and mathematics, first finding work on coastal coal ships, and eventually on sea-going craft. His skills at mapping and surveying were noticed, and he was asked to map the St. Lawrence River in preparation for General James Wolfe's assault on Quebec in 1761.

In 1768 Cook was appointed master on the exploration ship *Endeavour* and told to sail into areas barely known, down the west coast of Africa, then over the Atlantic to the east coast of South America, travelling down to the southern tip of South America (Cape Horn) and into the unknown South Pacific. His ship was 106 feet long and 29 feet wide, sailed at 7-8 knots, and carried 368 tons. (The *Sydney Star* was roughly six times as long, three times as wide, sailed at three times the speed, and carried sixty-eight times the weight.) On that small vessel Cook took along a crew of eighty, plus eleven scientists, notably botanists. In order to guard against scurvy during the long months at sea without seeing land, Cook took sauerkraut on board, and a live goat for its milk. Cook stayed away for three years and came back with a vast amount of information, even though he hadn't located the elusive southern continent everyone knew existed, presuming the globe was divided into two land mirror images of each another. In the years 1771-75, Cook undertook a second journey on an even smaller ship, the *Resolution*, and in 1776 he captained that same ship on a third journey, which first sailed up the west coast of North America to Alaska, but then drifted down into South Pacific territory once more. Alas, Cook didn't return from that third trip, as he was bludgeoned to death by Hawaiian natives.

As we sailed into the seas explored by Captain Cook, I saw islands on the charts named for Cook and his sailors and scientists. I contemplated the difference in ships from Cook's voyage to ours, and how typical it was of our era that we approached a stretch of three weeks without land with apprehension, whereas Cook willingly ventured to sea for three months or more at a time.

There were three weeks ahead with only the sea, sky, ship, and one another—thirty-six people in a hotel on a floating island. There was enough food, plenty of beer and wine, and our sleeping accommodations were more than adequate. But there would be no TV, telephones, Internet, golf, theatre, sports, live concerts, or shopping. Of the thirty-six people on the island, twenty-seven had a lot of work to do. You're allowed to be curious about their work, but you must be aware that you're not to interfere with it. The idle passengers must make their own arrangements to pass the time, and ideally they all get along and spend much of that time together. Johanna and I did three things: We explored the ship and learned more about its crew; we developed daily routines around mealtimes, exercise, reading, knitting, looking, and talking; and we set out to enjoy the company of the other passengers.

Aboard the *Ville d'Aquarius*, we began to think of ships as possessing personalities—they weren't just hunks of floating steel. We still think in terms of "our" first ship and "our" second ship. For a long time I put a photograph of the *Ville d'Aquarius* on my computer screen, fine daily company. No wonder we asked many more questions about the *Sydney Star*, for we knew better what might be interesting.

The *Sydney Star* was built in Bremen, Germany, in 1972 and made its maiden voyage in early 1973. It was then called the steamship (ss) *ACT 5* and was one of five or six ACT vessels built for the trade that links Australia and New Zealand with North American ports. These ships were the largest and most modern container transporters at the time, steamships that could reach well over twenty knots fully loaded. In 1987 the *ACT 5*, then fifteen years old, sailed to Yokohama, Japan, for a complete overhaul. The steam plant was replaced with a new turbo oil engine, and the ship was renamed motor vessel (mv) *Sydney Star*. Its cruising speed dropped to about 17.5 knots; however, its fuel consumption was cut by more than 50 percent, substantially decreasing its operating costs. The new engine, a Sulzer RTA 62, put out 15,320 horsepower @ 88 RPM, and drove a six-bladed propeller. The ship also acquired a bow thruster, a smaller engine at the front of the ship used for dockings and departures.

The *Sydney Star* was 217 metres long, smaller than the *Ville d'Aquarius* by about half the length of a football field. Its width was twenty-nine metres, three metres less than the *Ville d'Aquarius*, and the draft almost the same at eleven metres. Empty, the *Sydney Star* weighed just over thirteen thousand tons. It could take on a maximum load of about twenty-five thousand tons, just over half of what our first ship could carry. Its maximum container capacity was 1,334 TEUs, 694 stored below, and 640 above deck, about one-third of the number of containers that could fit aboard the *Ville d'Aquarius*.

While the *Sydney* Star could transport some bulk cargo as well, it was mainly designed to carry containers, about half of them reefers for the transport of perishable food. Reefers are cooled in two ways. Some have self-contained electric refrigeration units, while others are cooled by means of a constant stream of brine fed to them from the ship's central cooling system. One day, I saw Keith, the ship's electrical engineer, and two helpers (Glen and a regular reefer electrician, Juan) on the Working Deck fixing a container's refrigeration unit. Temperature gauges outside each container were monitored every day, for each container is set at a specific temperature, depending on its cargo. Apples are merely cooled, but ice cream must be kept frozen at -12 °C; if it's kept any colder than that, ice crystals form that decrease the quality, any warmer and the ice cream gets soft.

Ships must also reserve space for fuel, equipment, and supplies, which limit its paying cargo. The official capacity for fuel storage was listed as 4,158 tons on the *Sydney Star*'s documents, plus 110 tons of diesel oil, a higher grade used by the generators. Fresh water supplies weighed another three hundred tons, and ballast (the sea water in tanks for stability) another five thousand tons. The ship also carried many spare parts for its engines and other equipment, weight that further reduced the cargo capacity. I once asked Chief Engineer Nick what happens when the engine stops in mid-ocean, days away from land. He assured me that they had enough spare parts on board, and enough mechanical expertise, to get the ship to the closest port, even if at a greatly reduced speed. During my engine-room tour on the *Sydney Star*, I saw some of those parts, and also a collection of tools, big and small. I tried to lift some of the large tools and couldn't. Altogether the ship carried ten thousand tons before it took a container on board.

As a business, a ship is a floating box for transporting containers long distances for a fee. How much it costs per container depends on a number of factors. Reefers cost more than ordinary containers, and a 2-TEU container is more expensive than a 1-TEU one. The rates also depend on the distance cargo is to be transported and whether it's deemed to be "dangerous cargo," such as chemicals. The officers told us that the *Sydney Star* was no longer a very successful business. For its size and fuel consumption, it carried fewer containers than more modern recently built container ships. This ship was not only smaller than the *Ville d'Aquarius*, it was considerably less efficient. Though its tonnage was half, its container capacity was only about one-third, and it had twenty-seven paid bodies on board, versus only twenty-one on the *Ville d'Aquarius*. As a viable economic enterprise, this ship was doomed, as were its three sister ships plying the same waters.

This point was drive home to me one day early on in our voyage. Two of the *Sydney Star* officers, Glen, the reefer engineer, and Keith, the electrician, stood near me on our Boat Deck watching the *CCNI CHILOE* move through one of the three double locks at the Pacific end of the Panama Canal. I saw a brand new ship, much more modern than the *Sydney Star*. Its rust-free superstructure gleamed in the late afternoon sun as its mathematically precise layers rose straight up above the rear of the ship. At the back of the ship a shiny orange lifeboat pointed its nose towards a spot just beyond the ship's screw. The whole composition looked daring and innovative, clean lined and tidy. "That's a beautiful ship," I said. Both Keith and Glen looked at me. Then, not deferent towards passengers just because they pay to be on board, Glen said, "A piece of junk," and Keith added, "No home for sailors."

Right there and then I got a lecture, with a can of beer thrown in, about ships, cargo, people, and life at sea. Yes, the ship was spectacular. Yes, it was new. Yes, it was efficient. And yes, the more than twenty-five-year-old *Sydney Star* was ancient and rusty, and it carried less cargo per metre of length and width than its Panama lock neighbour. But less beautiful? "We don't think so." They impressed upon me that ships need to be more than merely efficient, more than just travelling machines making money. Ships have sailors on board and need to offer those human beings elements of grace and humanity, and at least a minimum sense of communal living. Meals need to be more than calories shovelled in to keep the body going, and cabins need to be more than sterile places with a bed and a toilet. Those on board need lounges and at least one deck for meeting places. All of those features were richly present on board the *Sydney Star*, which had been built with the well-being of the crew in mind. I was told to look more closely at the ship next to us. Everything was cramped and there was no deck for relaxation.

The *Sydney Star* was doomed, and both of them said so with pain in their voices. Their beloved ship and the line that had built it had long been part of the merchant shipping tradition, but the logo high on its stack and on the cap and shopping bag we had received, was already no longer a true indication of the line's ownership. The Blue Star Line was about to disappear from the globe altogether. Founded in 1911, almost a century ago, the line's roots went back even further, to the Vestey brothers, originally butchers in Liverpool in the late nineteenth century. Not satisfied with only one store, they opened new ones throughout England and became the first butchers in the UK to introduce refrigeration in their stores. Until then, meat was sold at discounts on Saturday afternoon as stores were closed on Sundays. Once they had enough outlets, the brothers looked for control of supplies as well, and eventually bought cattle ranches and a meat packing plant in Argentina. They then closed the circle by founding the Blue Star shipping line, mainly to transport meat to the UK and pick up eggs from China. The brothers bought other shipping lines, one by one, and expanded their operations to include ships that plied their trade between Australia and the United States. Over the years, most of their ships had "Star" in their names. During World War II, the British government chartered many Blue Star Line ships. Twenty-nine of these ships were sunk, with the loss of many sailors. After an initial post-war revival, the company began to sell off some of its divisions, and in 1998 it sold the route we were on, and the ships sailing it, to P&O Nedlloyd. That company had already planned to remove the four remaining Star ships from service even before we were on board.

Glen and Keith could accept that the ships wouldn't sail forever. Much of the rust could no longer be removed, and not all of the damage could be repaired. The equipment on board required plenty of maintenance and spare parts were becoming a real problem. Newly built ships may have been about the same size, but because of their tighter design they could often carry many more containers. Glen and Keith pointed out that newer ships had fewer crew on board, primarily because computers and other technology had changed sailing methods. For example, with satellite navigation a ship no longer requires a full-time navigator. With fewer sailors on board, the superstructure of a ship can be much smaller than that of the *Sydney Star*. Most new ships we saw only had "business space," the bare minimum to operate the ship, and the superstructure itself seemed small and squeezed between containers. Some ships had only one lifeboat, instead of the two on the *Sydney Star*. Many new ships are built with the measurement of a 2-TEU container as a base for the superstructure; all inside spaces are 40 x 8 x 8', or a multiple or fraction thereof, including the kitchen, lounges, and cabins. Everything is a rectangle, neat and tidy, dull and unimaginative, all steel and vinyl—so unlike the *Sydney Star*. All this and more I learned from these two highly competent and technologically savvy officers, who were yet old-fashioned and romantic sailors.

A day or so after we left the Panama Canal, the passengers were offered a tour of the engine room, with Chief Engineer Nick as guide. Most of his explanations were offered while we stood in the engine control room with its large bank of monitors, in front of glass windows that provided a view of the various pieces of noisy equipment. We wore our gloves and also donned ear protectors for walking through the noise. As we toured, Keith was busy watching dials and making notes in the control room. After our visit, I could never resist the temptation to look inside the Poop Deck door into that jumble of equipment, pipes, engines, and dials. I would smell the oil and steam, feel the heat, and marvel at the skill and stamina of the people

Martha, Keith, Nick, and I are in the engine room's office, deep in the bowels of the ship. Notice the ear protectors and gloves. Outside the office the noise was overwhelming and a thin oily layer waited for every touch.

who worked there daily. Almost all the passengers we met voiced the same awe for this ship's cardiovascular system and we were all impressed with the ease with which the various engineering sailors performed their tasks.

Early on in the voyage I discovered a connection between my heart and the rotation speed of the driveshaft and propeller. On a working ship you can hear and feel the propeller turning everywhere in the superstructure, which is built right over the engine room. The first few nights I went to bed on the *Sydney Star* I got worried. It seemed that my heart was beating much faster than I was used to. I wondered if something was happening to me as I felt the pronounced thumping in my chest. I didn't feel sick or out of breath, so I ignored the sensation. Then it dawned on me: the screw rotated at a rate just a bit above my normal pulse. It wasn't my heart that was beating 88 RPMs, but my bed in tune with the driveshaft.

After touring the engine room, I accepted the invitation to walk the "Burma Road," a narrow hallway at the very bottom of the ship that connects its fore and aft. It was a tricky walk in dim light past pipes and equipment, some of which I had to step over. The sea was just underneath me, perhaps no more than three feet away. The "road" ended at stairs that climbed up into the paint storage area, where I saw hundreds of cans of paint, right

Keith, Glen, and Apollo busy fixing an electric reefer motor. The white reefers behind their backs are not run with individual cooling motors but with circulating brine originating in the engine room. Glen is the one smiling.

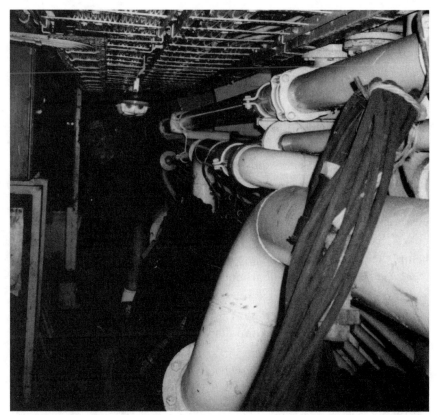

The start of the "Burma Road," a narrow way from stern (back) to stem (front) right above the keel of the ship. You walk through a gauntlet of wires, pipes, gauges, and unyielding steel.

underneath the foc's'le. I was surprised to come upon a large earth-moving truck chained to the floor in a separate compartment. It was unloaded in an Australian port while we were onshore, so I never did see where it went.

The engine room is one important place aboard ship; the bridge, the domain of the deck officers, is the other. The wheelhouse is the central command post and the ship's eyes. Here, all relevant information on the weather, other ships, and sea conditions is gathered and assessed, and decisions are made, communicated, and executed. It's also the place that most passengers want to see. Standing on the *Sydney Star*'s Monkey Island, we were surrounded by many of the ship's essential communication devices. Various radio towers and antennas, a radar tower, and satellite receivers for navigation and the Internet were all connected to the bridge beneath us.

The outlets for a number of ducts that connect to the innards of the ship, mostly ventilation shafts, exited the ship at this level. This was also where sailors hoisted and took down flags as we entered and left different ports: a company flag; the flag of the country whose harbour we were entering; and a flag to signal dangerous cargo, if such cargo was on board.

The wheelhouse was filled with dials and equipment. Two screens, one on either side, provided the information on speed, the distance to go, and changes in course required for the officers to safely guide the ship to the next port. The screens also showed the radar impressions of other ships, and shore features. In one corner, telex and short-wave radio provided a steady stream of information about the weather, time, ocean depth, and even reports of other ships' accidents and problems. The bridge "dashboard" had a lever for changing rudder speed, and a steering wheel, or helm. The steering wheel on the *Sydney Star* was very small and used only when entering or leaving a harbour. At these times, an AB would do the actual steering on commands from the captain and pilot. At sea the ship is on automatic pilot, even when changing course, for such a change has been programmed into the computer that both guides and monitors the ship's progress.

The rear side of the wheelhouse had no windows. A sturdy curtain separated the navigation compartment from the rest of the wheelhouse. Its most prominent feature was the chart table, where officers checked positions and plotted courses. No lights were switched on in the wheelhouse at night, except in this screened area, for the officers on watch needed efficient night vision. The bridge had open spaces on either end of the wheelhouse, with a small bank of controls on both sides. During rain or snow, a canvas top was fixed to the stanchions. From these open areas the captain and pilot kept a close eye on tugs and the shore while approaching or leaving a berth, calling out instructions to the helmsman and ship's officer inside the wheelhouse when a change of course or speed were required.

As we learned the geography of the *Sydney Star*, we also became more familiar with the officers and crew. On the whole the *Sydney Star*'s complement of officers and crew was quite similar to that of our first ship. Copies of the roster hung in prominent places on the ship. It listed full names and functions, as well as cabin numbers, emergency duties, boat-station duties, and boat-station assignment. On this ship, engine-room "oilers" were called "wipers," and the captain was also known as master.

The deck sailors consisted of the chief officer and the second and third officers, all of whom were Filipino, as was the rest of the deck crew. Also on board was a deck cadet, who was learning his chosen trade and who assisted all the other deck officers in their duties. The bosun supervised a deck crew of four ABs. Reporting to the chief officer were two stewards, a chief cook, and a second cook, for a total deck complement of fourteen.

The thirteen-man engineering staff was headed by the chief engineer, who was English. Reporting to him were the second, third, and fourth engineers, and an engineering cadet, all Filipino. Keith, the chief electrician, and Glen, the reefer engineer, were on board only for the first part of the trip. After they left, their places were taken by Filipinos they had trained. The engineering staff also included two wipers, two fitters, an OS (ordinary sailor, a rank below AB as an OS is not licensed), and an M/Man (motorman, an otherwise unlicensed but experienced engine-room assistant to the engineers).

While this was a much smaller ship than the *Ville d'Aquarius*, it had six more paid bodies on board. The presence of an extra cook and steward indicated that a bit more attention was paid to the comfort of everyone on board, just as there was more respect for maritime tradition in the dinner and bridge dress code. On the other hand, the bigger payroll may have also contributed to the fact that ships like the *Sydney Star* and its sisters had a hard time competing with newer freighters, and why a line like the Blue Star was on the verge of giving up on this route.

On this ship, too, safety was a priority. Every day at 1130 the fire alarm rang, and once a week the whole ship got involved in a more elaborate safety drill. On the muster hanging in the wheelhouse and in some of the hallways the passengers were also listed, and each assigned to a boat station with the following instructions appearing next to our names in the emergency duties column: "Don life jacket, wear warm clothing, headgear and stout shoes/boots."

After hearing the alarm, we would pocket our wallets, prepare ourselves as instructed, and report to one of the two lifeboats. In the meantime, all the sailors looked after their duties first, and then reported to their assigned lifeboat. At each station the officer in charge checked off all the names. The whole exercise took about thirty minutes, and everyone was serious about it. A fire or other disaster on board ship in the middle of the ocean is no laughing matter. Firefighting water pipes and hoses were checked constantly. When a pipe that ran the full length of the Working Deck sprang a leak, it was replaced immediately. The third officer, often assisted by the cadet, regularly inspected the lifeboats' systems and supplies. In an emergency on a ship there's nowhere to go except into the water or into a lifeboat, and lifeboats look tiny in waters that stretch out for days in all directions.

One day during his breakfast visit, the captain warned us that the ship was going to have a "man-overboard" drill, and since the crew had not been warned in advance we should keep quiet about it. As soon as the warning signal bellowed throughout the ship, we went to watch on the Boat Deck, where sailors were scanning the waves for a carton painted bright orange that had been thrown overboard by the captain to represent the "man overboard." Other crew and officers were on the Bridge Deck inspecting the sea with their binoculars. (Apparently there was a prize for the first one to spot the box, which was by now well behind us.) The ship slowed down and made a turning maneuver that would rapidly get it back on its previous course. In the meantime, two sailors had put on "jumping overboard gear" for the ultimate rescue, gear that obviously was also suitable for very cold water, even though we were close to the equator at this moment, with water temperatures around 28 °C. Johanna was greatly amused, though this was

The "man-overboard" exercise day was hot and muggy, close to the equator as we were. Pity the two sailors who wore elaborate diving suits. They walked with great difficulty, making Johanna laugh.

obviously a serious exercise. The box was spotted, and the ship passed by it closely, but didn't pick it up. Soon we were on our way again.

The mix of English and Filipino sailors aboard the ship got my attention, and I noted the presence of Filipino officers in senior positions, which hadn't been the case on the *Ville d'Aquarius*. On both ships, the Filipino crew had a lounge of its own and I noticed that the Filipino officers on the *Sydney Star* spent their social time with their countrymen, not with the other officers. I could see that the two nationalities worked well together professionally, but didn't often mix socially. It stands to reason that after a day of hard work it's more comfortable to be with those who share your first language, your culture, your mores and habits, your jokes, and your memories. However, differences in professional culture may also influence the social behaviour on board. Both the English and German officers seemed more ambitious than their Filipino colleagues. I'm sure that some Filipino merchant marine officers wish to become captain and chief engineer, and some already are, but the Filipino officers I met, without exception, indicated they didn't want that ultimate responsibility. Both the second engineer and the first officer on the *Sydney Star* had achieved much already, both were still young, and both were only one step below the top job in their profession. But when I asked how long it would be before they were promoted to captain or chief, neither seemed anxious for that next step, though their superiors assured me that both were professionally competent to take it. I wondered if this different level of ambition also kept the two nationalities apart. I had been told that the salary levels of Filipino sailors were well below those of German and British officers holding the same positions, yet Filipino sailors on both ships told me that their incomes were well above those of their countrymen with land-based jobs.

By the time our ship aimed its bow directly at Auckland, Johanna and I had already developed our routines on board. The *Sydney Star* didn't have the exercise facilities of the first ship, and so improvisation was called for. The walking deck was considerably smaller and the ship had no stationary bike or rowing machine on board. By the end of the journey I had completely circled the ship ten times, also climbing all the stairs I encountered, thirteen steps between floors. In a large bin close to the foc's'le I discovered damaged twist locks and a steel bar, perfect for lifting weights. When the walking deck was too wet, I didn't lift weights or walk, but simply ran the superstructure stairs up and down, by the end of the journey fourteen times in a day. Johanna walked the decks and swam regularly in the pool, which to her delight had been repainted shortly after we had left Savannah. When the winds or swells were strong, the pool would be emptied, and then a protective net was placed over it. Johanna loved the pool most when moderate rolling caused waves in the pool, but it didn't take much movement to cause the water to slosh all over the Boat Deck.

There was plenty of time between meals during these lazy sea days to fit jigsaw puzzle pieces, have conversations, visit the bridge, stand in the ship's nose, watch waves and skies, write, read, stare, swim, joke, and share. On three Sunday afternoons we had a brief and improvised Boat Deck prayer and sharing service with David and Jean, our Anglican friends. All these activities filled our days without trying, and in the end the whole assembly of trivia seemed to add up to something significant and lasting. Many times I experienced what I can only describe as deep-down happiness.

The *Sydney Star* had three communities on board: the British, the Filipinos, and the nine passengers, the latter being 25 percent of the bodies on board. Because of the long stretches at sea and the larger group of passengers than on our first ship, the shaping of a temporary community was inevitable. We came to recognize that the captain had a good deal to do with creating a welcoming social environment. He was truly the mayor of the village under his feet, constantly concerned for the welfare and happiness of the officers, crew, and passengers. One thoughtful gesture was the deck lunch while sailing the Panama Canal. The experience of sharing a well-stocked lunch table and the spectacular surroundings as we were floated through a technological marvel built a lasting camaraderie. We were strangers when we first met, but friends when we parted after four weeks. Something special happened, a sense of commitment to one another that made the outward bound trip a sheer joy for all of us.

Perhaps standing together on Monkey Island waving to the people in Savannah was a promising beginning. The daily passenger cocktail hour became another enjoyable meeting time. Our cabin steward, John, who we would often draw into our conversations, would stand behind the bar, serve drinks, and make sure the snack bowls were always filled. We quickly learned one another's drinking preferences as we told stories of what we had seen that day. We went off to dinner in a happy frame of mind, where we commented on the food and asked questions of the captain and chief engineer at our respective tables. As we got to know each other, we began to tease, quip, laugh, sense touchy areas in one another's lives, cross boundaries, and apologize. In short, we opened the doors to greater intimacy and discovered a high degree of goodwill and acceptance on the part of all.

Individual routines began to naturally dovetail with the routines of others. We became a group of nine, although within the group the three married couples had their private time outs. Soon after leaving the Panama Canal, Bill and Martha got into the habit of sitting together on the Boat Deck in midafternoon, each holding a large thermos tumbler from which they sipped. All of us knew it was a private couple time not to be intruded upon (although I would make an exaggerated detour around those two deck chairs when walking by). The four Brits also formed an almost daily subcommunity of their own, having tea together in the passenger lounge around the same time.

Perhaps the bonding occurred because all nine individuals had something in common. We were all confident and happy with our lives and looked forward to the future. Individual traits were quickly identified, verbalized, and often made the topic of gentle and respectful comment, sometimes in the form of teasing. Jean seemed to do laundry before breakfast each morning, and this was noticed by all. Soon she was nicknamed "washer woman." As an engineer, Michael was the most technically minded, and his sharing of what he discovered on the bridge soon made him the designated "passenger captain." Martha was looking for a party the moment she set foot on board—why else bring all those supplies? St. Patrick's Day provided her with an early opportunity and we were all invited to celebrate the Irish saint's birthday with special invitations. She not only organized parties, but her ebullient sharing of herself and her goodies led the Filipino crew to name her "Mama Martha." Her husband Bill had a Type A personality in a large body with a booming voice. He spent hours of effort doing nothing, hanging in a deck chair staring, dozing, brooding perhaps, and was surprised to find himself "hard at work doing nothing." Roberta was admired by all, for even the slightest movement of the ship brought on the threat of seasickness, and she constantly swallowed medicines that made her sleepy. Knowing her predisposition to seasickness, she had nevertheless chosen to make this trip, and she never complained. David loved his new role of grandfather, and we relished the pictures of his grandchildren, as well as his gentle smile and demeanour, and his knowledge of so many things besides pharmacy. Russ was both a private and community character. He told us that he had long wanted to take a sea voyage, but the inability of his wife to stand even the thought of the sea had stopped him until now. This trip would give him time to be alone, reflect, and perhaps write, but in company he was clever with words and gentle in teasing. He was also accident-prone, experiencing more scrapes and bruises than all the rest of us combined. Johanna was her usual sharing self, the "wise woman" Russ called her once. As for my contributions to this community—perhaps I would be labelled "the talker."

It didn't take long for one of us to begin a one-thousand-piece jigsaw puzzle that formed a single tricky pattern. The first puzzle we did was a waterscape, a peaceful little harbour full of boats. You know how it goes with puzzles—people say they don't want to join in but they pick up a piece, find where it belongs, and soon everybody has a hand in it. We did about six puzzles together during the trip. Martha, Bill, Russ, and I often played bridge. Martha became the eventual overall winner, but the scores were close and the games enjoyable, with plenty of good-natured teasing. Often Johanna knitted, and the Brits talked quietly in the lounge. By 2200 we'd all be in bed.

Martha organized a number of preprandial parties for whatever flimsy reason hit her fancy. She had even packed green serviettes in her boxes for the St. Patrick's Day celebration. Officers, British and Filipino, were invited, and they showed up in their dinner outfits. On April 1, we were watchful for pranks, although none came, but Martha announced that she would serve champagne during cocktail hour. After a couple of glasses each, we decided to make a joint tour of all the passenger cabins, just to see how the others lived. We were amazed at how the cabins differed from one another in colours, furniture, sizes, and ambience. There were lots of jokes and giggles as the nine of us jammed into the cabins, some of the single ones quite small. We actually lost the next day, and not because of the champagne we drank but because we crossed the Date Line and jumped from Tuesday to Thursday, leaving Wednesday to be celebrated twice on our return.

Whenever one of us spotted any sea life, we were quick to call the others. One day, the sea was in a turmoil when schools of fish came close to the surface. Birds flew in from all directions for a feeding frenzy, and a fishing boat sailed full steam to the spot for an abundant catch. Sadly, there were fewer wildlife sightings than we had hoped or expected to see and the sailors told us that there was less sea life than in previous years. There were fewer flying fish, they said, those delicate blue and brown sea creatures that are thrown up by bow waves and then fly in all directions, sometimes for a hundred metres and more, flapping their wing-like fins and floating on air over water, often in small schools. Johanna and I spent many pleasant hours watching for them at the bow tip. We also saw dolphins frolicking in the water, but perhaps no more than six pods during the whole voyage. Twice we saw the plume of a whale, and one day the tail of one, close to Auckland. One day, three swordfish sea-danced like dolphins, but with their swords splitting the waters at great speed. Twice, a large sea turtle swam by the bow right underneath the surface of the water. Both times we were about fifty sea miles from the Galapagos Islands, the closest we approached the place made famous by Charles Darwin, proponent of the theory of evolution, who had visited here as a scientist on board a British exploration ship in the nineteenth century.

There were fewer birds as well, so we were told. A few hours out of Panama, twelve boobies joined the ship, alternately soaring along looking for flying fish thrown up by the bow, or perching on the crow's nest. They had come from the Galapagos Islands. In flight, the boobies looked elegant with their pinkish-red socks trailing their graceful bodies, at rest they were ugly blobs. They were noisy, too, sometimes threatening us by flying very close, ready to bomb us with white excrement that soon covered the foc's'le deck. As we approached Pitcairn Island they disappeared one by one. One of them injured a wing and found a resting perch on a steel ledge on the Working Deck, from which it screamed abuse at all who came by. John, one of the ABs, took pity on it and got some frozen fish from the kitchen and tried to feed it. However, the bird's curved beak was designed to scoop fish out of the water and it had trouble picking up the fish lying flat on a steel ridge. Within sight of Pitcairn, John threw the bird overboard, hoping it would fly away and survive, either in the sea or on the island. The boobie scratched John's arm, but did fly away.

All of us spent a lot of time watching and talking, in twos, threes, or everyone together, usually with elbows leaning on some railing. Entering a harbour was always an adventure. As we approached the coast, we watched for the pilot boat and the channels marked by rows of green and red buoys, speculating on what berthing spot was reserved for us as the harbour came in sight. As the tugs approached and attached themselves to the ship, we admired the agility of the line throwers and rope pullers, then waited as this monstrous ship came to a complete rest and the ladder was let down for visitors to come on board. We'd wander to various spots on the ship for a better view and always ended up chatting and exchanging observations with someone else who had also chosen that specific spot.

While we were at sea, we also came to write together. Early in the trip, Russ had indicated his love for writing and told us of his membership in a Sacramento writing group. As a former publisher and writer myself, I became instantly intrigued and asked him if he would share some of his work, which he did willingly. I suggested that we both write and then share our writing regularly. He agreed, and as the conversation took place while watching the wake of the ship stretch out long behind us, I suggested we try a poem entitled "The Wake."

After four days we confessed to each other that we hadn't written our poems yet. Johanna became impatient with "these men," and promptly wrote a wake poem herself, sharing it to loud applause at cocktail hour. This led to the further suggestion that we all try our hand at writing some form of reflection on our shipboard life. The suggestion was met with hesitant and certainly not universal approval, but before the community began to disband in Auckland, seven of us produced one or more pieces, each one celebrated while drinking Martha's champagne in a public preprandial reading. Martha offered to enter all of the compositions into her laptop, and gave us each a disk. Our offerings were as varied as our personalities. Russ, Johanna, and I wrote several poems each, all reflections prompted by life on the ship. Bill produced a gentle piece of satire, a "journal" he imagined Jean had written about her laundry life on board the *Sydney Star*. He was also deeply impressed by the engine room and wrote an ode to it. David wrote a poem explaining why he really didn't want to write poems, while Jean wrote a piece that celebrated our crossing of the equator. Martha wrote a piece praising the excellent food on board, plus an ode to Elmer the cook.

No one had to write of course; however, the writing undeniably brought us closer together. Months later, Martha wrote to me: "[The] impetus for us to share in the joy and challenge of expressing ourselves through writing during the weeks together created a lasting memory that will be treasured for our lifetimes."

The officers, notably Captain Stephen, Chief Engineer Nick, Chief Electrician Keith, and Reefer Engineer Glen, made a huge contribution to our community. Stephen, Nick, and Keith were on board when we first boarded the *Sydney Star*. They were our hosts at dinner, and never tired of answering our questions, even if many of them merely showed our ignorance. They were quick to join in the teasing and repartee, and had many stories to tell about ships, previous passengers, peers, and cargos. All had been at sea for many years. To make sure that everyone mixed with everyone else, we changed our seating arrangements at Sunday evening dinner, and we all ate at both tables during our journey.

Most days, Captain Stephen Pridmore would come by at breakfast and lunch to pick up our comments and share weather and harbour information, but primarily to take the pulse of the group, I suspect. He was a gracious host at dinner and often generous with complimentary wine at meals. When pilots were on board, he preferred not to have us on the bridge, but he made us feel most welcome at all other times. A few days out of Panama we were scheduled to cross the equator at about 700, and he urged all of the passengers to assemble in the wheelhouse to watch one of the two radar screens that also constantly showed our longitude and latitude. We planned to cheer when the screen showed: 0.00.000, but it never did. The increments aren't in single digits, but jump three to five numbers at a time. One moment we were at N 00.00.003, and the next moment at S 00.00.002, but we cheered anyway and made jokes about having felt the bump as we crossed. Captain Pridmore issued a personal certificate to those of us who hadn't crossed the equator before, to prove that we had now done so. He also organized a tour of the ship, walking us by the kitchen, bridge, engine room, ship's office, and the food storage coolers and freezers. He provided each of us with a Blue Star company cap and a tote bag.

This albatross kept us company for thirty-six hours, swooping from left to right, sometimes dropping way behind the ship, and then coming up again. All the passengers made regular trips to the stern of the ship to see it.

Captain Pridmore also organized special events for the crew and passengers. There were three major parties on successive Saturday evenings while he was on board: a bingo, a barbecue, and a "horse race." The bingo and horse race evenings were held in the officers' lounge with all crew and passengers, free drinks included. The barbecue took place on the Boat Deck, and when we showed up for it in late afternoon, a surprise awaited us. The national flags of all the people on board hung along the railings beside the flags of some of our destinations: the United Kingdom, Holland, Canada, the United States, the Philippines, Australia, New Zealand, and Jamaica.

The horse race evening began at 1600 hours. During the days leading up to the race, we had all been asked to pick the name of "our" horse. That and other information had been assembled into an official program by the captain, who also acted as race secretary and bookmaker for the evening. In the middle of the race card we paused for dinner, a buffet with a huge roasted turkey as a centrepiece. Each race featured five painted wooden horses "running" along a track painted on a large piece of canvas spread out on the lounge floor. A horse's progress was determined by a large die thrown out of a bucket that entitled the "owner" to move it ahead the appropriate number of squares on the track. Each race had its own peculiarities and potential handicaps, eliciting lots of laughs. The winners of the first five races were entered in the final race to crown an overall champion. Martha won the

Saturday night live! Everybody on board (except the few on watch) are at the horse races. The village all together. It was a wonderful evening.

last race, and donated her winnings to the crew's benefit kitty. Entering a horse cost one dollar and everyone was also invited to bet on who would win each race. After betting closed, the captain figured out the odds, and the race got underway. The horse race was the last big event before Captain Pridmore left the ship in Melbourne for a well-deserved vacation back in England. The night before he left, he once more invited the officers, crew, and passengers to the officers' lounge for drinks. There was one more thing I'll never forget about Captain Pridmore: the conspiratorial look on his face as he announced at breakfast one morning that in a few days we would briefly stop at Pitcairn Island! None of us had known that this was possible, and we couldn't wait to see what was in store for us.

Chief Nick was the only British officer to make the whole round trip with the two of us. Johanna and I had the privilege of being his table guests for the first three weeks on board. He seemed utterly on top of his job, confident and energetic, and walked around the decks with a swagger of ownership. He never tired of answering our ship and engine questions. He also talked freely about the difficulties of being a husband and a father of a three-year-old son when away from home for months at a time. Nick told us a wonderful story about a vacation he took with his family and that of a close friend on a canal boat in England. They had boarded the boat at the rental place, listened to the instructions for managing it, and shortly thereafter had become stuck in the side of the canal. "What did you do?" I asked. "Sat down and drank beer," he replied. Nick wasn't aboard ship because of any romantic notions of the sea. While being trained as an engineer, he had decided that working for a large engineering firm and always reporting to a boss looking over his shoulder wasn't for him. Ships offered him freedom and allowed him to be his own boss. It hadn't taken him long to serve all his apprenticeships and he had achieved his rank at quite an early age.

Nick loved to sound mysterious when anything on the ship malfunctioned. One day, we encountered a hose tied to the Working Deck railing spouting water with force into the ocean. This went on for at least three days, the water obviously originating from the deep bowels of the engine room. We asked Nick if we were sinking or if the ship had sprung a leak. Nick, always with a smile on his face, offered a different explanation each day, always implying that the ship was in danger, but never fear, Nick is here. We never did find out what the trouble was. Johanna and I would often sit in one of the two alcoves (we called them gazebos) on the Working Deck, Johanna doing her crafts and I reading aloud to her. Then an irritating noise began to interfere with our enjoyment, an irregular loud clanging, perhaps coming from the steel contraption that held the lifeboat above our heads, as if someone was hitting it with a steel bar. We worried that a steel support was cracking, or shifting position, and that the whole assembly was about to collapse. After enduring the sound for two consecutive days, we asked Nick to take a look. He did, offered a number of outrageous possibilities, and also pretended not to hear it. We never caught him doing anything about it, but two days later the noise had disappeared. With a straight face we thanked him in public, and he pretended not to understand what we were talking about. He was a thoroughly likeable and cheeky host.

Until he left us at Brisbane, Chief Electrician Keith co-hosted the captain's table. Although he seemed a private man, he joined in to become a full participant in our parties and was an excellent storyteller. Reefer Engineer Glen joined us at the Atlantic side of the Panama Canal and stayed with us until our second landing at Auckland. He quickly became a passenger favourite—his storytelling expertise kept us laughing many nights at table and on other social occasions. He took on the role of bingo caller and track announcer, and on both occasions produced memorable one-liners. Although he sometimes went over the top, he had a thoughtful side that led to some serious conversations about life on ships.

We had less regular contact with the rest of the crew, especially on the way out. They ate their own food in their own dining room and in the evenings were together in their own lounge or in their private cabins. However, they did come to the captain's three parties and all the passengers mixed with them, as well as the British contingent. Moreover, just as on the *Ville d'Aquarius*, all of us were soon invited to their lounge for an evening birthday celebration for two of the crew. There was even a band at the party, with one crew member on the drums, and two others playing their guitars. We sang along to well-known pop songs and they even had some printed lyric sheets available. Even the captain joined in sometimes, especially for the singing of his favourite, "Rock around the Clock." After this birthday party, contact with crew members came easier, in smiles as we walked around the deck and passed them working, and sometimes in brief conversations. We became better acquainted with two Filipino crew members, John and Reynaldo, who found an opportunity to ask us about our faith and shared with us the difficulties they encountered being Christians on the high seas. John, known also on board as "St. John" and "Bible John," was the sailor who tried to rescue the injured booby. During our trip other crew members shared with us their stories of family in the Philippines, and relatives in Canada and the United States. All of them became a vital part of our experience.

I have no doubt that the ship itself, its age, its dignity, its wooden decks, taffrail and mahogany doors, and its spacious cabins and lounges, encouraged dignity and fellowship. But there's a remaining mystery here. Could any captain or shipping company guarantee the wonderful community we experienced by hand-picking compatible passengers and bringing them on board? Of course not, no more than any coach or manager can guarantee a sports team's positive chemistry before the season starts. Perhaps the magic should remain a mystery, one for which I'll be eternally grateful.

With our shipboard community firmly in place, we approached Pitcairn Island. Pitcairn may well be the most famous—and infamous—island in the South Seas. On his last journey, Captain Cook had a lieutenant on board by the name of William Bligh. After his return to England, Bligh was appointed captain of the *Bounty* in 1787 and instructed to sail into the South Pacific and collect breadfruit plants for delivery to the West Indies,

Pitcairn: a rugged bit of rock rising right out of the South Pacific Ocean. It is so small a speck that the Bounty *mutineers were confident that no one would ever find them there.*

where they would be planted to produce cheap and nutritious food for slaves. Most breadfruit of that region propagates not by seeds but by shoots, which Bligh planned to transport in carefully tended flowerpots on his ship. The *Bounty* and its crew set out in December 1787, but ran into frequent foul weather that sometimes damaged the ship. It didn't arrive in Tahiti until ten months later.

Captain Bligh experienced what Captain Cook also had encountered on these islands: Native women both attractive and willing. Bligh's crew easily and frequently succumbed to temptation in the months it took to gather enough shoots to make the trip worthwhile. By the time the ship finally left the island for the West Indies in early 1789, half the crew had contracted venereal disease. The voyage was barely underway, however, when some of the crew, led by First Officer Fletcher Christian, mutinied. About two hundred books have been written about this mutiny, and five major films produced, and still there is no trustworthy account that settles whether Bligh was truly at fault as a cruel captain, or whether Christian wasn't quite the righteous defender of the crew, but merely a selfish opportunist. Whoever was to blame, Bligh was put on board a launch with water and food and eighteen of his followers. (The suspicion is that more would have gone with their captain if the launch had been larger.)

With Christian now in command of the *Bounty*, the mutineers sailed to Tubuai Island, hoping to settle there with the local population. However, the Tubuai people were positively unwelcoming, and moreover, there was no meat on the island. Christian sailed to Tahiti again, where the ship picked up some of the women they had befriended, as well as livestock, mostly pigs. Back they went to Tubuai for a second try, and once more they were rebuffed. They then sailed back to Tahiti, but knew that staying there permanently would be risky. They didn't think Bligh would make it back to England to report them, but other British ships would likely come to the island to collect breadfruit. Christian's plan was to sail to Pitcairn, a small island on one of Cook's charts, and there strip the *Bounty* of anything useful and burn it. Sixteen of his mutineers preferred to stay in Tahiti. A few years later, many of these men were taken prisoner, most convicted of mutiny, some pardoned, and some hanged. Christian and nine sailors, plus twelve Tahitian women, six Tahitian men, and one child sailed to Pitcairn, which he found even though the map he used was off by at least one hundred sea miles. That cartographic error explains why the British ship *Pandora*, which was sent to find them, never did. Captain Bligh managed to reach Timor,

3,618 nautical miles away from where the mutiny had occurred, with the loss of only one life. His journey is still recognized as one of the greatest feats of sea navigation and survival in history. From Timor he made his way back to England on a Dutch merchant ship. A London Board of Inquiry completely exonerated him.

The story of Christian and his followers is a sad one. One sailor committed suicide, some died in accidents on the rocky and treacherous island, and many were murdered. In 1808 the American ship *Topaz* was the first to discover that this thought-to-be uninhabited island was in fact populated. The only mutineer still alive was John Adams, whose stories were the only ones available for accounts of what had happened after the mutiny. But how reliable are they? For one thing, his name doesn't appear on the original *Bounty* roster. Had he changed his name? Or was he someone already living on Tahiti who had joined Christian? Or was he Christian himself, a smart man who realized that he would be a target of prosecution for as long as he lived? Many of the *Bounty* mysteries will never be solved. It wasn't until 1814 that British ships arrived at the island, the *Briton* and the *Tagus*, and in 1817 the *Sultan*.

Pitcairn, this two-square-mile piece of craggy rock, has intrigued many generations, as small islands tend to do. There's something in many of us that longs for a perfect place away from it all, an anchored ship so to speak, where life is simple, needs are few, community is assured, and the surrounding sea is a barrier against both intruders and temptation. Because of the many books and films about the island, Pitcairners have had to deal with many requests from prospective settlers. They have allowed a few, some of whom have written books about their experience. One such settler is Dea Birkett, a young English woman who lived on the island for a few years in the 1990s and wrote *Serpent in Paradise*. Hers is a fascinating story. She booked a working passage on a Norwegian tanker after having been given permission to come to the island. The ship stopped long enough to drop her off. Her first surprise was that the islanders were less interested in her than in whatever they could get from the ship, especially from bartering with the ship's cook. She soon realized that the island is totally dependent on passing ships for many essential foodstuffs, since the island can only grow a limited amount and variety of food. To get off the ship she had to climb down a rope ladder into a longboat dancing on the water, always in danger of smashing to bits against the steel of the tanker. Once everyone boarded the longboat with their supplies, it took off for the island, which had no harbour, only a jetty. To get to it, the longboat had to wait for the surf to lift it over a barrier.

At first Birkett's island life seemed all that she had dreamed of, and the people welcoming and interesting, but she also learned to cope with limitations. The most important cash-producing enterprise was selling items to ships' crews and tourists: bananas and papayas; wood carvings; carefully worked baskets woven from dyed plant materials, with PITCAIRN embedded in decorative patterns; painted leaves; stamps and postcards; and T-shirts. Since the island doesn't produce wood for carving, its most lucrative product, the islanders have to take their two longboats to Henderson Island to harvest and bring back suitable logs. Henderson Island is an uninhabited coral island some 110 sea miles away, a dangerous trip in these puny craft full of islanders and supplies.

Pitcairn is a religious island, its roughly forty inhabitants all members of the local Seventh Day Adventist church, on its pulpit the original *Bounty* Bible. Officially, drinking alcohol is taboo, but some islanders indulge. Although there was a fresh water spring on the island when Christian landed, it's now virtually dry and the islanders depend on rain, carefully caught and stored in cisterns. In her book, Birkett also describes the health of her island friends. Obesity, diabetes, and heart disease are gradually gaining ground. After living on the island for awhile, Birkett discovered that she was not, and would never be, a real islander, as others discovered before her. Pitcairn may look like a paradise, but it's a closed community with secret codes and language that demand the surrender of all individuality to the group. Once she realized that, she left, and wrote her book.

That Pitcairn isn't a paradise was vividly demonstrated in a recent court case (2005) in which six Pitcairn men were accused of sexual abuse and incest. Tried in Auckland under British law (officially Pitcairn is still British), five of them were convicted and sentenced to jail terms, a vital blow to this island so dependent on muscle power to manage the longboats and other physically demanding island tasks. Part of the defense was that "we have always done it this way, and everyone knew." Not everyone did—there's no mention of this behaviour in Birkett's book, although knowing it now one perhaps could read hints of it between the lines.

We arrived at Pitcairn Island at 0530 and simply drifted. We were amazed how small it was, simply a multicoloured rock rising out of the ocean. Soon after our arrival, a longboat headed out to us from its shore. A longboat is a small open vessel for the transport of people and cargo over short distances.

It may be rowed or pushed by a screw operated by an outboard or inboard motor. The boat we saw approaching had an inboard motor, a big tarpaulin covering most of the boat, and some people sitting on the small fore deck and in the aft. To us the sea looked calm, but the boat bobbed up and down, the people on board rising and falling with it. Welcomed by the captain, and with the help of sailors who threw down rope ladders from the railing, about a dozen of the longboat's passengers climbed on board, carrying bags and boxes. Out of these came their tourist wares wrapped in newspapers, which were then displayed in the officers' lounge. We looked at the goods, talked to the islanders, and purchased a number of small baskets as gifts for our children, as well as a big one that Johanna still uses to store and carry wool for knitting. We bought stamps and postcards, and also a small dolphin woodcarving. After about two hours, the islanders climbed back down and returned to the island. We waved goodbye to them and they waved back to us. The *Sydney Star* lifted anchor, and to our delight sailed right around the island before taking off in the direction of Auckland. Clearly the stop at Pitcairn Island had been a treat for the passengers, but whether the captain had any other reason for this interlude we never discovered. When we broached the subject of our visit in the days that followed, he told us he had no idea what we were talking about, that his log showed no such visit, and that we must have dreamed it. Had he done something against the letter of his shipping company's rules but entirely in keeping with the spirit of being master of this ship? Whatever it was, all of us passengers were grateful.

As we neared Auckland, New Zealand, we became very aware that our fellowship was about to dissolve. We exchanged addresses and voiced promises about future contacts, and even visits. Everyone was aware that links after travel aren't guaranteed, not even likely. Yet, we observed the rituals of eternal friendship, partly because one never knows, and in fact I'm still in contact with some of our fellow passengers several years later. Our farewell rituals included two elaborate parties, both organized by Martha with the assistance of Captain Pridmore, who made the ship's cook available to prepare nibbles now that Martha's supplies had run out. The first party was to say goodbye to Jean, David, Michael, and Roberta, the night before we landed in Auckland. It was also the night that Martha shared her writing with all of us and Bill read his engine-room poem. We would have another party a few days later before we said goodbye to Bill and Martha in Melbourne.

We met at breakfast together for the last time the next morning and said goodbye to our four friends. Later that day we saw Jean and David, who had booked into a downtown hotel, in a little postal station where we bought stamps and mailed letters and postcards. That's the last we saw of them. It's safe to predict that if we ever meet again, we'll see the memory of that four-week voyage in one another's eyes, mostly the unexplained magic of it.

CHAPTER TEN

Auckland to Savannah

Auckland marked the end of the long stretch across the South Pacific, which had been interrupted only by our short visit to Pitcairn. For the next few weeks the legs between stops would be shorter, from one to four days, until we returned to Auckland and made the return journey to Panama. Our passenger community was about to disperse, and our attention turned more to the ports we visited.

Although Auckland is by far the largest city in New Zealand, it's not the capital. That honour belongs to Wellington, which is much more centrally located. The first European to find and use this land (for sweet water and other supplies) was Abel Tasman, a Dutch explorer who landed here in 1642. Cook came by in 1768 and after him whalers and sealers. It's estimated that around twenty thousand Maoris lived in what is now the Auckland area in the early nineteenth century, as the land was fertile and the waters provided plenty of fish. In 1840 Britain entered into a treaty with the indigenous population, and soon more British immigrants and other Europeans came. The governor, William Hobson, wanted Auckland to be the capital of this new acquisition, but the more centrally located Wellington eventually prevailed. Auckland is built on an isthmus and has the unique distinction

197

of having two separate harbours, one to the east in the Pacific Ocean and the second to the west in the Tasmanian Sea. It has a still rapidly growing population of over one million, and its citizens enjoy a moderate climate, even warm enough to grow citrus fruits. Many islands dot the surrounding waters, some with cone-shaped centres that provide clear evidence of the area's volcanic past.

After our goodbyes, Johanna and I walked towards the Auckland port gate for a day of sightseeing and a visit with a distant cousin of Johanna's. Pieternella Dijkgraaf started work at a downtown tourist shop at ten o'clock, but we arranged to meet her for a morning coffee. The store was close enough to walk to in the fine mild weather, and when we met it struck me how much the two women looked alike. Pieternella suggested we take a two-hour tourist bus trip around the inner part of the city. Auckland is built against a range of hills that circle the inner city and harbour, and as the bus climbed the hills, we could often see our ship's distinct stack emblazoned with the company symbol. After the tour we walked around, bought a newspaper and some magazines, and sat on a bench in a square simply watching the city go by. Auckland was still in the grip of the recently completed America's Cup yacht races, and many store windows featured special displays and souvenirs. A little after 1600, Pieternella's husband, Walter, who was already retired, picked the three of us up and drove us to their home on the outskirts of the city. We spent an enjoyable supper hour with Walter and Pieternella and their son in their home and beautiful garden, complete with orange tree. They drove us back to the ship in plenty of time for our late evening departure.

The day in Auckland brought home to us that the ports on this trip would be less exotic than those we visited aboard the *Ville d'Aquarius*. Almost every port still on the itinerary was a typical large Western city, with downtown areas dominated by office towers, which were rendered bereft of citizens come nightfall. Downtown areas do offer daytime entertainment: museums, restaurants, and department stores, but they were all similar and distinguishable only in minor details. While the *Sydney Star*'s passenger lounge resources included plenty of tourist brochures for various ports, much of the focus was on restaurants and shopping malls, or on attractions impractical for our allotted time. Such brochures were composed for tourists who arrive on airplanes and have at least a two-day plan. When you arrive on a ship like ours and are totally new to a city, you lose precious time deciding where to go and finding out how to get there, as ports are sometimes far from tourist areas. When you're in a new country for the first time, you also need time to find a bank or cash machine for local currencies. The cities we visited on our second trip didn't latch onto our memory the way Malta, Singapore, Shanghai, and Pusan did. We found nothing remarkable about Auckland as a city. It was a Western city with Western people and Western ideas, its British history still very much present. If it had an underbelly of poverty, homelessness, and neglect, we didn't see it. We could quite easily have been in Toronto, Winnipeg, Minneapolis, or Buffalo. Of course, each city has unique features, but overall you walk in familiar territory, and after a day of it we'd had enough.

That night we left Auckland for Melbourne, sailing first north, then west around New Zealand's North Island, and then southwest towards the bottom of Australia's mainland. As we sailed south, the weather cooled considerably, as we were now rapidly sailing further away from the equator towards the southern hemisphere's fall and winter. The colder water ended Johanna's daily swim; moreover, the sea was full of persistent swells that made the ship roll constantly.

A few days out from Auckland a pair of albatrosses came in sight. With a wingspan of three metres (ten feet), these amazing birds soared behind the ship above the wake, from right to left, left to right, dropping back for hundreds of metres, then gaining on the ship, and all without flapping their wings, simply using the ship's wake and updrafts from waves. Only their wing tips trembled a bit. They were a spectacular sight. We leaned on the Poop Deck railing and marvelled at the wonder of this life form. One stayed with us for thirty-six hours.

In just over four days we reached Melbourne, where Bill, Martha, and Russ would leave us. After drifting for a few hours outside a bay leading into the port, we finally berthed at night. After saying a final goodbye to our three friends in the morning, we took a taxi, which dropped us off in the centre of the city close to the central railroad complex. Melbourne was founded in 1835 by British settlers on the north shore of what is now Port Phillip Bay, through which we sailed on our way to the port. The city hugs both sides of the Yarra River, a wide ribbon of water now home to many pleasure crafts. The city grew rapidly during and after the Victoria gold rush in the 1850s and served as Australia's capital from 1901-27. (Canberra is now the nation's capital.) The city's current population is approaching four million. As is the whole of Australia, Melbourne is renowned for its interest in sports. It hosted the 1956 Summer Olympics and every year all the top tennis professionals gather for the Australian Open, one of the four major tennis tournaments (the French Open, Wimbledon, and the US Open are the other three).

Our cab driver told us that Melbourne offered a tourist tram that looped around the inner city. After getting enough Australian dollars at a bank, we took the tram on a one-dollar ticket that allowed us to get off and on at will. We had a most enjoyable time in a marvelous botanical garden, full of unfamiliar trees and shrubs, some interesting birds, and a wonderful hothouse full of flowers. From there the tram took us to the state government buildings, which looked typically Victorian in their stonework and architecture and reminded us that Australia, like Canada, was once a British colony. At noon many employees were sitting on the deep green lawns and eating their lunch. The weather was gorgeous, sunny and not too hot.

After completing the tour, we made our way to the Yarra River, bought something to nibble on, and sat by the river watching the many small craft leisurely plying its waters. A cab took us back to port and our ship, and later that afternoon we slowly sailed underneath a high and spectacular bridge, an important commercial link between Melbourne, its surroundings, and the rest of the country. It reminded me of the Bridge of the Americas in Panama. We continued through a developing industrial area with many large oil storage tanks. As we entered Port Phillip Bay on our way to the ocean, I couldn't even locate the small exit channel until we were very close to it. Once we passed through it we were on our way to Sydney, about one day's sailing away.

In preparation for our visit to Australia's largest city, we had come across a brochure on the ship with information about the Flying Angel, the welcoming house for sailors right in the heart of Sydney. Remembering the helpful people at the Houston centre, we asked our cab driver to drop us off there. On the way, he pointed out several sites in various stages of construction in preparation for the Olympic Games that year. When I asked him about his expectations for the games, he was surprisingly negative. No, he didn't expect to make extra money because of the Olympics, quite the contrary, for traffic would be snarled. And no, he didn't appreciate the games upsetting the life of his city.

When we entered the Flying Angel, we were warmly welcomed and given coffee. The staff quickly assembled maps, brochures, and discount tickets to the Sydney Aquarium, which they highly recommended we visit. They informed us that their van toured various port areas three times a day and

For many sailors, seaman's centres are shore havens, giving opportunity for shore talk, telephone calls to family, sometimes divine worship, and a time to forget life on board, which is always hard. This one in Sydney was also kind to us passengers and a prompting for us to become volunteers in a similar institution in Montreal some years later.

the driver could have easily picked us up, thus saving us a twenty-dollar cab fare. The no-charge service was also available that afternoon to take us back to the ship, and we decided we would take advantage of it.

The aquarium complex was a twenty-minute walk from the Flying Angel. Johanna was intrigued by the many school classes on a visit to it, all the girls in neat school uniforms reminding her of Madeline, the heroine of one of our favourite picture books. Inside was a spectacular oceanarium with panoramas of Barrier Reef life, the deep ocean, and a harbour bottom with an old row boat, an anchor, and other debris. We descended into the exhibits and walked through transparent Plexiglas tunnels, surrounded by water and the sounds of sea creatures. Walking beside or beneath a gigantic stingray, an equally menacing white shark, and all sorts of fish, some singly, some in schools, with only the thin Plexiglas between us and them, gave us both an eerie feeling.

We exited the complex just before noon, and walked to the internationally famous Opera House, which reminded me of the billowing sails on a fast-moving sailing ship. On the way we passed an office tower with an enormous canvas hanging down its street side that portrayed a bookcase full of books. The "shelves" and "spines" were clearly visible. We're both book lovers and craned our necks for a long time to drink in the scene. We didn't enter the Opera House, but simply walked among the many tourists to the front door, looking at it from various angles. From the inner harbour site, surrounded by expensive condominium and apartment buildings, we got a good look at the Sydney Harbour Bridge. For a fee, people can walk right over its span and a group was in the process of doing just that. Slowly sailing in the bay was a ship that would have looked familiar to Captain Cook some 250 years ago: small, three-masted, and square-rigged, with a prominent forecastle, and beautifully painted.

We saw signs that pointed us to the Royal Bontanic Gardens, an enormous botanical garden, far larger than the one in Melbourne. As the garden clearly wound its way back to where we had come from, we explored it. Once again we spotted unfamiliar plants and birds. After we left the garden, we passed a large downtown church that had its front doors wide open with a number of people exiting. We climbed the stairs to take a look inside, and the minister welcomed us warmly, asked us who we were, where we were from, and about our own church. He was full of enthusiasm and interest in our lives, both on the ship and at home.

By the time we returned to the Flying Angel we were tired and our feet

We could hardly believe our eyes finding this canvas "library" on the side of an office tower right in the heart of Sydney. It was hard to find the right angle from which to take this picture.

were sore. The centre was full of history, with models of old and famous ships, traditional ship artifacts like brass clocks and lanterns, many photographs, and items for sale. At 1630 we got in the van, which was loaded with sailors, and took off for the two ports it serviced. I was lucky enough to sit next to the volunteer driver, and we talked all the way. His enthusiasm and love for his work remained with us and provided the impetus for us to consider doing similar volunteer work once we arrived back home.

While walking around Sydney's harbour site, we had seen a number of freighters going in and out, and I began to wonder why the container port was so far outside the city at Botany Bay when this port and a large harbour were right in Sydney. Nick told me that traditional ports, built for general cargo ships and around which cities were built over the years, often couldn't be transformed into container ports. The larger ships, the extensive container storage areas, and the space requirements of the enormous unloading and loading equipment made newly built container ports a necessity. Hence, this container port at Botany Bay, so named by Captain Cook when the botanist on board found a wealth of plants on this site. Long before Sydney and its harbour were constructed, Botany Bay was the place where convicts from England were unloaded. The two words "Australia" and "convicts" are closely linked in the minds of many people, but what's often overlooked is that the British government shifted its transports to Australia only after colonists in what is now the United States successfully objected to convicts being shipped there.

On our return to the ship we discovered that we were no longer the only two passengers on board. An elderly couple from Sydney, quite recently married, had joined us. They were on their way to visit friends in Auckland and preferred this mode of travel over flying. Tony had been at sea all his life, mostly in the British navy, but spent his last working years as a captain on one of Sydney's regional ferries. His wife, Thelma, was an active member of the very downtown church we had visited. But they weren't the only newcomers on board; we had a new captain, Colin Mundy, who had also brought his wife Jeanette.

That afternoon we left for Brisbane, a bit more than a day away. We docked near Brisbane on a Friday evening at a container port some distance from the city. Brisbane, now capital of the Australian state of Queensland, began its life as a penal colony in the 1820s and for a century grew slowly. It now has almost two million inhabitants, and its buildings follow the Brisbane River, one of the most meandering major rivers I have ever seen. Like the rivers in Sydney and Melbourne, it's preserved for all its citizens, easily accessible, and a delight for small crafts, motorized and paddled. During World War II, Brisbane served as South West Pacific headquarters for General Douglas MacArthur.

We were closer to Wynnum, a small town a short cab ride away, from which we could board a commuter train for the hour's journey to Brisbane. The ship spent two days in this port, mainly resting. We learned that Australian ports close down for the weekend, probably because of strong stevedore unions and hefty overtime charges. On Saturday we took a cab from port to Wynnum, and then a train, which took us to the heart of the city in just under an hour, where we boarded a bus for a two-hour guided tour. Afterwards, we walked along the river on its extensive boardwalk, flanked by apartment buildings, boutiques, shopping centres, and restaurants. After the train dropped us back into Wynnum, we walked the length of the village, just to look around and to locate a church for Sunday worship.

The next day we got up early and took a taxi into Wynnum, where we found a Presbyterian church with a service already in progress. We entered anyway, in time for a familiar hymn and then a sermon. As soon as we sat down we were handed hymnals and a Bible opened at the Isaiah passage that would be read. After the service we were invited for a cup of coffee in the churchyard and chatted with members of the friendly congregation. After leaving the church we walked along Moreton Bay to Manly Harbour village, three kilometres away, for a Sunday fair with a market, music, and other entertainment. We spent about four hours there, eating fish and chips and listening to a small jazz band from a nearby private high school. We watched children playing in the playground in the park along the water, and throwing frisbees on the small beach. The three Australian cities we visited, and Wynnum also, were built around harbours or rivers and have preserved their waterfronts as assets for everyone to enjoy, not just individual home owners and developers.

When we arrived back to the ship, we discovered that three other passengers had come aboard: Americans John and Marcia, and German-Canadian Gerhard. We welcomed them to cocktail hour, and acquainted them with some of the other shipboard routines.

From Brisbane, the ship sailed southeast towards Wellington, New Zealand, 3.5 sailing days away. Unfortunately, our time in port was so short that a walking visit to this small city wasn't feasible. One notable landmark at the edge of the port area was a large rugby stadium, Westpac Stadium, which reminded us of New Zealanders' devotion to that sport and their successful team, the All Blacks, with their Maori war dance before each international game. The next stop was Port Chalmers, the most southerly container port of the country, about a day's sailing away. We landed very early in the morning, and were told that we wouldn't sail away until early evening, even though the number of containers to be unloaded and loaded was small.

Johanna and I decided to visit Dunedin, a forty-minute bus ride away. We walked around after getting off the bus and came upon a marvelously refurbished but little-used railroad station. It had a coin-operated public toilet that was completely washed down after each use, including the walls and floors, with the toilet seat automatically rotating. In a city square called Octagon, we discovered a gathering of the Studebaker club of South Island; there were about fifty cars from the 1920s to the last ones built. The proud owners were ready to show off their babies to anyone who showed the slightest interest. After the bus ride back, we spent some time in Port Chalmers, a one-street town with the port on one end, and only some short dead-end streets to both sides. We loved the little Anglican church on the hill just outside the town itself. We walked up, but the building was closed, although the door sign indicated that it was still in use for worship. With its massive gray stone walls and tower visible for miles around, it looked as if it had been moved here from a small English town.

Once we arrived back at the *Sydney Star*, we had plenty of time before departure. I saw a couple fishing from the quay on the other side of the harbour and decided to saunter in that direction. They were a married couple of Dunedin university professors who lived in Port Chalmers. When they learned that we were passengers on the ship across the harbour, they offered to drive Johanna and me to the breeding grounds of the albatross, an hour away. It was a kind and generous offer, but we had not enough time to take them up on it.

From Port Chalmers it took two days to sail back along the east coast of New Zealand to Auckland. There we said goodbye to Tony and Thelma, with whom we had spent many pleasant hours of conversation. Tony, especially, had many stories to tell. He had been orphaned at a young age, and the British navy had become his parents and family for most of his life. We had only part of a day in Auckland, but Pieternella and her daughter took us to a local market, where we bought some souvenirs. When we got back to the *Sydney Star*, we gave them a tour of the ship before they returned home.

On April 25, we set out on our return voyage across the Pacific. Our first stop was Pitcairn Island, but this time for official duties. The Blue Star Line ships on this route were also the official supply ships for the island. In Auckland, three containers loaded with supplies had been placed on board in a strategic place for easy unloading, and in Auckland a passenger bound for Pitcairn Island had come aboard. Vulla Young, a descendant of the mutineers, had spent three months with her daughter in Auckland, but was now on her way back to her home. The Auckland pilot aboard as we left port was the same one we had seen twice before, a stereotypical sailor with grizzly reddish hair and blue eyes. We wondered if he had been born in Holland, as he looked like a Friesian, and spoke Dutch to him just to find out. He wasn't.

The relatively short time between the Australian and New Zealand ports had pushed to the background an obvious change in the atmosphere on board. The new captain was a very different master than the first had been, and he soon made changes in the ship's routine. For one thing, cabin steward John told us he was no longer permitted to serve drinks and snacks in the passenger lounge for our cocktail hour, and we would have to make our 0600 coffee ourselves. The new passengers didn't seem interested in the social routines we had experienced on the way up. The American couple chose to have drinks in their cabin, and Gerhard seemed to want to be on his own most of the time.

Dinner table arrangements had changed also. With fewer passengers, and Keith and Glen gone, one large table was deemed sufficient, with enough room for Captain Mundy, Jeanette, and Nick. At first Nick, Johanna, and I continued the type of table talk we had enjoyed before, but soon conversations became formal, polite, and only occasionally interesting. Towards the end of the journey, Nick seldom bothered to show up anymore, and some nights the captain and his wife didn't bother either, eating in their cabin. Some nights the captain's body language indicated that he merely tolerated our presence, yet other evenings he would be a most gracious host, full of conversation and stories from his thirty-five-year career as a sailor. His changes in mood were hard on all the passengers. As for parties, they were few and far between. Jeanette invited all of the passengers and officers to her birthday party in the officers' lounge. It was pleasant enough, but the ambience was formal and much less congenial than similar events on our trip out. On another occasion the captain invited the passengers for drinks, and he clearly had commanded all of his officers to be present as well. The captain's wife did mix with passengers a bit, because she used the Boat

Deck facilities and shared the pool with Johanna. She organized morning on-deck Tai Chi sessions for the three women, but only Johanna accepted her invitation. There were no barbecues, bingo, or horse races, even though Saturday evenings were available for socializing. The change was regrettable, but no captain has any obligation to socialize with his passengers or crew. Passengers are promised a cabin, food, and access to some of the ship's space and amenities, but entertainment is their own responsibility. Some ships are just more friendly places than others, depending on the individual captain.

The change in leadership also made my daily visits to the bridge uncomfortable. When the captain was present, his body language often seemed to indicate that passengers weren't welcome, and I began to avoid going there when he was on the bridge. One thing that did improve was the food. It had already been more than adequate with the first cook, Elmer, but his replacement, Nestor, came from a family who owned a chain of bakeries in Manila—and could this man cook! Some of his creations, notably lamb and pork, were as good as in any fine restaurant. Every dinner featured four courses: soup or salad; an appetizer of meat or fish and garnish; a large main course; and dessert. The quantity of this splendid food led some of us to skip the main course, preferring dessert after having already been filled by the first two courses. Our reluctance to eat all four courses prompted Nestor to ask the captain if we didn't like his cooking. Through the captain, and directly to him, we assured Nestor that it was, in fact, the excellence of his cooking that had done us in. He seemed reassured. I often played ping-pong with Nestor in the crew's lounge after dinner, and he beat me every time.

Given the changed circumstances, Johanna and I simply shrugged our shoulders and organized our lives aboard ship in different ways. We knew that we'd be at sea for three weeks, the only interruption being a day at Pitcairn Island. Johanna and I continued our routines of exercise, reading, walking the deck, talking, and mingling with the other passengers when it seemed the thing to do. We spent many hours simply sitting on the Boat Deck in one of the gazebos, Johanna crafting something, and I reading aloud to her from *Adam Bede*. The gazebo was a must, for the weather remained cool and the trade winds were strong. The ship was constantly in motion in all directions because of the winds and the persistence of long swells.

We also began to learn more about the crew. I got into wheelhouse conversations with the chief and second mates, and Johanna and I made more evening visits to the crew's lounge, even though the heavy smoke bothered us. Instead of going to the lounge before dinner, we'd take our drinks outside to the portside of the Poop Deck. We were sailing in an almost eastern direction, with a few degrees north to it, gradually approaching the equator again on our way to Panama via Pitcairn. Every night at around 1800 we watched the sun go down behind us, clearly visible because of the angle of the ship's progress. We hung over the railing together, or sat on convenient bollards, to watch and photograph the spectacular cloud shapes and colours, every night a different panorama. Usually some ABs detoured on the way from deck work to their cabins to say hi and chat a bit. Joel was an especially engaging fellow, young, handsome, strong, and full of stories about his family back home in the Philippines. We came to look forward to his Poop-Deck visit, and when he realized this, he made sure to come by for a chat.

Watching the sailors more closely, it struck us how conscious they were of the threats to life and limb in their workplace. A ship is a steel box filled with machines and tools, with moving parts in greasy engine rooms, and ropes and cables that snake and wind across decks and up and down the ship. Below and to the sides looms dark deep restless water, upon which ships often move in mysterious and irregular ways. It all adds up to danger for the worker. I watched ABs repainting the superstructure of the *Sydney Star* sparkling white. Each sailor hung in a safety harness as he sat on a sturdy board that hung from ropes attached to the top of Monkey Island. After scraping off the rust, they painted, mostly with rollers. I watched as they prepared for the work by stringing strategic ropes and fitting and attaching harnesses. They carefully and insistently assisted and supervised one another. Though they spoke Tagalog, the main Filipino language, it was easy to understand the drift of their conversations. They took time to guard against accidents and prevent damage to the ship.

Each day the sailors performed preparation rituals at the beginning of the morning shift, and each time they resumed their shifts after the midmorning coffee break, lunch, and midafternoon tea break. They remained cautious and watchful every time, not rushing their work, checking and rechecking for one another. At one point they began chipping rust and repainting the foc's'le, making it off limits for Johanna and me for a number of days. Joel hung in a harness high above the ship, restoring the crow's nest mast to a gleaming white. When he was finished, the whole ship looked the better for it. The crew had also filled the scupper holes along the

On the home stretch between Auckland and the Panama Canal my wife and I stood at the railing every night to watch sunsets. Don't I look utterly relaxed?

working deck with cement. Those holes, placed a strategic distance apart in the Working Deck sides of the ship, drain any water flung on board by waves. As we could see on many ships, those streams of draining water create pathways of rust down the sides of the ship. In some ports we saw sailors hanging in harnesses repainting the ship's sides. Apparently our captain had decided that refinishing the decks, which would take on more water without the scupper holes, would be easier than constantly repainting the ship's sides. But he had created a problem for us. On this leg, with winds constantly in the three-to-four range, enough water came over the railings to cover the Working-Deck path for days on end. For about half the journey we couldn't walk that deck anymore. The first officer would regularly tell us where work would be done that day and ask us to stay away from those areas. The decks were spray-hosed for cleaning regularly, which also made them out of bounds for awhile.

Several other events provided a diversion from the break in our daily routines. One day, the *Sydney Star* sailed towards a small sailing boat bobbing up and down on the waves. The ship slowed down while the captain talked to the sailors—a father, his two sons, and a son's girlfriend. They were on a two-year sailing trip and hadn't seen a ship or another human being for two weeks. They had recently spent a lot of time along the west coast of South America and were now on their way to Alaska. When our ship resumed speed, they were out of sight in ten minutes.

One day, water suddenly appeared in the hallway outside our cabin, only kept out by the high ledge between the cabin and hallway. Our cabin steward, John, used a vacuum cleaner to get rid of it, but the next day it happened again. Clearly something was leaking steadily, apparently refrigeration units somewhere behind the laundry area. It took two ABs two days to fix it, using cement and working in a cramped space where they couldn't stand up. This wasn't the only mechanical problem aboard the *Sydney Star*. In Auckland one of the on-board cranes used for bringing supplies on board had given off high screeching sounds that clearly indicated a malfunction. Once we were underway, and under the direction of Chief Nick, two engineering sailors dismantled the crane and discovered that its main bearing had given up the ghost. While the two sailors removed the bearing, almost welded to its housing because of long use, Nick scouted the airwaves for a replacement to be flown to a port where it could be picked up, but this type of crane was so old that no replacement could be found, at least not while we were on board. The crane remained dismantled during the rest of our trip, further evidence that this ship was becoming obsolete.

In Auckland a load of fresh lumber had been stored on the Poop Deck, and we wondered why. After about six days at sea, three ABs used some of the lumber to build a wooden platform where a winch was located on the starboard side, about halfway down the Working Deck on its portside. The platform was built on a spot left open between reefers, partly because of various pipes and other equipment normally to be found there. It had to be carefully molded around obstacles, with many measurements and many stud and plywood cuts. On the third and final day of this carpentry project, my curiosity got the better of me, and I stopped my walk to ask, "What are you doing?" The answer came back swift and sure, "Pavarotti is going to sing here." I saw the broad smiles on the sailors' faces and began to laugh. Soon we laughed together long and loud; it was a wonderful moment. For the rest of the journey those three sailors and I would exchange a special smile whenever we met on the ship. On that day, just ahead of reaching Pitcairn, we also passed Rapa Island, which is still owned by France and home to about four hundred people. On the way out we had missed seeing it, for it had been shrouded in mist. It was much longer and larger than Pitcairn and rose steeply out of the ocean with a jagged silhouette that seemed to indicate that it had been the product of a volcanic eruption.

Although I had many conversations about island life with Vula Young (who is mentioned in Dea Birkett's book), she didn't tell us much about the Pitcairn community. In her seventies, Vula didn't mix much with the other passengers, partly because she was diabetic and had problems climbing stairs so didn't always join us for meals. On our first visit to Pitcairn, I had spoken with a young Pitcairn woman who told me she was both the police officer and the nurse on the island. She also told me about the recurring problem of Pitcairn's water supply; Pitcairn's methods of storing rainwater, and that little rain had fallen over the last few months, causing a water shortage. In the first days on our way to Auckland the winds had been consistently high and the skies cloudy, with frequent rain squalls all around and over the ship. While I thought about the needs of the islanders, and once seeing a massive black cloud formation that seemed aimed straight for the island, I composed a poem, a prayer of sorts for the parched island, which I showed to Vula, and for the first time she became animated in her talk. She suggested I show it to that same young woman when we reached Pitcairn, as she would surely come aboard again. I did so, and she told me it had rained buckets a few days after our departure, and the island cisterns had filled up.

The day before our arrival at Pitcairn, we had asked the captain if we could visit the island. He told us that going ashore would depend on the roughness of the sea and warned that islanders would charge us $25US each for the simple privilege of visiting, and another $25US each for transporting us twice in their longboats. Although we realized that sources of cash income for these people were few, and that perhaps our contribution would help them, we decided not to go ashore. As it turned out, when we arrived the captain decided that the seas were too rough, even though from the *Sydney Star*'s perspective they seemed calm enough. We did get our passports stamped as proof of having been within the territorial waters of the island—for $5US each!

We anchored at Pitcairn Island at 0600, some distance from the island. All cargo had to be lowered into longboats by means of winches, a dangerous and tricky job in an open sea that never rests. Unloading began by about 0800. The three containers for the island were first unloaded on the specially built platform, and then loads in nets were winched down to one longboat. The cargo lashed on the Poop Deck, including lumber, was lowered into the other longboat using the remaining on-board crane. We watched the heavy and risky work for most of the day, until it finished at about 2030. We saw building materials, including windows, for a house; four small red all-terrain vehicles; and a used Massey Ferguson tractor.

The first officer was in charge of unloading cargo from the Poop Deck. As they worked, the crew members talked to one another in Tagalog, but

After being loaded with the help of a winch on board of the Sydney Star *at anchor, the islanders take a load back to their island home, one of many that day. This was a calm sea, so we were told!*

again it was clear to me that safety was uppermost in their minds. I shuddered as I saw the lumber swinging across the Poop Deck, hung in ropes attached to hooks on a crane, which then lowered it into a longboat (so small in comparison to the *Sydney Star*) that danced up and down in the waves. But the sailors took their time, always weighing the dangers of not tying the ropes just right, or lowering the hook at the right time. I noticed how the first officer didn't simply assert his superior status, but worked with the other sailors as one of the team. The whole of it was a demonstration of skill as the crew looked out for themselves and one another, and for the two islanders below them in the longboat. One load of lumber did get loose and fell down into the sea and the boat; fortunately it missed the two longboat crew members. Some items couldn't be unloaded from the containers before total darkness halted the proceedings and were kept on board for off-loading on the way back to Auckland in a few weeks.

While all this was going on, the *Sydney Star* crew members who weren't involved with unloading the cargo used the time off for fishing. They held loose lines between their fingers, the hooks baited with small pieces of fish. The results were phenomenal: at least thirty fish, some as large as ten pounds. Nestor did wonders with them over the next two days. Three times a two-to-three-foot shark got hooked, but three times he wriggled off and away. John the electrician appeared to be the most accomplished fisher. He also pointed out a bird flying high up with a small fish in its beak, dropping it, diving after it, and catching it again, three times before swallowing it. We wondered if it was play, or if the bird was positioning the fish for easier swallowing.

It was after 2000 hours when the *Sydney Star* lifted anchor and sailed away from Pitcairn towards our next stop, the Panama Canal. We crossed the equator once more, but this time no attention was paid to it on board. We attended another crew member's birthday party where Johanna was asked to sing a song using printed music, a sentimental pop song she knew anyway. I spent many hours rearranging the library in the passenger lounge, sorting the books by type, and within each category alphabetically by author. We had brought on board recent tourist brochures from all the cities we had visited and renewed the folders in the lounge.

On May 12, we arrived back at the Panama Canal. At the canal, we went through the three locks during the day, with the weather sunny and warm. I watched a gleaming white cruise ship, two locks ahead of us, eighty-five feet up in the sky while we were still at sea level. It seemed impossible.

Also at the canal two P&O experts were brought on board to update the ship's computer software. One was Bob Lucas, an engineering supervisor from London, the other a software technician from Rotterdam named Kees Oosterhout. They would sail with us to Philadelphia. We had drinks with Kees in our cabin every afternoon before dinner, and talked about Rotterdam, political and social conditions in Holland, soccer (his son was a promising striker), changes in shipping and port procedures, and jazz, and we told him a bit about our sailing experiences.

A day after clearing the locks on the other side of the Panama Canal, we arrived in Kingston, Jamaica. We had been unsure about visiting this city, for we were a bit anxious about reports of crime; however, Jeanette organized a tour for the passengers and herself. We were picked up by a guide in his roomy van. The first thing I noticed was that he wore a heavy gold chain around his neck. He was a large man who had to worm his way into the driver's seat, and warmly welcomed us to the island in his strong bass voice. He first drove us past a hospital to drop off one of the Filipino sailors who was in need of medical attention and then took us on a tour. He showed us both sides of Kingston, the very rich and the very poor, driving us through areas he told us were filled with guns and violence, and pointing out an area where a gun battle between a drug gang and the police had taken place a week before. (He assured us we were safe with him.) On this Sunday we also saw many people on their way to church, mainly women and children dressed up in colourful attire, the women with elaborate hats, even in the poorest and most wretched areas. He took us up a hill that overlooked the city, and pointed out the national soccer stadium where Jamaica's team, the Reggae Boys, had scored so many triumphs in the previous few years. The guide's love for his country was obvious and deep. We all agreed that the tour was a disturbing experience, yet one we wouldn't have liked to miss.

After Kingston, we landed in Philadelphia and Norfolk, before heading to our final destination, Savannah. We reached Philadelphia in the middle of the night, and were roused out of bed to meet US customs and immigration officers. The next day we walked into the city, passing the *United States*, a formerly glorious transatlantic passenger liner, now sleeping and rusting away in an obscure corner of the harbour. We saw the Liberty Bell in a park. We drank coffee in a café. We ate lunch in another. And then, we grabbed a cab and went back to the ship. Frankly, we were Western-citied out. However, after dinner, we were invited to come along to the downtown Philadelphia Seafarer's Center, and we were jammed into a large van with a group of sailors. We spent a few pleasant hours in that smoky, loud, and bustling place and then took the first "delivery" van back to the ship.

We didn't even bother trying to get off the ship at our next stop in Norfolk, but were impressed by the major US naval fleet based there. We had a good look at huge aircraft carriers, supply ships, and other mighty ships of war, but we were too far away to see any on-board activities.

We arrived back in Savannah on May 22. There we said goodbye to the crew and other passengers. Our dining steward, Lito, had packed sandwiches for us when he heard that we'd be driving the rest of the day, but the customs and immigration officer who checked us and our passports told us we couldn't take them. A taxi van drove the two American passengers to the Savannah airport, dropped off Gerhard at a hotel, and then took us to our car.

It took us two days to drive home. The air conditioning wasn't working and the weather was brutally hot, so we drove many miles with our front windows open. As we rolled along the highway heading north, it was difficult to accept that the adventure was over. Our conversation on the way home was filled with recollections of Nick, Martha, Glen, David, and our other shipboard friends. We both remembered the good times, as we do to this day. Even though the last three weeks of our second trip had been less fulfilling than the rest of our container-ship experiences, our love for this mode of travel has not cooled.

Eight years later, we're still easily tempted to tell the tales of our two voyages. When I look at the many photographs and other mementos we still treasure, the journeys come back to me most vividly: ships, sailors, laughter, languages, fellow passengers, ports, landscapes, storms, waves and swells, fish, skies, seas, maps, histories, and stories.

CHAPTER ELEVEN

Quo Vadis?

As I look back on our voyages, one thing becomes clear: Johanna and I travelled when the real impact of container shipping was about to take on gigantic proportions. I have simply endeavoured to relate what I experienced as a passenger on container ships, and what I was most curious about. Yet, somehow the story seems incomplete without adding a bit more about recent developments in container shipping and their potential impact on passengers.

In some ways the container ship *Sydney Star*'s design still represented older modes of shipping, in the same way that early automobiles looked like horse carriages. The *Ville d'Aquarius* was already a number of steps away, more like automobiles of the 1930s, perhaps. Newer ships are technologically a different breed altogether, and their design changes determine port design. Both have their impact on the lives of human beings.

Kees Oosterhout told me about the changes at his home-base Rotterdam container port. The port was already experimenting with computer-controlled container transfer to and from temporary storage areas by unmanned cranes. Those cranes loaded containers on train cars in the right sequence

Yet another ship: sleek, powerful, fast, huge. Johanna and I stare at the photograph and sigh, "Oh, for one more trip ..."

for loading onto ships. When we travelled, bugs in the system were still being worked out, but it's now in full operation with computer operators overlooking the terrain from towers strategically placed throughout the dock area.

The day will come when computers will control the cranes that load and unload containers on and off ships, so Kees said. Already each container's place and numbers are in a database well in advance of its placement on board ship, assuring that it's loaded in the correct sequence. Once cranes and containers are equipped with the proper sensors, computers can control the crane's actions. This will eliminate the high-priced help needed in the crane cabin, and the drivers of trucks loaded with at most two containers. Kees didn't like that idea, since his son was training to become a container crane operator, a well-paid and highly skilled, though stressful, profession.

Container ships will continue to get even bigger, and perhaps also faster. Several new Maersk ships have a capacity of close to 10,000 TEUs, and it's possible that container ships of up to 20,000 TEUs will be constructed that sail only on major routes between the primary producing and consuming regions. Those ships will seek the most efficient ports for trans-shipment of containers to and from smaller ports in surrounding regions. Singapore and Hong Kong are two such ports already. Key factors include not only the size of a port and its equipment, but also the cost of harbour labour, and how long it takes from sea to berth. Compare Hamburg and Rotterdam, for example. Hamburg is well inland, and it takes ships over six hours to reach it from the North Sea at slow speed through a river of limited width. Rotterdam's Europort, on the other hand, is right at the sea's edge.

Many traditional seaports have problems similar to Hamburg. Philadelphia is more than seven hours' slow sailing from the Atlantic, Norfolk close to three, Savannah close to four, and Houston four. Moreover, all ships coming into or leaving these ports require a pilot on board both ways, plus one or more tugs. It all adds up to considerable cost. The additional problem is one of access for huge ships. What's the maximum draft and width of a ship for a specific channel, canal, or river? The *Sydney Star* carried its containers eleven wide, the *Ville d'Aquarius* thirteen, and that Maersk ship seventeen. Can ships go to nineteen? Twenty-one? More? Perhaps using smaller ships for containers only destined to travel to and from river and inland ports would be cheaper and more efficient in the end.

A recent media report from Hamburg's port authority argues that Hamburg has advantages over Rotterdam and Antwerp—specifically that land and river transportation to its hinterland is shorter and cheaper. However, the report adds that, in order to realize this advantage, "the Elbe River shipping channel will need to be further developed in the coming years to cater for the ever-increasing traffic volumes as well as the next generation of container ships."

Other ports cope with similar challenges. Antwerp and Rotterdam, traditional European ports of entry for Northern Europe's population, know that they're in for fierce competition. A number of years ago, the Dutch government built a super-rail line from Rotterdam into Germany for its port goods, at stupendous financial cost and with significant environmental worries, not to speak of the loss of valuable and fertile agricultural land, including many orchards. Our two trips made me more aware of news items pertaining to global shipping, and I smile when I read periodic accounts of which port is now the biggest, best, fastest, cheapest, or most up to date. The items read like sports news, but they cover very serious economic and environmental concerns. In major ports, tens of thousands of people are dependent on the shipping industry for a living.

Ports will need to change as ships get larger. A container loading crane is a massive steel structure constructed to have a thirty-ton weight at the end of its long arm for placement at the far end of the ship. But how long can an arm be before the whole structure topples over? Huge ships already have nineteen or even more containers in one row. Will the time come when such ships will need to be loaded and unloaded from two sides by two different cranes? If that happens, it will force the construction of brand new container ports.

This trend towards bigger and faster ships is also affecting the Suez and Panama canals. Neither is able to accommodate supertankers anymore, those huge behemoths, 250,000 tons or more, with their environmentally dangerous loads. Taking also into consideration the high canal tariffs of tens of thousands of dollars per ship, and up to a hundred thousand or more for modern cruise ships, many large ships now find it more economical to use the old precanal routes around the southern tips of Africa and South America.

The Suez Canal is clearly no longer as vital to shipping as it once was. In fact, the Suez Corporation offers special discounts to ships contemplating the longer journey around Africa. In the early 1980s, over twenty thousand ships used the canal annually, but now fewer then fifteen thousand do and annual revenue is stagnant at two billion dollars. It seems sad that this is so. Perhaps like some nineteenth-century idealists, I wish that life in Egypt could improve for the many millions there who live in poverty and for whom canal revenue is a promise. For me, still, Egypt is a land of magic.

The Panama Canal also faces challenges. When we travelled through it, it could only accommodate ships up to 295 metres long and 32 metres wide, with a maximum draft of 12 metres, 65,000 maximum tons, and a maximum container load of 4,750. The *Ville d'Aquarius* wouldn't have been allowed in the canal because of its width. According to a relatively recent *Globe and Mail* article, there are plans to refashion the Panama Canal by building new locks that will accommodate ships up to 385.8 metres long, 49 metres wide, and with a maximum draft of 15.3 metres, a maximum weight of 150,000 tons, and carrying a maximum load of 12,500 containers. The construction problems are enormous, requiring a second massive construction miracle. In addition to the construction of new locks, new channels have to be dug, requiring the removal of vast quantities of earth and rock—130 million cubic metres by one estimate. There's also the question of whether there will be enough water to maintain the current system of using the massive rainfalls for the operation of the locks. The estimated $13 billion US construction cost is another huge obstacle.[3]

As touched on in Chapter 9, new trends in container shipping also affect the staffing of ships. Gottfried, the second officer on the *Ville d'Aquarius*, told me that the much bigger Maersk ship that followed us out of Singapore harbour carried only about fourteen sailors on board, versus our ship's twenty-one. Yet, it was built to carry up to 6,600 TEUs, compared to 3,900 on the *Ville d'Aquarius*. Gottfried didn't know the precise makeup of the crew, but suspected that many more functions were controlled by on-board computers, and that the ship had a computer expert on board to handle any software adjustments and hardware repairs.

In conversation with Kees, I wondered aloud how these larger ships would be maintained with smaller crews. Chipping rust and painting is a labour-intensive job, and if it isn't done a ship may not last long. He told me that on such a ship the crew keeps systems going, and when more major maintenance is required, "flying squads" come on board. Alternatively, such maintenance is scheduled while the ship is in port. Another consideration is that ships today aren't built to last very long. At over twenty-five years old, the *Sydney Star*'s days were numbered, and ways had been found to cut down on standard maintenance, for example, cementing the scupper holes closed. A ship like the *Ville d'Aquarius* was built with a life expectancy of eight years. If a ship isn't expected to last very long, maintenance is reduced, and the owners will be less demanding on the quality of its initial building. The hull of the *Ville d'Aquarius* was likely to have been considerably thinner than that of the *Sydney Star*, so Chief Nick told me, perhaps eleven milli-metres versus seventeen millimetres. Other construction shortcuts would be employed also, which could pose a safety problem for sailors on ships of lesser quality, especially when these ships are of gigantic proportions. In the early days of supertankers, a number of accidents pointed to just such dangers, not only to the men on board but to coastal environments.

This brings me to the human element. If the shipping industry contin-ues to exploit technology in order to replace bodies with machinery, what's the human cost? If all of the jobs disappear, then what happens to people earning a living in shipping? More than one officer told me that the num-ber of port stevedores is steadily shrinking as new technology makes them

---

[3] Mark Brooks, "The Bigger Ditch," *The Globe and Mail*, 23 July 2005, p. F6; see also Maurice Bijo, "Panama Canal Expansion: Context-Cost & Benefit Analysis—Proposals," *fenix Panama* (28 March 2006).

redundant. In conversation with a shipping expert, I was told that some longstanding customs will disappear over time. For instance, on both ships we sailed on, two sailors manned the bridge at night, an officer and an AB. If something had happened to either one—a sudden illness, a heart attack, or an accident—the other would have been able to immediately take steps to ensure the safety of the ship. But why not adopt the long-established train system of a "dead man's" button or pedal? The ship normally sails on automatic pilot, guided by computers. A supervising officer could push a button every ten minutes; if he failed to do so, an alarm system would warn the captain that something might be amiss. Gottfried thought it likely that the Maersk ship was already using such a system on the bridge and in the engine room, thereby eliminating two bodies.

What's driving this explosion of container shipping? One captain I talked to at the Mariners' Centre in Montreal said that he feels part of a system that mercilessly pushes all its participants—manufacturers, distributors, and transporters—ever bigger, faster, and cheaper. I had long conversations with that captain, who pointed to the world of instant gratification we live in. Goods must arrive just in time to fill up depleted store shelves, and manufacturing parts to keep the production lines going.

The captain had come from a British seafaring family, and from childhood, there had never been any question of what career he would follow. He grew up in Liverpool when its thriving port was the heart of its economy. Now it's being transformed into a different city, for when ships come in for only a few days instead of a few weeks, local labour and spending is vastly diminished. Competition, speed, and cost controls make for small crews and sailors who have to perform too many tasks for which they may not have been trained properly. "Too many jockeys on the sea," the captain said. That includes bridge officers. Moreover, no one wants to be a cadet for long, or serve multiple years as third, then second, then first mate, before becoming master. It must all happen quickly, or the sailors will quit and look for faster moving careers onshore. The captain said he had had pilots on board who clearly didn't know what they were doing, and who endangered the ship. I asked him how he handled those situations. He replied, "I arrange it so that I learn the tricky parts of what's ahead, and then I give the orders. And I closely watch other ships when they sail close to us. You never know."

That conversation in Montreal brought back memories of my talks with Bob Lucas, who had come on board the *Sydney Star* in Panama to train the engineering staff in the use of the newly installed computer software. He was forty-nine years old then, had always been with the Blue Star Line, and felt himself a true "Blue Star Man." His career had begun in 1967 at the age of sixteen, with three years of specialized training as an apprentice engineer. After graduation, he took a job as a junior engineer in 1971, and began to climb the steep and slow ladder towards his initial target: chief engineer.

For many years he sailed on general cargo ships, ten-to-fifteen-thousand-ton ships that had forty to forty-five sailors on board (and from which, he said in passing, about 10 percent of each cargo got pilfered in various ports). He reached the level of third engineer when he was twenty-three, became second engineer two years after that, and was made chief engineer at age thirty-six. It had taken him twenty years. When I mentioned Bob's history to him, the captain said that about half the cadets he saw today, deck or engineering, would quit after their first trip, having realized how much they had to learn and how long they would be away from home and the comforts of home. Most young people from the West don't want sea-going jobs anymore. The top officers of many shipping lines still come from traditional Western seafaring nations, but their numbers are going down. Many ships already have complete crews from nations now emerging as the shipping labour pool, the Philippines and India in particular. Two of the captain's senior officers, both from Indonesia, sat with us and their nods confirmed what he was saying.

During our volunteering stint in Montreal I also spent a few evenings in the officers' lounge of a Dutch ship, a specialized carrier of heavy loads, like train engines, with a complement of about twelve sailors, six Dutch officers and six crew from Cape Verde Islands. I first told them about my own schoolboy feelings about Holland, the sea, ships, history, and daring adventures. Then I asked the first mate, "Do you feel proud of, connected with, the generations of Dutch seafarers who have made a name for themselves?" The answer came swift and sure. "No." One officer blamed the Dutch government for letting the industry leave Holland for flags-of-convenience countries. (I've also heard American, Canadian, and British sailors say the same thing about the shipping industry in their respective countries.) They told me that at one stage Holland had more than ten schools for sailor training. Now there's only one left. These sailors had a job, and perhaps they liked the sea, or the travel, or their father or grandfather had been a sailor, or they simply wouldn't want a 9 to 5 job back home. But there was no residue of pride in being part of a national tradition. I could understand these experienced sailors, but I was also a bit disappointed.

I'm not sure if it was connected, but those Dutch sailors were waiting for orders to have their ship towed to a Quebec shipbuilding company for extensive repairs to their bow. They had collided with an oncoming freighter in the St. Lawrence Seaway outside Montreal. I wondered if it was the fault of the pilot on board, or perhaps inadequately trained sailors on the other ship.

I once asked *Sydney Star* Captain Mundy what the major difference was between a sailor's job when he started as a teenager some forty years before, and today. What did he like about the changes? "Nothing much," he growled. When I prodded him, he told me two things. Container ships had severely restricted shore time. When he started with the Blue Star Line, he sailed on ships that brought sheep carcasses from Australia and New Zealand to England. The ship tied up close to an abattoir, and for three weeks the sheep were killed, dressed, and hung in the ship's coolers, until these were full. Only then did the ship depart. In the meantime, the sailors had shore time and many made local friends. Containers put an abrupt end to that. His second grievance was the control over his on-board life. According to maritime tradition, a captain, once underway, is in total control of his ship. Now those onshore dictate, aided by satellite communications systems that mean there's no place for a captain to hide anymore. Captain Mundy was close to retirement, and his periodic grumpiness may well have had something to do with his current job conditions.

The British captain I talked to in Montreal also said that shore time is shrinking. In some ports no one leaves the ship, and even when sailors can go ashore, they may only have a few hours. He praised the various seaman's clubs for the work they're doing, and gave me a jar full of Canadian coins, more than fifty dollars' worth, left over from previous trips, as a donation for the Montreal centre where Johanna and I were volunteering. He said that lack of shore time makes for increased tensions on board. All sailors ever see is ship and cabin and lounge and sea and engine and bridge. It's not enough to keep the mind and spirit alive. I asked if he blamed the shipping companies and their profit-driven hurry. Yes, he said, but in turn the public drives them. North Americans and Europeans want to be able to lay their hands on whatever they want the moment they want it, and at a price they don't have to think about paying. The shipping industry floats on the insatiable demands of consumers to deliver goods on their terms.

In *The Sea*, a publication of the London, England-based the Missions to Seamen (now called the Mission to Seafarers), I came across an article by

Michael Grey. Even though conditions on board have improved considerably since Captain Cook's time, Grey argues that the "modern containership is a miserable place for her crew, with every last square inch of deck allocated for the stowage of revenue-earning boxes." No more "open deck to walk on, to play deck games on, to lounge about on, and on which to watch films screened under the stars." For exercise, "a grim steel-shrouded obstacle course is available ducking under locking bars in the narrow alleyways outboard of the hatches and under the deck stack of boxes. It has about the same charm as walking about a multi-storey car park."

No wonder, the article argues, there's a manning crisis, and it won't do to simply get new bodies on board from areas of the world with high unemployment. Those bodies have to be trained first. The article concludes: "If people are to be persuaded afloat . . . there must be more consideration given to the quality of life at sea."[4]

I asked a lot of questions about ships and shipping, and saw and heard both good and disturbing things. The *Sydney Star* had been an old-fashioned ship, kind to its sailors and passengers. But she's gone now. I picked up the final obituary in the business section of our newspaper in early 2003, when the last one to be cut up for scrap was the *American Star*. That year England issued a commemorative set of stamps featuring the *Sydney Star* at anchor at Pitcairn Island. The route is now being serviced by other ships and other shipping company names. The memory of this line is being kept alive only by a Blue Star Line website by means of which sailors that served it keep in touch.

The *Ville d'Aquarius*, though already a next generation ship with plastic instead of wood and with smaller decks for recreation, still had a swimming pool on board and fine large cabins for the crew, officers, and passengers. She would now be ten years old, two years older than the eight years for which she was built. As Glen and Keith had pointed out, newer ships were more like the ones Michael Grey's article described, and they loathed them. I wondered how long it would take before these two highly skilled and experienced sailors packed it in and found a job onshore.

Is there a future for passengers on these new freighters? In 2006 I telephoned TravLtips again and asked them if the business had changed since we booked our second trip with them. They told me there were fewer trips of the kind we took and sent me copies of their magazine, so I could look

---

[4] Michael Grey, "Compensations needed for life at sea today," *The Sea* (March/April 2000): 4–5.

for myself. I compared two issues, one from January/February 1999 and the other from January/February 2006. I was pleasantly surprised. It was true that the earlier edition featured more voyages of the kind we took, trips of fifty or more days, but both issues included a feature article written by a passenger about just such a trip, and they read much the same. The 2006 issue featured an account by Elaine R. Edson of her voyage on the *Rickmers Tokyo*, a multipurpose cargo ship that took a little over four months to cover the globe. Her descriptions of facilities and life on board sounded encouraging, and the costs were comparable to what we paid. TravLtips also reports that 2007 freighter-ship travel opportunities were similar to 2006. It's clear that the days of freighter travel aren't over, but perhaps more than ever the axiom "buyer beware" holds true for prospective passengers.

Johanna and I still think back on our two trips and the cargo ships we sailed upon whenever we see a container truck on the highway with a familiar company name, or pick up a product manufactured or grown across the ocean. We'll never forget the sheer unencumbered happiness of our voyages and the many ways they enriched our lives. Sailing on a freighter is a unique experience that brings you in touch with places, conditions, cities, people, nature, and also yourself, in ways that are constantly surprising. And there's the sea itself. Sometimes I thought about the sea as a threat, sometimes as a symbol of human life, always restlessly on the move. All those who board a freighter will have their own kinds of thoughts. The sea asks questions of those who sail her.

To any readers whom this book has inspired to undertake a similar journey: Bon Voyage!

Appendix: Freighter Travel Tips

For anyone now ready to seriously consider becoming a passenger on a freighter, this appendix will provide enough information to get the process started. The very first step is to find a travel agency that will provide information and arrange bookings. We discovered that ordinary travel agents don't usually have the necessary contacts. Here are three that do:

The Cruise People
1252 Lawrence Avenue East, Suite 210
Toronto, ON
Canada M3A 1C3
Tel: 1-800-268-6523
Fax: (416) 447-2628
Website: http://www.thecruisepeople.ca

TravLtips
PO Box 580188
Flushing, NY
USA 11358-0188
Tel: 1-800-872-8584
Email: infor@travltips.com
Website: http://www.travltips.com

Strand Voyages
1 Adam Street
London, UK WC2N 6AB
Tel: (44) 020 7766 8820
Email: voyages@strandtravel.co.uk

We used the Cruise People and TravLtips. Here are some of the key areas they will alert you to, before and as you book.

Costs

We paid the following amounts for our two trips:

Ville d'Aquarius (1998):

Travel (includes travel aboard ship only)	$16,427
Trip cancellation insurance	$550
Health and accident insurance	$900
Estimated amount spent on board and in ports	$1,500
Total	$19,377

For the sixty-five-day journey, the cost was just under $150CDN per person per day. However, to this figure must be added the costs of getting to where you'll board the ship, and going home after the journey. We had already been in Holland for awhile and were within easy reach of Hamburg for this journey.

Sydney Star (2002):

Travel (includes travel aboard ship and two Australian visas)	$14,500
Trip cancellation insurance	$600
Health and accident insurance	$1,100
Estimated amount spent on board and in ports	$1,200
Transportation and hotel costs—Ontario to Savannah and back	$800
Total	$18,200

For seventy-three days, this worked out to about $125CDN per person per day.

Travel Documents

A passport valid for six months after your planned return date is essential. While you're on board, the captain will have it in his possession, and he will give it back to you any time you go ashore. The travel agents provide information on the countries where visas are needed. TravLtips arranged for Australian visas using photocopies of our key passport pages. For our first journey, we needed a visa for China, which took time and money to acquire from the Chinese embassy.

Health and Immunization

For both journeys we needed a document signed by our family physician about the state of our health, including the names and dosages of the prescription drugs we were taking. As most freighters have no elevators and many stairs, a reasonably good physical condition is essential.

We were also required to get vaccinated against diphtheria, tetanus, and polio, and bring our immunization certificates on board. Actual inoculation requirements depend on travel destinations, and travel agents will provide specific information about what is needed. For example, if you plan to travel to African ports you would also need a yellow fever inoculation.

If you're on medications, calculate the quantity of drugs you'll need on board, and pack more than you think you'll need. Bring some Gravol—you may not need it but you'll be on a dancing ship.

Insurance

For both journeys we purchased three types of insurance. Included in the cost of the travel is an insurance policy that will indemnify the ship's owners for any costs incurred because of passenger illness or accident that forces an interruption of the journey.

The cost of travel health insurance depends on your age and health status. Don't rely on your provincial health care programs only!

As we booked well in advance of sailing, and considering our age, we also bought trip cancellation insurance.

Departure Arrangements

Unless you live in the departure port city, you should get to the port location at least one day in advance of the planned boarding and have a place to stay for one or more nights. We phoned the local agent every day during the week before departing, just to make sure that the ship hadn't sunk or was otherwise in trouble. Both travel agents provided the names, addresses, and phone numbers of local agents, and the agents were helpful and patient. If you need to fly in, or come by train or bus, make sure that your return journey's date is flexible.

What to Bring on Board

Currency

We brought on board both US cash and US traveller's cheques. Neither ship accepted credit cards or personal cheques. In most cities we were able to pay taxis in US dollars, but of course the cab drivers set the rate. As none of them were really expensive, we paid what they asked. The agent in Shanghai provided us with enough Chinese money for the long taxi ride into the city, in exchange for a $50US traveller's cheque. For additional money, we quickly found a bank for a supply of local currency. We didn't use bank debit cards then, but probably would now. Advancing money on credit cards is expensive.

Clothing

If laundry facilities on the ship seem adequate (that information should be provided by the travel agent), don't bring too much clothing. Much depends on the ship's itinerary; both our ships covered 750-1000 km per day, so variations in climate were expected. If you'll be visiting colder areas during your journey, bring at least one warm winter coat or jacket, and a hat or toque. It can get cold on deck! Bring at least one pair of work gloves. They save your hands and wear out fast.

Shoes

Bring a pair of sturdy flat-soled shoes for daily use on deck, slip-on sandals for inside the ship, and a pair of slippers for inside your cabin. That may seem cumbersome, but ships are very dirty, and you can easily pick up a blob of grease or oil on deck, and carry it inside to dirty the ship's hallways. We also liked to keep our cabin as clean as possible.

Electrical Appliances

The travel agents will provide information about the ship's voltages for your personal appliances (hair dryers, shavers, etc.). Some appliances automatically adjust to variations in voltage, but for those that don't, electrical or travel stores sell voltage converters. Some ships have rounded plug prongs instead of the North American flat ones, and there are adapters for those as well.

Books and Other Pastimes

You'll have plenty of time to read—and to knit, crochet, do crossword puzzles, or play board games. Plan what you need to bring. On our first trip we took along a short-wave radio, but made little use of it. On our second trip we carried on board a small radio/CD player and about forty of our favourite CDs, which was a much better idea. However, life on board a ship has its own rhythm, and we had no problem filling our days with deep satisfaction.

While we didn't, you may wish to take your laptop along, as well as a cellphone, iPods, and perhaps other electronic equipment. Specialized travel agents will provide information on what might be useful and usable on board, as well as what might not be. I know that using the ship's telephone (employing satellites) was very expensive when we sailed, something like $10US per minute!

Miscellaneous
- The ship provides bath/shower towels, and its slop chest will have tooth-paste and other sundries, even Aspirin. We could also purchase writing paper, envelopes, and postcards on the ships.
- We brought our own toiletries, including a small supply of washcloths and two small towels we could use wherever we wanted to.
- Bring sunglasses, sunscreen, and your optical prescription if you wear glasses (just in case—a ship is full of unyielding hazards).
- Pack a sewing kit, tissues in small packages, pens and pencils, Scotch tape, and paper.

Other Things to Think About
- Dietary restrictions. Of course, caloric intake is your own decision, often based on will power. You may need the latter if the food on board is as good as we found it on both ships. And with alcohol being cheap on board, gaining weight from drinking is easy. Consult your travel agent if you have extraordinary dietary requirements. We have a daughter with celiac disease (absolutely no gluten is allowed in her diet), and from what we observed, no ship's cook could cater to such a person. The travel agent will also be able to tell you whether vegetarians and vegans may be accommodated.
- Water. We were strongly advised against drinking the ship's tap water and always bought bottled water, available in 1.5-litre bottles at a decent price.
- Medical care on board. At least one officer on board must be trained in emergency medical procedures, and consulting doctors are always within reach of the ship's radio to instruct him in specific cases. However, common sense dictates that you don't climb aboard ship with any condition that regularly flares up and needs a specialist's care.
- Bring a positive attitude with you. Not every ship may offer as good a journey as both of ours did. The lessons we have learned in life were richly confirmed on board: People will treat you the way you treat them.

Tipping

Tipping the people on board is a minefield without a clear path. Container ships aren't like cruise ships. Our travel agents gave us no guidance, and captains were reluctant to spell out specifics. On the *Ville d'Aquarius* we gave our steward, Ariel, all the foreign currency we had left over from various port visits. I would guess it added up to the equivalent of about $100US. On the *Sydney Star* we gave $120US to John, the steward who cleaned our cabin daily and who served at mealtimes for about two-thirds of the seventy-three-day journey. He also brought our luggage from the quay to our cabin. We gave $50US to the cabin/meal steward, Lito, who took over from John and who helped us with our luggage when we left. Both these gentlemen seemed pleased, and Lito gave some indication that it wasn't even expected. I suspect that, unlike on cruise ships, the actual wages of stewards don't reflect tipping expectations. I have no idea what's right or wrong, but offer my experiences anyway.

Glossary of Maritime Terms

AB (or A/B): Able-bodied seaman; a member of the deck crew who is certified after a minimum of three years' experience.

Aft: Near or towards the stern (rear) of a vessel.

Amidships: The middle portion of a vessel.

Astern: Behind a vessel or going in a backward direction.

Automatic Pilot: The instrument that controls the vessel's steering gear automatically when set for a course.

Ballast: A heavy substance used to improve the stability of a vessel; most ships use water held in tanks at the bottom and to the sides of the vessel.

Beam: The width of a vessel.

Bosun: Boatswain; the foreman of the deck crew who usually reports to the first officer.

Bow: The foreward end of a vessel.

Bow Thruster: A small engine at the lower bow used to help control the vessel in tight harbour spots.

Bulk Carrier: A ship designed to carry large quantities of such cargos as sugar, sand, ore, etc.

Charter: The hiring out of a ship by its owner.

Chief Engineer: The senior officer licensed to and responsible for the workings of all machinery on board.

Chief Officer (or Chief Mate): The deck officer with the highest rank below captain; second in command of the vessel.

Complement: A term that encompasses all the workers on a vessel, officers and crew.

Crew: All of the workers on board below the rank of officer.

Derrick: A certain type of crane on board a vessel.

Draft: The depth of a vessel below the waterline.

Even Keel: When the draft of a ship is the same fore and aft.

Fiddley: A wooden rim around dining room tables that may be raised to protect dishes from sliding off in a storm. (The *Sydney Star* had them, the *Ville d'Aquarius* didn't.)

Flags of Convenience (FOC): The official registry of a ship in any country that offers such registry without many regulations.

Fore: The area towards the front of a vessel.

Forecastle (or foc's'le): The front section of a vessel, which in earlier times used to look like a castle and served as living quarters, as well as a platform for attacks on other ships. It's now often used as a storage area, while its "platform" serves as an anchor-launching location and a place from which strong ropes are attached to shore.

Gangway: A platform or set of steps used to get off and on a ship from dockside.

Hatch: An opening in the main deck (or working deck) into the holds of a vessel.

Helm: The tiller or wheel found in the wheelhouse or bridgehouse that is used to turn the ship's rudder.

Helmsman: The AB operating the helm.

Hold: Any compartment below deck for cargo.

Keel: The very bottom of the ship.

Knot (short for nautical mile): The unit of speed per hour at sea. One knot equals 1,852 metres per hour.

Main Deck (or working deck): The area directly above the holds. Sailors and stevedores move on it while loading and unloading ships.

Master: Another name for captain.

Monkey Island: A deck built over the wheelhouse.

MV: Motor Vessel.

Officer: A licensed member of the ship's complement, either "engineer" or "deck."

Oiler: An unlicensed member of the engine-room staff; one who oils and greases bearings (but now often only checks on automated lubrication systems).

OS: Ordinary seaman; a rank below AB.

Pilot: A shore-based licensed seaman who comes on board to assist the captain in getting his ship in and out of ports.

Poop Deck: The deck above the stern of a ship.

Port: The left side of a ship when facing the prow.

Prow: The bow of a vessel, its foremost part.

Reefer: A ship or container with refrigeration capacity.

Ship's Agent: A shore-based representative of the corporation that operates a particular ship.

Slop Chest: The on-board supply of items for sale to both sailors and passengers.

SS: Steam Ship.

Starboard: The right side of a ship when facing the prow.

Stevedore (or longshoreman): Dock workers who take cargo off or load cargo onto ships.

Taffrail: The wooden top part of a ship's railing.

TEU: Twenty Foot Equivalent Unit, meaning a container twenty feet in length. (A 2-TEU unit is forty feet long.)

Time Zones: At the equator, Earth's circumference is about 40,000 kilometres. As Earth travels around the Sun in twenty-four hours, it makes morning and night occur at different times of the day in different places. For international organization, our forebears created twenty-four times zones, each a little over 1,650 kilometres wide. With both our ships basically travelling parallel to the equator (the *Ville d'Aquarius* just under one thousand kilometres every twenty-four hours, the *Sydney Star* about 750), we regularly changed our clocks on both ships, each time one hour forwards going east, backwards going west. Canada, large as it is, has to contend with no fewer than five time zones.

Ton (or tonne): One thousand kilograms.

Watch: A four-hour period in which designated members of the engineer and deck sections are on duty.

About the Author

Photo by Johanna Peetoom

At the age of nineteen, Adrian Peetoom emigrated from Holland to Canada on a small freighter converted to emigrant carrier, which pitched and rolled its way across the Atlantic in March 1954. After obtaining a B.A., he began a thirty-one-year career in publishing in 1961. Adrian served in sales and editorial functions and authored a number of professional books for teachers. Always an active participant in Christian church life, he is currently writing a journal account of twelve months in the life of an Anglican parish. Having raised six children, Adrian and his wife, Johanna, did very little travelling until after retirement, when they discovered an article on taking passage on container ships. They embarked on the treasured cargo journeys related in this book in 1998 and 2000. Since 2005, Adrian and Johanna have lived in Edmonton, Alberta, close to three lively and literate grandchildren. In addition to their six children, the couple have thirteen grandchildren.